Rock-a-Billy Rebel

Known and Unknown Stars I've Known

MACK ALLEN SMITH

Rock-a-Billy Rebel

Copyright © 2012, by Mack Allen Smith.
Cover Copyright © 2012 Sunbury Press.

All rights reserved, including the right to reproduce this book or portions thereof in any form whatsoever. For information contact Sunbury Press, Inc., Subsidiary Rights Dept., 50-A West Main St., Mechanicsburg, PA 17055 USA or legal@sunburypress.com.

For information about special discounts for bulk purchases, please contact Sunbury Press, Inc. Wholesale Dept. at (855) 338-8359 or orders@sunburypress.com.

To request one of our authors for speaking engagements or book signings, please contact Sunbury Press, Inc. Publicity Dept. at publicity@sunburypress.com.

FIRST SUNBURY PRESS EDITION
Printed in the United States of America
December 2012

ISBN 978-1-620061-55-8

Published by:
Sunbury Press
Mechanicsburg, PA
www.sunburypress.com

Mechanicsburg, Pennsylvania   USA

Dedication

Sam Phillips, who did more than anyone in the world to change the course of music, made the following statement: "The gap between success and failure is so small at times, and there are so many artists who deserve to be remembered.

With this in mind, I dedicate my book to known and unknown stars everywhere.

Also, I dedicate this book to my wife, Lois B. Smith. Not only for her typing and editing, but for her love, support, and hard work in keeping the Smith Clan afloat for over fifty years.

Table of Contents

PREFACE

CHAPTER

1	DADDY, MAMA, AND TWO UNCLES	1
2	J. Z. GEORGE FFA BAND & KENNY MINYARD BAND	3
3	MACK ALLEN SMITH & THE FLAMES	5
4	WARREN SMITH	13
5	BARRY SMITH	15
6	BILLY WAYNE HERBERT	16
7	DURWOOD HERBERT	20
8	TERRY HERBERT	21
9	OLE MISS DOWNBEATS	24
10	RED McGREGOR	27
11	JIM RORIE	29
12	JERRY JAYE	31
13	BOBBY NEAL	33
14	ELLIS HOPPER	34
15	SANFORD HORTON	36
16	DAVID LEE COX	38
17	JAMIE ISONHOOD	40
18	JESSIE YATES	42
19	LANEY O'BRIANT	44
20	JAMES KEITH WORRELL	45
21	ARTHUR BROWNING	47
22	HARDIN BROWNING	48
23	THE CASUALS/KASUALS	50
24	MAGNOLIA BLUE	51
25	MURRY MOORMAN	52
26	TONY BROWNING	53
27	STEVE McGREGORY	54
28	ACE CANNON	57
29	DOMINIC FRATESI	59
30	JAMIE WINTERS	61
31	STEPHEN WINTERS	63
32	BOB TIMMERS	65
33	MARTIN HAWKINS	67
34	LARRY ROGERS	69
35	THE CONTINENTALS	71
36	THE REETS	72
37	CURB SERVICE	73
38	BUDDY MILLETT	74
39	LAWRENCE STACY	75
40	GARY LEE WORSHAM	76
41	JOHNNY VINCENT	77

42	QUINTON CLAUNCH	78
43	PETE BARTOSCH	80
44	STONE BLUE	81
45	RAY HALL	82
46	BENNY RIGBY	83
47	GEORGE THOMAS	85
48	RICHARD McLAUGHLIN	87
49	JENKINS RUSCOE	88
50	GROVER NEAL DUKE	89
51	TWO SONS OF GROVER NEAL DUKE	91
52	JIMMY GILREATH	92
53	THE NITE-LITERS/JOHN MIHELIC	94
54	WILLIE NARMOUR AND SHELL SMITH	95
55	JOHN HURT	98
56	DOC HERBERT	99
57	BILL WALKER	101
58	DON CHANDLER	103
59	JAMES GOVAN	105
60	SUSIE JAMES	107
61	DENNIS JAMES	109
62	SONNY BURGESS	110
63	CHARLIE FEATHERS	112
64	BENNY BARRENTINE	114
65	ERNIE BARTON	116
66	JUMPIN' GENE SIMMONS	117
67	SHYLO	118
68	DOUG STEEN	119
69	THE RED TOPS	120
70	THE GANTS	122
71	JOHN HUGHEY	124
72	KENNY LOFTIN	126
73	JAMES O'GWYNN	127
74	RICK, JIMMY, & DAN	129
75	RAY & HERSHEL	132
76	RICKY MABRY	134
77	EDDIE LEE ALDERMAN	135
78	BOBBY ALFORD	136
79	ROBERT ALEXANDER	137
80	RICHARD CORDER	138
81	JERRY MASTERS	139
82	LISA COOK McNAMARA	140
83	OTHER KNOWN & UNKNOWN STARS	141
84	WINDING IT UP	152
	BIOGRAPHY	153
	DISCOPGRAPHY	156
	PHOTO SECTION	174

Preface

When I decided in June, 2009, to write this book, my primary objective was to write a book that was substantially different from others I had read. Specifically, the books I'd read were about singers, musicians, producers, etc., that the authors hadn't known personally prior to starting their books. In two instances, the authors were from overseas and their only connection to the American artists they were writing about was hearing their records on the radio. Their books were only about artists with records, and were based on several years of interviews and in depth research of studio files.

On the other hand, my goal was to write about people I'd known for many years who I had performed with on stage or in the recording studio or, at least, knew them personally and had first-hand knowledge of their careers in music. I also wanted to include their day job careers whenever I could. Having played or sang on a record was not a criteria for getting a spot in my book. Hence the title: "Known and Unknown Stars I've Known." Some are known throughout the music world for their accomplishments. Others never made it big in the music business, but, nonetheless, are stars to me.

My main fear when I started was that I might forget some who should be included in my book. I hope that didn't happen, but, like they say, ain't nobody perfect.

To everyone included in this book, I hope you will approve of what I wrote. If by chance I forgot to include anyone who should have been included I can only say: "Please forgive me."

Research sources included information in my memory bank, information from a questionnaire I sent to known and unknown stars I've known, information obtained from phone calls, personal interviews and finally some information on known stars was obtained from the internet (primarily Wikipedia, the free encyclopedia).

Chapter 1
Daddy, Mama and Two Uncles

Malcolm (Mack) Alonzo Smith was born August 31, 1912, in Carroll County, Mississippi. He died March 22, 1988 at Carrollton and is buried in Evergreen Cemetery near North Carrollton.

Fannie Mae (Herbert) Smith was born September 26, 1911, in Carroll County, Mississippi. She died July 19, 2003, at Golden Age Nursing Home in Greenwood, MS. and is also buried in Evergreen Cemetery.

Jimmy Herbert (Uncle Jimmy) was born November 1, 1907, in Carroll County, Mississippi. He died May 15, 1964, at Greenwood and is buried in Odd Fellow Cemetery in Greenwood.

Archie Herbert (Uncle Archie) was born August 5, 1919, in Carroll County, Mississippi. He died March 28, 1966, at North Carrollton and is buried there in Evergreen Cemetery.

My daddy didn't play a musical instrument and his father, mother, nor any of his seven siblings (5 brothers and 2 sisters) played a musical instrument. He did whistle and sing old Roy Acuff songs and gospel songs. Still, he supported me and, while he was a deacon in Carrollton Baptist Church for many years, he probably didn't approve of my singing in the honky-tonks. Nonetheless, he never said anything to me.

Mama, on the other hand, was a very talented guitar player and she had two brothers who played musical instruments for many years. Santa Claus brought me a Gene Autry guitar when I was ten years old, but I never played guitar. Mama kept it tuned and played it a lot more than I did. I just wanted to sing.

My early exposure to country music came from the Herberts when I was around four or five years old. My mother (Fannie Mae) played guitar and sang old Jimmy Rogers songs, while her brothers (Jimmy and Archie) both played guitar, fiddle, and bull bass and sang all the country songs that were popular at the time. It didn't seem like there were very many people living close to us, but on Saturday nights the old log house where we lived and the porch were packed with people dancing all over the place while Mama, Uncle Jimmy, and Uncle Archie were picking and singing. The old log house belonged to my grandparents (Lum & Sally Herbert) and is located in the Hickory Grove community of Carroll County. There was no electricity, running water, or indoor plumbing, but no one seemed to mind. The house is now owned by Uncle Archie's son, Terry Herbert. And, I might add, Terry and his family have all the modern conveniences. Times have changed. Unlike my singing in the honky-tonks years later, alcohol was not allowed at these old Herbert gigs. Mama hated alcohol so much she should have gone on a sobriety tour.

Uncle Jimmy lived in Greenwood, and I remember when he arrived for the old country dances there would be a big bull bass strapped to the top of his car, and the back seat and trunk were filled with musical instruments. Since we had no electricity, there was no need for amplifiers. The Herberts made enough racket with their acoustic instruments for everyone to really have a good time. There was always excitement in the air when Uncle Jimmy arrived.

In the summer of 1947 after finishing third grade we moved to Carrollton where Daddy opened a grocery store. We had living quarters in the back of the store. We now had electricity, running water, and indoor plumbing. Before moving to Carrollton we lived at Camp McCain in Elliott, Mississippi and I entered third grade in Grenada. Camp McCain was where I was first introduced to electricity and also indoor plumbing. Also, at Carrollton, we had an electric radio which mama would turn on each Saturday for us to hear Uncle Jimmy and his band playing at a radio station in Greenwood. One song I remember him singing on the radio was "Bubbles in My Beer." Uncle Jimmy had now gone electric and besides being on the radio, he and his band played at the Greenwood VFW and other clubs during the late '40s and early '50s.

To my knowledge Uncle Archie never played the honky-tonks like Uncle Jimmy did; however, he moved his family from Hickory Grove to North Carrollton and kept on playing. With us in Carrollton this worked out good for me because I used to go by his house and he would play the guitar while I sang Hank Williams and Carl Smith songs. I remember when Hank Williams died on January 1, 1953. Someone recorded a tribute song and I would sing it while Uncle Archie played the guitar.

Beside country, Uncle Archie could play the blues. John Hurt was a good friend of his and would drop by the bus shop where Uncle Archie was manager, and they would play for hours. Uncle Archie had those John Hurt licks down pat. I loved his John Hurt pickin' better than anything else.

In 1954 Rock-A-Billy hit with Elvis Presley, and he came out with the song "That's All Right, Mama," so country music took a back seat. But, I'll never forget Uncle Archie and all those times he played the guitar while I sang those country songs.

To my daddy, mama, and two uncles, I just want to say thanks for everything. God bless you and yours. May you rest in peace.

Chapter 2
J. Z. George FFA band and the Kenny Minyard Band

I choose these two bands for Chapter Two because the FFA Band was the first band I ever sang with, The Kenny Minyard Band was the second band I ever sang with, and it was the first band I sang with in the honky-tonks. I had been singing for several years with Uncle Archie playing guitar, but these were my first with bands.

J.Z. GEORGE FFA BAND - FFA stood for Future Farmers of America; however, some of us called it Future Something Else of America. This was all in fun, and done with much affection.

In 1954, while in my junior year at J. Z. George High School in North Carrollton, Mississippi, I became lead singer in my first band (The J. Z. George FFA Band). The state FFA association had just started a statewide hillbilly band contest, so we were formed to compete with other bands throughout the state. Rock-A-Billy had just gotten started with Elvis Presley ("That's All Right, Mama;" "Blue Moon of Kentucky;" "Good Rockin' Tonight" and other recordings on Sun Records in Memphis), so I wanted to do some Elvis songs. However, I was told that it was a hillbilly band contest and Elvis songs were not allowed. Therefore, I sang some Hank Williams and Ray Price songs. Before Elvis, Hank was my number one man and I admit to crying when I heard about his death on January 1, 1953. Next to Hank, I liked Carl Smith.

The FFA band consisted of me (lead singer), Charles Martin (lead guitar), Alton Alderman (rhythm guitar and harmony vocals), Sidney Nabors (rhythm guitar and harmony vocals), Junior Bailey (harmony vocals), and Clovis Harbin (bass tub). The J. Z. George band won the state FFA Band Championship two years in a row (1955-56). I also played bass tub since Clovis Harbin had graduated the year before.

My junior year (1954-55) was when Mississippi started having the state FFA Band Contest and I am truly proud and honored to have been in the bands that won the first two state championships (school years 1954-55 and 1955-56). Our trophies were in the trophy case at J. Z. George and I suppose they perished when the school burned in 1958. If they were, by chance, saved, and if anyone knows where they are, I would surely love to see them again and, if possible, take a photograph of them.

The Kenny Minyard Band - Kenny Minyard was born December 13, 1923, in Carroll County, Mississippi. He died February 4, 2009. Kenny is buried at Mt. Pisgah Cemetery in Carroll County.

In 1956, while in my senior year at J. Z. George High School in North Carrollton, Mississippi, Swinton and Virginia Minyard took me dancing at the Greenwood VFW. Swinton had an uncle, Kenny Minyard, who played there every other Saturday. I'll never forget that first night. Swinton knew about my singing in the FFA band, so he talked me into singing with Kenny's band.

I wanted to do some Elvis songs, but Kenny had a hillbilly band and they weren't doing any Elvis stuff. However, the lead guitar man (Alton Cheek) said they could probably follow me on an Elvis tune. I asked Alton if he had heard "That's All Right, Mama," and he replied, "Yeah, it starts off with some cat strumming the guitar, don't it?" I said, "Yeah, man, just start strumming in the key of "A" and I'll jump in." I was shocked and surprised when the group erupted into applause. I guess Kenny was surprised, too, because he hired me to sing Elvis songs with his band whenever he played at the Greenwood VFW. I sang about two months with Kenny before forming my own band.

Kenny's band in 1956 was comprised of Kenny Minyard (bull bass, rhythm guitar, drums, and singer), Alton Cheek (lead guitar), Eddie Lee Alderman (steel guitar), and Bob Dickerson (rhythm guitar and singer).

I'm not sure how long the Kenny Minyard band played after 1956. Music changed and clubs were booking more Rock-A-Billy and rock & roll bands. I think he played into the '60s before hanging it up. Nonetheless, Kenny knocked them out for a long time and even made a come-back when he turned 80 years old.

I played for a surprise 80th birthday party for Kenny in 2003. It was at this party where he started singing and playing guitar again when he took the stage with Good Time Express. A couple of years later I was on a show with Kenny at Teoc. He played guitar and sang and the crowd (old and young) went crazy. He still had that magic even in his sunset years.

I have a picture and newspaper article when Kenny played at the American Legion in Greenwood on November 3, 2008. This was just three months before he died on February 4, 2009. I will gladly include this picture in the photo section.

James Minyard, Kenny's nephew, told me that at his gig three months before he died Kenny did "Milk Cow Boogie Blues" and brought the house down. Band members that final gig are as follows: Kenny Minyard (rhythm guitar and singer), James Minyard (fiddle), Bobby Alford (rhythm guitar and singer), Glenn Walker (banjo), and Jimmy Hamilton (rhythm guitar).

Kenny Minyard was a good man who was loved by all who knew him. I will never forget that he gave me my first job singing in the honky-tonks. But, more than that, he was a true friend of mine for over fifty years

Chapter 3
Mack Allen Smith and the Flames

In this chapter I will attempt to list the different groups of Flames by time period starting with 1956 when we were formed and bringing it to the present time. I hope I don't forget anyone. This chapter will be used loosely as a point of reference throughout the book since a number of Flames will be highlighted in subsequent chapters.

The Appendix (Rockabillyhall.com) will also be used as a point of reference. The narrative portion of my biography and the complete discography, as shown on the internet, are presented in the Appendix. The discography shows all songs we recorded over the years, along with release dates of records, record labels, where recorded, and the names of musicians who played on the records plus what instrument or instruments they played. In most instances the producer is shown and some also show the engineer.

<u>1956:</u> After singing with Kenny Minyard for a couple of months, I formed a band called The Carroll County Rock & Roll Boys which consisted of me (lead singer and rhythm guitar), Ellis Hopper (lead guitar), and Billy Wayne Herbert (rhythm guitar). For the rest of the summer we performed on a radio program each Saturday afternoon which was broadcast from the Greenwood VFW. It was at one of these Saturday afternoon radio shows where I met my wife.

Besides the radio shows, we performed at a ballpark in Greenwood with Sun Record artists: Warren Smith, Sonny Burgess, and Charlie Feathers. Joe Gary joined us on drums for this gig and he did a great job. We were the warmup band and, even though we were unknown rednecks, we still got a good response. In fact, Bob Neal, a popular disc jockey from Memphis who promoted the show, talked to me about coming to Memphis for an audition at Sun Records. Ellis Hopper tried to get me to forget college and for us to go to Memphis and try to make it in this new Rock-A-Billy revolution that was sweeping the nation. I probably should have gone to Sun Records for an audition, but I didn't. They had some good artists on Sun, and I may or may not have gotten a contract. Nevertheless, it wouldn't have hurt anything to give it a try.

Shortly after entering college at Holmes Junior College in September, 1956, we performed at a variety show in the Holmes Junior College auditorium. The variety show performance led to a write-up in the college magazine where the writer talked about how the girls screamed as I sang and wiggled my right leg. After the show Ellis Hopper again approached me about postponing college and us going to Memphis for a shot at making it as Rock-A-Billy artists. When I rejected this idea again, Ellis quit the band.

After Ellis quit the band I hired Eddie Lee Alderman from Carroll County to play lead guitar. He also played some steel. I also hired Charlie McCarty from Kosciusko, Mississippi, to play drums and Clyde Campbell from Carrollton to sing Pat Boone and

Fats Domino songs. I did all the Rock-A-Billy songs. At this point we changed the name of the band to Mack Allen Smith and the Flames. Rusty Hobgood from Holcomb, Mississippi, became our manager.

Mack Allen Smith and the Flames performed on weekends at the 51 Club in Durant, Mississippi, and the VFW in Kosciusko and Greenwood, Mississippi. During the week we played some at a local spot called Grapes Court in Pickens, Mississippi.

It sounds like I had fun while attending Holmes Junior College and I must admit I did. There was a little problem, though. I was having so much fun I stopped going to class. My parents were sacrificing so I could go to college, and I wasn't even trying to get an education. At least, one that would lead to a degree. Finally, President Branch called me into his office and told me that Holmes Junior College was not a boarding house. He said if I stayed I would have to attend classes. I told Mr. Branch I was paid up to the end of semester and, if it was all right with him, I would stay until then and decide what I needed to do. He agreed to let me stay on until the end of the 1956 fall semester.

President Branch told me that he hoped I would make the right decision which, in his opinion, would be to stay in school, apply myself, and get a college degree. Of course, I didn't take his advice, but he was right. Instead, I made a really bad career move. I quit college and joined the Marines. Clyde Campbell and Rusty Hobgood both joined with me, and we were off to sunny California.

1959 & 1960: In January, 1959, I completed my tour of duty with the Marines and returned to Carrollton, Mississippi. After a couple of weeks I had re-formed The Flames and was back on stage. The group included me as lead singer, Keith Worrell (lead guitar), Red McGregor (rhythm guitar), and Durwood Herbert (drums). At our first gig (a variety show at the J. Z. George gym), we met David Lee Cox who was playing piano with a group from Winona. We talked him into joining The Flames. I consider these five (me, Keith Worrell, Red McGregor, Durwood Herbert, and David Lee Cox) the original 1959 Flames. Later in 1959 Laney O'Briant (lead guitar) from Durant and Jessie Yates (rhythm guitar) from Kosciusko joined The Flames for a few months. They quit after a couple of months and formed a band with Jessie singing lead. With the Flames, I hogged the microphone and didn't let anyone sing much except David Lee Cox. He was so good on the piano that I had to let him sing some.

During the summer of 1959 I finally got around to auditioning for Sun Records. We recorded four songs with me singing: "Sandy Lee," "Kansas City," "Mean Woman Blues," and "Young Dreams". The Sun producer, Ernie Barton, wanted me to come back into the studio and record with the studio band. Red McGregor told me to do it, but David Lee Cox wanted to try another studio and see if someone would use the band, too. Guess what my decision was? Another bad career move. I went along with David Lee, but we never got a deal elsewhere.

I went back to Sun Records to accept Ernie's offer, but he had moved to Little Rock, Arkansas, and no one knew where the master tape was. Several unsuccessful attempts were made over a 40 year period to locate the master tape. However, I am happy to report that the master tape has been found and is in my possession. The long lost Sun recordings were released on CD in December 2010 on Redita Records in the Netherlands.

Our gigs in 1959, besides the variety show, included the Vaiden gym, VFW clubs in Greenwood and Grenada, the Community House in Carrollton, The Wagon Wheel in Jackson, Mink's Supper Club in Greenville, and a number of parties at various country clubs, high schools, and colleges. I also had two day jobs in 1959. I worked five months at Supreme Electronics in Greenwood and one day at Medart Lockers in Greenwood. At Supreme I was a drill press operator, and at Medart I hung doors on a line before they entered the paint room. I sure wished I had stayed in college.

The original 1959 Flames stayed together throughout 1960. The sixties started out like the fifties ended with me singing at night and sleeping most of the day. Additionally, I was eating Mama's good cooking. I was eating good and didn't have to pay Mama and Daddy a penny for food or rent. I had it made in the shade, but that all ended on April 10, 1960. Lois Bennett and I got married. After a two-day honeymoon in Winona, I had to start looking for a day job to supplement my singing money.

After the Winona honeymoon, we moved into a one bedroom cottage on West President Street in Greenwood. After settling in for a few days, I got a job at Fisher Stationary Company as a typewriter and adding machine salesman. Here I was overnight, all domesticated and everything.

During the first part of December, 1960, Warren Smith joined my band for a number of shows and dances in North Mississippi. Warren was a big Sun Records star, and we were honored to have him with The Flames for several months. He was a great singer and performer. Warren will be highlighted in the next chapter (Chapter 4).

<u>1961 & 1962:</u> The original 1959 band began breaking up in 1961. Keith Worrell and Durwood Herbert left for college at Ole Miss, and David Lee Cox moved to Jackson. After trying out a couple of guitar pickers (Gilruth Johnson and Ellis Hopper), Arthur Browning replaced Keith Worrell on lead guitar, and Buddy Millett replaced Durwood Herbert on drums. Later, Harding Browning joined The Flames on piano, and my brother, Barry Smith, joined The Flames on bass. Red McGregor and I were the only remaining members of the original 1959 band.

The new group of Flames, me (lead singer), Arthur Browning (lead guitar), Buddy Millett (drums), Hardin Browning (piano), Red McGregor (rhythm guitar), and Barry Smith (bass), were The Flames when we recorded our first two records in 1962 at Hi Studio in Memphis. Doug Steen played sax on one side of our first single and Durwood Herbert played drums on both sides of the first single and on one side of the second. In addition, John Michelic and Johnny Baker played trumpets on one side of the second single, and Johnny played harmonica on one side of the second single. The first two records were released by Dominic Fratesi on Vee-Eight Records. For complete details of these first two single records see the Appendix (Rockabillyhall.com).

As for my day jobs, I left Fisher Stationary in April 1961 and took a job managing a music store on Carrollton Avenue in Greenwood. Then in 1962 I changed day jobs again. I started work at Staple Cotton Association in September when the cotton started coming in as a temporary seasonal worker, but it turned into a permanent job that lasted four years. I continued singing at honky-tonks throughout the Delta, and we usually played five nights a week. On Tuesdays and Thursdays we played after Bingo at the Greenwood VFW, and on Wednesdays and Fridays played after Bingo at the Greenwood Moose Lodge. Then on Saturday nights we alternated between several clubs (Cleveland American Legion, Greenville American Legion, Delta Supper Club in Helena, Arkansas, and the Greenwood clubs, to name a few). We also played a lot of gigs at The Community House in Carrollton.

It's hard to imagine fifteen or twenty minutes sleep doing a person much good, but when I worked at Staple Cotton and sang five nights a week, I would go home at lunch and sleep fifteen or twenty minutes. Then, Lois would wake me up and I'd go back to work. My take-home pay from Staple Cotton was $38.00 dollars a week, so we really did need the $10.00 dollars I made singing each night.

When the cotton started rolling in the fall, I had to stop singing during the week because I worked 95 hours a week at Staple Cotton. Even with all those hours you still couldn't make much money because, instead of paying time and half for all hours over 40, they had a sliding scale where the more hours you worked, the less you made per hour. I made minimum wage of one dollar per hour, but after 40 hours, it started sliding down. By the time I reached 95 hours, I was lucky if I made fifty cents per hour.

Some people I've told this thought I was lying. Looking back, I don't think it was legal. Of course, everyone wasn't on the sliding scale. Just the ones who did the work. Reportedly, officers who were sitting on their behinds in the offices downstairs were enjoying salaries as high as $100,000 per year, or more. Perhaps that's why they needed a sliding scale for the ones who did the work. Kinda like Robin Hood in reverse. Instead of robbing from the rich and giving to the poor, they were robbing from the poor and giving to the rich.

The year 1961 was a super year because of one important happening. On January 29, 1961, my sweet darling, Cynthia Alan Smith, was born. We decided to call her Cindy. She was pretty and smart and a genuine blessing, not only to us but to her grandparents. My daddy always called Cindy his favorite granddaughter. She was, of course, his only granddaughter.

1963-1969: During this period Mack Allen Smith and The Flames were as follows: Mack Allen Smith (lead singer), Murry Moorman (lead guitar), Barry Smith (bass), Buddy Millett (drums), Hardin Browning (piano), and Bill Bole and Terry Jenkins on trumpets. Sonny Strohm from Grenada was our sax man for a while in 1963 and played on one recording session in Muscle Shoals, Alabama. Bill Tackett from Jackson also played sax for a while.

In 1963 we started recording for Dominic Fratesi at Fame Studio in Muscle Shoals, Alabama, with records released on Statue Records. We recorded eight songs for Dominic resulting in four Statue singles. We also cut songs during the sixties that were released as singles on Mariteen, Cynthia, and Jab (a subsidiary of Atlantic). In April 2009 Fat Possum Records re-released on their subsidiary (Big Legal Mess Records) 21 songs that were recorded from 1962 thru 1967. In the sixties I recorded a total of 33 songs at Muscle Shoals and Memphis. A number of these cuts were also released on albums overseas during the seventies and have wound up on CDs overseas. We did a lot of recording in the sixties; however, I see no need to list all the sessions, songs, and who played on them because that information for the most part is detailed in the Appendix.

This sixties band (63-69) was the best butt-kicking band I was ever associated with. In my opinion, that band replaced the 1959 band as the butt-kicking band of all time.

I think the instruments we had being a perfect fit for the soul music and rock and roll of the sixties had a lot to do with it. And, we were all fairly young (even me and Buddy Millett).

In 1966 I changed day jobs again. In September, with my newly acquired cotton classing license in hand, I left Staple Cotton to class cotton for the federal government. Classers with the government worked at GS-9 rate which was a much better base than Staple Cotton and, unlike Staple Cotton, there was no sliding scale. It was time and one half for hours over 40 and double time on Sunday. Man, that fall was great. Lois was even able to buy a few steaks at the grocery store and ensure Cindy some good stuff from Santa Claus.

In 1967 there was another important happening. On March 11, 1967, my son, Malcolm Allen Smith, Jr., was born. He has always been called Allen. Like Cindy, he was welcomed by parents and grandparents alike and has been a real blessing in our lives.

The fall of 1966 was encouraging. I was making good money classing cotton. Then Jim Bickerstaff from Memphis released two songs I had recorded at Muscle Shoals ("Big Silver Tears" and "Not Strong Enough"), and they were getting good air play at stations in and around Memphis. Dewey Phillips, who had broken Elvis' first record, was playing both sides on his radio show at a station in Millington, and George Klein was playing "Not Strong Enough" on WHBQ. Dewey Phillips got us booked on George Klein's TV show and on Eddie Bond's TV show. We also played at Eddie Bond's club. Jim opened a recording studio (Lyn-Lou) on Chelsea Avenue with Larry Rogers and convinced me that Memphis was where I should be. I had planned to enroll at Delta State University for the 1967 spring semester. Then, bad career move three. I decided to move to Memphis instead.

I needed a day job to supplement my singing money, so Jim helped me get a job as an assembly line supervisor at Pace Corporation. At night I was in the recording studio trying to come up with a hit record, and on weekends I traveled back to Greenwood for a short visit with my family and a weekend gig at some honky-tonk.

Again, there is no need to furnish information in this chapter regarding recordings at Lyn-Lou in Memphis with me singing, as they are all detailed in the Appendix. I did put out a few records on other artists. How did they do? What can I say - I lost money. Like Mack Allen Smith records, they started off slow then tapered off. Dick Stevens from Isola, Mississippi, and I put out a record "Why Can't Time Stand Still" on the Reets from around Cleveland, Mississippi, that I thought was real good. The Reets were a great group and Larry Rogers did a good job of producing and engineering for us on this session. We got air play on some Mississippi stations, but we didn't have the know-how or the money to do a record justice.

The summer of 1968 was nice. We sold our house on Barton Avenue in Greenwood and moved the family to Memphis. No longer was I in the studio at night drinking whiskey, flipping pills, and trying to cut a record. I was so happy to be with the family that I stopped going to the studio all together.

We moved back to Greenwood in August 1969 and rented a house on West Jeff Davis. Lois got a job with the Leflore County School District, and I went to work as a salesman at Delta Chevrolet. We were both working, the band was cooking, the children were healthy and growing, and the sixties were looking much better toward the end than they had before. I spent most of the sixties chasing a dream. Like the old saying I saw somewhere: "I feel much better now that I've given up." Irrespective of my dream chasing (in the sixties), Daddy and I still got in some good bird hunting and we didn't miss many of Mama's Sunday meals.

The sixties ended with me selling cars at Delta Chevrolet and singing in the honky-tonks at night. The sixties were gone but not forgotten, and they never will be.

<u>The Seventies</u>: When 1970 began, I was still working at Delta Chevrolet and I was still singing in the honky-tonks. That butt-kicking band from the sixties was no longer intact, but we were still rocking. The horns were gone, Hardin Browning was gone and replaced by Larry Blakely on keyboard, later by Jessie Yates, and Buddy Millett had been replaced on drums by Lawrence Stacy.

We purchased our second and last home in January 1970 at 814 West Claiborne Avenue in Greenwood, Mississippi. This has been the Smith residence for over forty years.

In November 1970 my day job changed again. I left Delta Chevrolet to run an insurance debit for Life of Georgia. My day job changed again on May 1, 1971, when I opened Mack Allen Smith's Town & Country Night Club on Highway 49 South in Greenwood. Except for a few months, this was our base of operation until September 1976.

As in the sixties, I recorded through the seventies, with records released in eight of the ten years in the decade (1970, 1972, 1973, 1975, 1976, 1977, 1978, and 1979). For details see the Appendix.

After saying goodbye to the Town & Country, we began playing in Vaiden, Mississippi, where we played almost exclusively the last seven years of my honky-tonk career (1977-1984).

Major changes to our band occurred in the summer of 1974. By then, Lawrence Stacy had moved to Texas and Murry Tingle was my drummer. Murry Moorman was gone and Laney O'Briant was our lead guitar, and Barry Hopkins from Kosciusko was on keyboard. My brother, Barry, had also left the band and we had a new bass player, Olan Crout, from Kosciusko.

After changes in the summer of 1974, band members were as follows: Mack Allen Smith (lead singer), Laney O'Briant (lead guitar), Sanford Horton (bass), Gary Lee Worsham (drums), and Steve McGregory (keyboards). This group stayed together for two and a half years (through the end of 1976). This was another butt-kicking band for sure.

A recap of musicians during the seventies is as follows: <u>Lead guitar</u>: Murry Moorman (two tours of duty), Roger Wade, and Laney O'Briant. <u>Bass</u>: Barry Smith, Laney O'Briant, Olan Crout, Sanford Horton, Prentiss McPhail, Van Cooke, and Paul Melton. <u>Keyboards</u>: Larry Blakely, Jessie Yates, Barry Hopkins, Steve (Reno) McGregory, and Larry Acy. <u>Drummers</u>: Lawrence Stacy (two tours of duty), Murry Tingle, Gary Lee Worsham, Charlie Davis, and George Thomas.

In 1975 I signed a contract with Johnny Vincent, owner of Ace Records. This resulted in four record releases (one single in 1975, one in 1976, one in 1977, and an album in 1979). Details of the Ace sessions are presented in the Appendix. Johnny

Vincent was a real class act, and I consider it an honor to have known him and be listed on his roster of Ace recording artists. Johnny also became a good friend of mine.

It was at Ace Records in 1975 when I met Martin Hawkins from England. I signed a contract with Martin to try and get some releases overseas. This resulted in one single and three albums in England and one album in Holland (see Appendix for details). Martin is also a writer and he wrote a number of articles trying to promote my career. Martin also booked me on a two-week tour in England in July 1979. Jessie Yates from Batesville, Mississippi, went with me to sing harmony, and he really was a big help. The Roger Humphries Band that backed us was fantastic, and Jessie and I had a blast.

During the 1979 tour of England, we performed at several clubs, as well as an annual outdoor concert which was attended by over ten thousand people. Besides the shows, I did radio interviews throughout England and even got to do a little sightseeing. Martin Hawkins took Jessie and me to see Buckingham Palace and Big Ben in London, and he took us to Canterbury where we went through Canterbury Cathedral. Then, Roger Humphries took us to see Leeds Castle one day when we were performing in that area. I don't remember exactly where Leeds Castle is, but it was pretty neat. There was water all around the place with ducks swimming on the water. We were told that Franklin Roosevelt and Winston Churchill once held a summit there.

The most important accomplishment during my two weeks in England in 1979 was obtaining a contract with Charly Records for an album release. Charly Records is one of the top companies in England and has released numerous records on Sun Records' stars. Needless to say, I was proud to join their roster of artists.

In the summer of 1973 I went back to college at Mississippi Delta Junior College in Moorhead, Mississippi. I went straight through summer, fall, spring, and summer again to receive my Associate Arts Degree. Then, I started at Delta State University in the fall of 1974 and continued straight through. I graduated in May 1976 with a degree in accounting.

With a degree in accounting, I got another day job. I worked as an auditor with the State Tax Commission for six months, then the Internal Revenue Service for six months. Then, in June 1977, I got a job with the federal government examining savings and loan associations. I continued this job for sixteen years and three months - by far my longest day job. I was never home, but the money from my government job, my singing in the band, and Lois working for the Leflore County School District sure helped feed, clothe, and educate my two children.

My daughter, Cindy, graduated from high school at Pillow Academy in 1979 and went to Mississippi Delta Community College on a dance scholarship. She got married and wound up going only one semester. Like father, like daughter, only she didn't join the Marines like I did. On the serious side, though, Lois and I are quite proud of Cindy Boo. She has done well without a college degree, and the two grandchildren she gave us are priceless.

The seventies ended with my son Allen (of whom I am well pleased) being just two months and eleven days away from being a teenager. The decade also ended with the England tour fresh on my mind and my looking forward to the release of my album by Charly Records.

<u>1980-First Half</u>: Mack Allen Smith (lead singer), Laney O'Briant (lead guitar), Paul Melton (bass), Larry Acy (piano), and George Thomas (drums).

<u>1980-Last Half Through the End of 1982</u>: Mack Allen Smith (lead singer), Laney O'Briant (lead guitar), Tony Browning (bass), Chris Mims (keyboards), and George Thomas (drums).

<u>January 1983 to October 20, 1984</u>: Mack Allen Smith (lead singer), Laney O'Briant (lead guitar), David Lee Cox (keyboards and bass), and David Lee Cox, Jr. (drums).

On October 20, 1984 (my 46th birthday), I hung up my Rock-A-Billy shoes and retired from the honky-tonks. It seemed only fitting that my honky-tonk career end with David Lee Cox, who had been a member of the original 1959 band, being with me at the end, along with his son, Junior, on drums, who wasn't even born in 1959. And, of course, icing on the cake was having Laney O'Briant, who also played with me for a while in 1959, playing lead guitar for me when I finished my singing career in the honky-tonks.

<u>October 2002 to the present time</u>: After an eighteen year retirement from singing in a band I came out of retirement in October 2002 for a performance at the old school house in Black Hawk, Mississippi. My brother, Barry, talked me into starting back. He said they needed a rock-a-billy singer. Also, he told me it didn't pay anything. "Just doing it for fun," he said. Well, I did it then and I'm still doing it and I'm having fun. I do occasionally stumble across a paying gig, though. But not at Black Hawk.

We've also played old school houses in Carmack and Gore Springs, community houses in Carrollton and Winona, the Elks Lodge in Greenwood, and the Carroll County Market in Carrollton. Additionally, we have played a lot of benefits and festivals in various locations. Everything is gone except my vocal chords, but I thank God every day for keeping my vocal chords working like they should.

The current Mack Allen Smith and The Flames (some say Ashes) consist of the following: Mack Allen Smith (lead singer), Laney O'Briant (lead guitar), Barry Smith (bass), Jamie Winters (rhythm guitar, Benny Rigby (piano), and Stephen Winters (drums). Others that play from time to time are: Bill Walker (rhythm guitar), Murry Moorman (lead guitar), Steve McGregory (piano), Sanford Horton (bass), Gloria Hathcock (harmonica), Jamie Isanhood (piano), Randy Williamson (drums), and Michael Bole (drums).

I have also purchased about 200 karaoke CDs and do performances alone at nursing homes in Greenwood, Grenada, Vaiden, and Kosciusko. Further, I do one man shows for family reunions, birthday parties, class reunions, private parties, churches, etc.

Praise the Lord, I'm having fun. Please don't let it end anytime soon.

Chapter 4
Warren Smith

Warren Smith was born February 7, 1932, in Humphreys County, Mississippi, near Yazoo City. He died January 30, 1980, in Longview, Texas. Warren's parents divorced when he was young, and he was raised by his maternal grandparents in Louise, Mississippi, where they had a small farm and dry goods store.

In early December 1960, my telephone rang and when I answered, a voice on the other end of the line said, "Hi, this is Warren Smith." Initially, I thought it was a joke. I didn't recognize the voice but figured someone in my band had gotten someone to pull a prank. I decided to play along, so I said, "This is Mack Allen Smith, how may I help you." He said, "My wife, baby, and I will be staying here in Greenwood at my mother's house on West Adams for a few months so I'd like to hook up with a good band for a few gigs." He further stated, "I have been told that you have the best band around these parts."

After a little more chitchat he asked if I could come to Angelo's Cafe on Carrollton Avenue so we could talk about him joining me and The Flames. He said he would be sitting in a booth beside the front window. I told him I would come on down. I knew I would recognize him because we had played a show with him in 1956, and I had seen his picture a number of times in the Memphis and Greenwood newspapers. When I parked my car and stepped up on the sidewalk I looked through the front window and, sure enough, there in a booth beside the front window, was Warren Smith.

To make a long story short, Warren joined me and my band, and we played gigs throughout North Mississippi for three months. When he joined us he had already left Sun Records and had a big country hit on Liberty Records entitled, "I Don't Believe I'll Fall In Love Today." Before he left us and headed back to California, Liberty released his second single, "Odds and Ends, Bits and Pieces." It also went to the top of the national chart.

During the three months I was privileged to share a stage with Warren Smith, we played around 20 gigs. We played VFWs in Greenwood and Grenada, Moose Lodges, stage shows in Corinth and Columbus, and many other locations.

Warren Smith was without a doubt the best singer and entertainer I ever shared a stage with. I can still see Warren taking the stage and knocking 'em dead. This three month period was a magical time that I will remember as long as I live.

Warren and I became good friends, and I'll never forget when my daughter, Cindy, was born January 29, 1961, he came by our house with a present. He said, "You think you're the only one that ever had a baby, don't you?" Warren had a big boy about two years old at the time so he told me that anyone could have a girl. He told me that if I wanted a big boy like his, I would really have to keep my mind on what I was doing. What a crazy person! What a great singer, performer, and recording artist! Thank you, Warren, for causing our memory banks to be filled with really special and precious memories that linger. We miss you a lot.

Pertinent information about Warren Smith and his career is presented as follows:

Warren joined the Air Force in 1950 and while stationed in San Antonio, Texas, he learned to play the guitar to accompany his singing. After his discharge he moved to West Memphis, Arkansas, and got a gig singing at the Cotton Club. Stan Kessler, who was playing at the club, liked Warren's singing so much that he got him an audition for Sam Phillips at Sun Records. As they say: the rest is history.

Sam Phillips also liked Warren's singing. For his first single Phillips chose "Rock 'N' Roll Ruby," backed by "I'd Rather Be Safe Than Sorry." Warren Smith recorded "Rock 'N' Roll Ruby" on February 5, 1956, and by May 26, 1956, it had hit number one on the local pop charts. This first record for Sun outsold the first Sun releases by Elvis Presley, Johnny Cash, and Carl Perkins. "Rock 'N' Roll Ruby" went on to become a worldwide Rock-A-Billy classic.

Other Sun Records, besides Sun 239-"Rock 'N' Roll Ruby/ I'd Rather Be Safe Than Sorry": are: Sun 250-"Ubangi Stomp/Black Jack David" (September 1956), Sun 268-"So Long, I'm Gone/Miss Froggie" (April 1959), Sun 286-"Got Love If You Want It/ I Fell In Love" (1957), and Sun 314-"Goodbye My Love/Sweet Sweet Girl" (1959).

Besides the Sun recordings, Warren Smith recorded eight singles and one album for Liberty Records, one single for Warner Brothers, one single for Mercury, and three singles for Jubal Records. In addition, Bear Family Records in Germany released two CDs of Warren Smith recordings. The first was the Sun recordings, 1956-1959, (Bear Family BCD 15514), and the second was the Liberty recordings entitled "Call of the Wild" (Bear Family BCD 15495).

On August 17, 1965, Warren had a serious car accident in LaGrange, Texas. He suffered serious back injuries, which took him a year to recover from. By this time, his contract with Liberty had expired, and they chose not to renew it. After this, his addiction to pills and alcohol held him back. Finally, Smith's drug problems led to an 18-month term in an Alabama prison for robbing a pharmacy.

In 1977 with the Rock-A-Billy revival in full swing, Warren was invited to appear at London's Rainbow Theatre on a bill featuring Charlie Feathers, Buddy Knox, and Jack Scott. To his shock, Warren was received in London with standing ovations. His reception in England boosted his spirits and upon his return to the U.S., he began to perform with new found vigor. In November 1978, Warren and fellow Sun alumnus, Ray Smith, toured Europe, again to great success.

In 1980, while preparing for another European tour, Warren Smith died of a heart attack at 47 years of age.

References:

Extensive research by Martin Hawkins and Colin Escott has resulted in two books about Sun Records artists, including Warren Smith. They are "Sun Records" and "Good Rocking Tonight."

Additionally, much information can be found on the internet. One good source is: Warren Smith (Singer) - Wikipedia, the free encyclopedia.

Chapter 5
Barry Smith

Barry Smith was born January 25, 1940, in the Hickory Grove community of Carroll County, Mississippi, known as Little Texas. He graduated from J. Z. George High School in North Carrollton, Mississippi, in 1958 after which he attended Holmes Junior College in Goodman, Mississippi.

Like me, Barry's first exposure to music was listening to the Herberts (our mother, Fannie Mae Herbert Smith, and our two uncles, Jimmy Herbert and Archie Herbert). Also, when we went to town on Saturday, we would often stroll close to the railroad tracks in North Carrollton so we could hear blues music that was coming from black cafes on the black side of the tracks. Barry is the one who inherited the Herbert musical talent because all I could do was sing. Some call it hollering.

In 1961, Barry started playing bass in my band, Mack Allen Smith and The Flames. He played with me 12 years (1961-1973) and was the bass player on every song I recorded during that period of time. All total, Barry played bass on 43 songs that I recorded during that 12-year period.

I have to rate Barry as the best bass player to play with me throughout my singing career. He also plays guitar and sings and does a good job on both.

In the summer of 1947, we moved from Camp McCain in Elliott, Mississippi, to Carrollton, Mississippi, where Daddy opened a grocery store. This was just prior to my starting fourth grade and Barry second grade. We had living quarters in the back of the store. We didn't have a yard to play in, so we considered the whole town our playground. Barry and I both went to the Carrollton graveyard at night and put a quarter on the angel head so we could become full-fledged members of the two chase two gang. This led to many fun times for Barry and me. These fun times are described in more detail in my book, *Looking Back One Last Time - A Memoir*.

Regarding day jobs, Barry has worked for telephone companies since 1964. These companies are: Southern Bell, South Central Bell, Bell South, and now AT&T through Byars Engineering. He had a small stint as a cattle farmer but stated that it didn't take long to figure out that cattle farming was not for him.

Barry stated that his hobbies are hunting and fishing and playing music (country and gospel). I hope he will keep playing music for many more years. He's 15 months younger than I am, so he's got to keep going after I quit.

Barry has been married to Judy Acy since January 12, 1970. He has three sons, five grandsons, and one granddaughter. Barry and Judy live in Black Hawk, Mississippi, where monthly gigs are held at the old Black Hawk school house. Since it only takes Barry about five minutes to get from his house to the school house, he has no excuse not to keep pickin' and grinnin'.

Chapter 6
Billy Wayne Herbert

Billy Wayne Herbert, the son of Archie Herbert and Gladys (Vance) Herbert, was born on November 28, 1939, in the Hickory Grove community of Carroll County, Mississippi, known as Little Texas. He died July 4, 2007, at a hospital in Memphis, Tennessee. Billy Wayne had a home on a lake near Hernando, Mississippi, when he died. He had been living there about 25 years.

Being the son of Archie Herbert, who played guitar, bass, and fiddle, Billy Wayne got plenty of exposure to music at an early age. He sat in a corner with me and my brother, Barry, at those old country dances where the Herberts (my mama, Fannie Mae; Uncle Archie; and Uncle Jimmy) played on Saturday nights.

Before getting into more music stuff, I want to tell about an experience Billy Wayne and I had with people coming out of graves at Hickory Grove Cemetery. I was in the second grade and Billy Wayne was in the first grade. Each day I waked two miles from Granddaddy and Mammie Herbert's house, where I lived, to Hickory Grove Church where Billy Wayne and I caught the school bus to Carrollton. Billy Wayne lived about 100 yards from the bus stop, so he would wait for me and we'd walk together to the bus stop.

Billy Wayne and I were passing through the cemetery on our way to the school bus stop when we saw a man's coat come flying out of an open grave. As it turned out, the man was a grave digger who was digging a grave for some dearly departed, but Billy Wayne and I thought it was a dead person who was digging himself out of his grave. We turned and ran back to Billy Wayne's house and told Aunt Gladys that dead people were digging themselves out of their graves. Aunt Gladys said I was the spokesman for the duo and that our eyes were as big as saucers.

As noted in Chapter 3, Billy Wayne played in my first band in 1956. He also played on the 1959 Sun recording where we recorded four songs with me singing ("Mean Woman Blues", "Sandy Lee", "Kansas City", and "Young Dreams"). Billy Wayne also wrote "Sandy Lee."

After graduating from J. Z. George High School in North Carrollton, Mississippi, Billy Wayne went to Ole Miss on a NROTC scholarship. Not only did Billy Wayne get the Herbert musical talent, he also got the Herbert smarts. In fact, he was salutatorian of his 1957 graduating class at J. Z. George. As for me, I graduated near the bottom of my class in 1956.

At Ole Miss, Billy Wayne joined the Ole Miss Downbeats on lead guitar. In 1959, after returning from the Marines, I went to several Downbeat dances with Billy Wayne, and they were without doubt in the same league with the best around. Details of this group will be presented in Chapter 9 entitled: Ole Miss Downbeats - 1954-1966.

Billy Wayne graduated from Ole Miss in 1961 and under the terms of his NROTC scholarship, he was required to serve six years as an officer in the Navy. During this six year period, he always managed to have a band. He served in Corpus Christi for most of his term and after his discharge in 1957 remained there for three more years to work a job in civil service. His playing in a band continued, and they must have been good because they were the opening act for a number of big stars at large halls and coliseums in Corpus Christi and surrounding areas.

In 1970, Larry Rogers, who had been a classmate of Billy Wayne's brother, Durwood, at Ole Miss persuaded Billy Wayne to quit his civil service job in Corpus Christi and move to Memphis and become a studio musician (on guitar and harmonica). Billy Wayne was building government retirement on his civil service job, and his six years in the Navy counted toward his retirement. Billy Wayne told me that he had to think long and hard before making the move but, in the end, his love for music won out.

When Billy Wayne moved to Memphis from Corpus Christi in 1970, two of his musicians came with him: Pete Bartosch (bass) and Ronnie Korner (drums). Besides working at Lyn-Lou Studio, they started playing at the Airport Lounge. This group, which was called "The Revelations," added Don Chandler on organ. Later, they added James Govan (singer) and changed the name of the group to Stone Blue. Details of this group will be presented in Chapter 44 entitled: Stone Blue-1972-80. I booked Stone Blue at my club in Greenwood, Mississippi, in 1973 for a Battle of Bands with me and my band (Mack Allen Smith and The Flames). If my memory serves me right, I think Stone Blue kicked our butts.

I'm not sure when Billy Wayne stopped working as a studio picker at Lyn-Lou Studio in Memphis, but in checking my Discography I found no sessions of mine after 1972 with Billy Wayne playing. I moved back to Greenwood in 1969 but continued recording at Lyn-Lou through 1981. In 1975 Shylo (Ronnie Scaife, lead guitar; Danny Hogan (bass); Butch Carter (piano); and Perry York (drums), started playing on my sessions whenever I used the studio band. Whatever happened between Billy Wayne and Larry Rogers I don't have a clue. I do know that Larry started doing studio work in Nashville and for several years he split his time between Memphis and Nashville. My records show that in 1980, I started recording my demos at the Billy Herbert Studio in Memphis and later at the Billy Herbert Studio near Hernando, Mississippi. According to Jim Rorie, he, Billy Wayne Herbert, and Maurice McGehee formed a group in 1971 called Black Gold and leased the Lyn-Lou Studio from Larry Rogers for a while. They also had Song City Music Publishing Company. Song City Music Publishing has one-half publishing on two songs I cut at Lyn-Lou in 1970, "I'm Not Drunk I'm Just Drinking" and "Do It To Them First." Not only did Billy Wayne play on these two songs, he produced the recordings.

While recording with artists in Memphis, Billy Wayne was fortunate enough to land some decent recording gigs. Specifically, he played bass on an album by Tony Joe White (the Polk Salad Annie man), and in 1975 Jerry Reed recorded Rooster Jones, a song co-written by Billy Wayne Herbert and Jim Rorie. As for his live shows while in Memphis, Billy Wayne has shared the stage with just about everybody (from Steve Cropper to Chuck Berry).

When Stone Blue broke up, Billy Wayne started doing a one-man show. He played lead guitar and harmonica, and he had an electric drummer and bass to keep the beat.

He also did the singing. Billy Wayne continued doing the one-man show for 27 years until he died on July 4, 2007.

Since Billy Wayne had his own recording studio the last 27 years of his life and recorded lots of songs that were never released because of his three year battle with cancer and other reasons perhaps, no one really knows for sure how many songs he wrote and recorded that were never mixed down to CD format. Jim Rorie, a friend of Billy Wayne's, estimates that it could be as many as 100 songs or more. Jim said that even when Billy Wayne was sick he wrote and recorded a song almost every day. This is possible because he had a studio and he played all the instruments.

I have six CDs that Billy Wayne recorded in his basement studio near Hernando, Mississippi, as follows:

Title	Number of songs
"Big Money"	15
"A Hollywood Night"	13
"Lay With Me"	15
"Delta Moon"	17
"Mostly Mississippi"	16
"Southern Style"	20

I am also aware that Billy Wayne recorded a gospel CD entitled, "Home Coming". He wrote all of the songs, and three were played at his funeral.

He recorded CDs to sell on his gigs, and I have been told that he sold quite a few. If a major label with worldwide distribution could get a hold (with estate permission) of all the songs Billy Wayne wrote and recorded, they might just find some treasures in those jewel cases and un-mixed masters.

Besides the Billy Wayne Herbert CDs, Billy Wayne recorded and played all the instruments on two Jim Rorie CDs, "Memphis Blues," and "One More for the Ditch." Both CDs have 12 songs each. "One More for the Ditch" was released by Scana Records in Sweden. For more information about Jim Rorie see Chapter 11.

Billy Wayne's gigs as a one-man band included The Hollywood, Ramada Inn on Brooks Road in Memphis, casinos in Tunica, Mississippi, river boats, and private parties. The last gig Billy Wayne played was at the Community House in Carrollton, Mississippi, on June 2, 2007. I'm happy to say that I was there because one month and two days later Billy Wayne died on July 4, 2007. At that final performance I believe he sounded better than I had ever heard him. When Billy Wayne headed for the stage, I told him to go break a leg. But, I believe the Lord looked down and said, "Son, I'm with you and I'm gonna see that your final performance is your best ever." And, it certainly was.

I sent Larry Rogers in Nashville a copy of the newspaper article that Susie James wrote about the show, then later I sent him a copy of Billy Wayne's obituary. I got a letter from Larry saying, "What's going on - you send me an article about Billy Wayne knocking 'em out at the Community House in Carrollton, then you send me his obituary." Larry talked a little more about Billy Wayne then he asked, "Was Billy Wayne happy and content with his life?"

I remembered asking Billy Wayne several years ago if he ever wished he had stayed with his government job. I said, "You could be retired now with 40 years of service time and drawing a big check each month." Billy Wayne said, "If I had stayed with the federal government I would be better off financially today, I suppose, but I don't want to start second guessing my decision this late in the game. Besides," he said, "I've been doing what I love to do for a long time now."

Then, I remembered Billy Wayne's last gig at the Community House again. During his performance, he said, "You know, most people have jobs and they get up and go to work each day. But, as for me, I just go out at night and sing and play my music." Why he said this in the middle of his performance I don't know.

When I answered Larry's letter, I said, "Yes, Larry, I think Billy Wayne was happy and content with his life. He owned a house on a lake with a recording studio in the basement. And he lived there with over 50 guitars. And, besides that, he sang and played his music until the end."

Billy Wayne Herbert was one of a kind. From the time he moved to Memphis in 1970 until he died 37 years later on July 4, 2007, he never worked a day job. He just went out at night and sang and played his music. And, I might add, he did it well.

Chapter 7
Durwood Dale Herbert

Durwood Herbert (my first cousin) was born December 26, 1942, in Carroll County, Mississippi. He died October 13, 1963, and is buried in Evergreen Cemetery near North Carrollton, Mississippi.

Durwood attended J. Z. George High School in North Carrollton, Mississippi. He graduated in 1961. After high school, Durwood attended Ole Miss at Oxford, Mississippi. He was a junior when he got killed in a car wreck between Clarksdale and Greenwood. His major at Ole Miss was pharmacy.

As discussed in Chapter 3, Durwood played drums in the original 1959 Mack Allen Smith and The Flames band. He played drums on the 1959 Sun Studio recordings and came back from Ole Miss to play on the first two singles we recorded for Vee Eight Records in 1962.

When Durwood quit my band in 1961 and left for Ole Miss we really struggled for a while. To say that Durwood was hard to replace would be an understatement.

At Ole Miss, Durwood played bass with The Confederates and drums with the Ole Miss Downbeats. Durwood's older brother, Billy Wayne, played with the Dowbeats before Durwood arrived at Ole Miss and, like Billy Wayne, Durwood did the Herbert name proud by carrying on this quality tradition.

I'll never forget the phone call I got from my daddy at 5:00 AM on October 13, 1963. I was half asleep when he said that Durwood had been killed in a car wreck. I thought at first that I was dreaming. I wish I had been. That phone call is one I will never forget, and Durwood Herbert is one person I will never forget.

Chapter 8
Joseph Terry Herbert

Joseph Terry Herbert was born October 8, 1948, in the hospital at Grenada, Mississippi. At that time, the Herbert family lived in the Hickory Grove community of Carroll County, Mississippi. He is known by everyone as just Terry Herbert. Terry graduated from J. Z. George High School at North Carrollton, Mississippi, in 1966. After high school, Terry attended Holmes Junior College in Goodman, Mississippi, where he received an Associates Arts degree in 1968. Then, Terry attended Ole Miss at Oxford, Mississippi, for one and one-half years. Terry had a 30-year career after college with the federal government's Soil Conservation Service.

Since Terry's brothers (Billy Wayne and Durwood) are highlighted in Chapters 6 & 7, I decided to highlight Terry here in Chapter 8.

The Terry Herbert story is as presented to me by Terry, after his wife Cathy did her edit and rewrite:

"As a ten year old boy raised in a household of musicians, I was often in awe of the talent. Not only did my father and two brothers play, but cousins Mack Allen Smith and Barry Smith played as well.

In his youth my father, Archie Herbert, played fiddle and guitar throughout Carroll County for country dances. He also was known to have jam sessions with John Hurt, a well-known blues artist. My father taught me the first chord on a guitar when I was fourteen. He taught me the basics of chord progression. He had no formal training and did not know some chords; he just made them up until they sounded right. I never developed that ability. I, too, never learned to read music and play totally by ear.

Both of my brothers, Billy Wayne and Durwood, played in Mack Allen's band. In 1959 Durwood, who was only sixteen, played drums with Mack. I remember listening to Mack's band practice either at their house or ours. Durwood played with Mack Allen until he left to attend Ole Miss in 1961. I was just fifteen when tragedy struck our family. On October 13, 1963, Durwood was killed in an automobile accident south of Webb, Mississippi. Just before Durwood was killed he had started to play bass guitar. He owned a Silvertone bass that I inherited, and my love for playing music was solidified.

When I was a junior in high school a classmate, George McCrory, was putting together a FFA (Future Farmers of America band) for a talent contest. The contest was held at Tallatchie County school. I know very little about the bass. George was a guitar and bass player, and he showed me the basic runs and note patterns. The FFA band members were George McCrory on guitar, Ronny Smith on drums, Kenny McCrory on trumpet, Ronnie Turner and Freddy Mullen on vocals, and me on bass. If memory serves me correctly we placed second in the talent contest.

In 1965 I was contacted by the Costilow brothers, Felix and PeeWee, about playing in their band, The Lost Chords, an appropriate name for a group of teenage musicians.

After suffering the loss of my brother, my mother, Gladys Herbert, was not pleased that I, too, wanted to join the music business. Against her wishes I joined the band anyway. The British invasion was in full swing during this time and we played songs by the Beatles, Rolling Stones, and others. Our first paying gig was at the Youth Center in Greenwood, Mississippi. We agreed to play for "the door." I believe our net earnings for the night were $5.00. We were not discouraged; we thought we had become PROS. The Lost Chords members were PeeWee Costilow on vocals, Felix Costilow on rhythm guitar, Warren Lee McNeer on lead guitar, Butch Buck on drums, and me on bass. The band was finally booked to play at a nightclub in Canton, Mississippi, called The Stork Club. I was seventeen years old; PeeWee was eighteen; Felix was fifteen; Warren Lee was sixteen; and Butch, who had been in the Navy, was in his early twenties. I still do not know how we were booked in that club at our age; I guess they just didn't ask. I remember walking into that club and feeling petrified. I had never been inside of a nightclub and did not know that sort of atmosphere existed. The air was thick with smoke; the lights were dim; beer cans were everywhere; and the ladies were dressed for temptation. I remember my first thought was, "Mother would kill me if she knew where I was." I saw my first bar fight that night, which did not help the state of my nerves any. The Lost Chords played several more gigs before we broke up, including a talent show at Holmes Jr. College. Our final gig was at my high school prom, a picture of which is in the J. Z. George School album.

In 1970, the Undertakers, another appropriately named band, needed a bass player. I agreed to play with them. We practiced a lot but did not play many dates. The band members were Frank Montgomery on rhythm guitar, Kenny Whitfield on lead guitar; Dave Belcher on drums, and me on bass guitar. Our last gig was the Community House in Carrollton, Mississippi.

I spent several years away from the music business, and during this time I met and married my wife, Kathy Downs, in 1976. Kathy and I became parents in 1982. Our twin daughters, Josie Lee and Jessie Lynn Herbert, were born. Sadly, Jessie Lynn died at birth. One of my fondest memories of Josie's early childhood is of my playing guitar and she and I singing together. In 2002, I, along with Under the Gun, performed for Josie and her husband, Lee Bidwell, at their wedding reception. What memories this life has given me.

While our children were small, a lifelong friend of mine, Jackie McIlwain, another guitar player, and I would get together for weekend jam sessions. In 1967 I met Carl Hopkins at a tee ball practice where his son and my daughter were playing. I learned that Carl sang and sounded a great deal like Randy Travis. He soon joined our weekend jam sessions. In 1992 Jackie asked his friend, Allen Malone, a lead guitarist, to come sit in with us. Things evolved from weekend jam sessions to the formation of a band. I switched to bass guitar, Jackie on rhythm guitar, Allen on lead guitar and vocals, and Carl on vocals. All we needed for a complete band was a drummer. I bought an electric drum machine and we named it "Freddie". Freddie had a mind of his own but sure didn't talk back much. The Rockin' Rhythm band was formed. The band played for class reunions, the Carrollton Pilgrimage, and even played on the C&G railroad train from North Carrollton to Greenwood, Mississippi. That was the last time passengers rode the train before it closed in 2002. Rockin' Rhythm changed its name several times. It was also called C.C. Junction for a short time.

In 1995 the band's present name, Under the Gun, stuck. The original band members were Jackie McIlwain, Allen Malone, Carl Hopkins, me, and a few different drummers including Michael Boles, who is the current drummer for the new popular band Crossin' Dixon. In 2002 Under the Gun decided to broaden the venues we would play to include nightclubs. At this time Carl decided to leave the band. Allen asked a fellow musician, Ken Spencer, to join us. Ken came on board as a guitarist and a vocalist, and Robbie Browning was hired on drums. The band became very busy very quickly. We were booked at clubs, festivals, and weddings almost every weekend. In late 2000 Robbie left the band and Alan Abbott was hired on drums. I also left the band at this time and Scottie Winters was hired to play bass. In October 2001 Abbott left and Scottie switched to drums. I returned to play bass. My first gig back was to play for the dedication of the Carrollton Community House. This gig was special because both of my brothers and I had played there in our younger years. It was also the place my twin sister, Sally Mary, and I chose to host our family reunions called "The Herbert Down Home Pickins," a time when all family musicians such as Billy Wayne, Mack Allen, Barry, and me, along with Under the Gun, shared the stage. A short time later I returned to the band after Allen Malone left and Robert Ray was hired.

Under the Gun has had the pleasure of opening for a number of national acts such as T. Graham Brown, Trick Pony, Percy Sledge, Billy Joe Royal, and popular group Crossin Dixon. The band also played numerous festivals including Grenada, Mississippi, Whittington Park in Greenwood, Mississippi, Ham Jam in Philadelphia, Mississippi, and Delta Jubilee in Clarksdale, Mississippi.

A long time goal of the band was to play casinos. It proved to be difficult to break into that circuit but not impossible. Under the Gun has been booked at the Isle of Capri casino in Lulu, Mississippi, the Jubilee and Lighthouse casinos in Greenville, Mississippi, and with the help of a booking agent, we played Bally's in Tunica, Mississippi, resorts in Tunica, and Harlows in Greenville, Mississippi. Playing the casinos afforded a small town band some great experiences. I met and joined Ronnie Milsap for lunch at Harlows.

During all of these musical endeavors I also maintained a "day job". In 2006 I retired from the federal government with thirty years of service. At that time I decided to throw my hat into the political arena and in 2007 was elected as a county supervisor for Carroll County.

In the fall of 2009 I announced my retirement from Under the Gun. I wanted to spend more time with my grandson, Caleb Leflore "Boone" Bidwell, born in June of 2008. One of his first words was guitar. He loves to visit and sit on Pop's knee to play my guitar. I am hoping he will continue the musical traditions that run so deeply through my family.

As for me, I will continue to be involved with music in some way - whether on stage or as Boone's biggest fan."

I want to add that Terry is a fine bass player and I have enjoyed singing with Terry and Under the Gun a number of times since I came out of my eighteen-year retirement in October 2002. Also, Terry left Under the Gun at the end of 2009 and has since played rhythm guitar with me.

MACK ALLEN SMITH

Chapter 9
The Downbeats / Ole Miss Downbeats
(1954 – 1965)

Ed Forsythe, a member of the original Downbeats, wrote an article for inclusion in the book: "History of Montgomery County, Mississippi," copyright Curtis Media Corporation, 1993. Ed sets the record straight about when the Downbeats were formed. (Some writings I've seen show 1959 was when they were organized; this is not correct according to Ed Forsythe, and he should know since he was there.)

The Ed Forsythe article entitled the Downbeats is presented as follows:

"This band was organized in August 1954 and original members were Ed Forsythe (drums), Sam Waldrup (saxophone), Guy Fisher (saxophone), Buddy Flowers (piano, arranger, and acknowledged leader), Tommy Gray (trombone), and Hershel Slaughter (bass)."

The group's first public appearance came as a result of a broken PA system. A dance was held at the Community House in Winona after each home football game and the music was provided by a record player connected to a PA system. The class sponsoring the dance was notified that the system was not working, and this prompted the sponsor to contact the Downbeats about playing for the dance. Since the PA system was rented for $25.00, that amount was paid to the band.

At the time the band was organized, Buddy Flowers was a student at Ole Miss. The other members attended Winona High School. After graduating high school in the spring of 1955 three members Ed Forsythe, Guy Fisher, and Tommy Gray joined Flowers at Ole Miss where they recruited five additional members and quickly became one of the most popular bands in the state.

The band operated under the name Downbeats until 1965 and during that time (1954-1965) had 33 different members."

I want to thank Buddy Flowers' sister (Lillian Kent McFarland) for all the pertinent information she provided.

The two original members that I knew best and had some contact with over the years have passed away.

1. Buddy Flowers (piano, arranger and leader) - Born: January 8, 1935, in Kilmichael, Mississippi; died March 19, 1993 in Syracuse, New York. After the Downbeats Buddy did some one-man gigs at local lounges, country clubs, etc. He also played some with Grover Duke and the Cavilers before moving to New York. Buddy is buried at Oakwood Cemetery in Winona.

2. Ed Forsythe (drums) - Born: March 19, 1937, in Memphis, Tennessee. Later the family moved to Jackson, Mississippi, before finally setting in Winona, Mississippi; died November 6, 2007, in Winona, Mississippi. After the Downbeats, Ed returned to his

hometown of Winona where he had a long and distinguished career in the insurance business. Ed is buried at Oakwood Cemetery in Winona.

When I returned from the Marines to Carrollton, Mississippi, in January 1959, the first person to call me was my first cousin, Billy Wayne Herbert. He called to tell me about this great band he was playing lead guitar with at Ole Miss. He talked about how they were kicking butt everywhere and that I just had to come hear them. Well, to make a long story short, so to speak, I did go hear the Downbeats, and they were everything Billy Wayne said they were and then some. Like ole Dizzy Dean said many years ago: "If you can do it, it ain't bragging." I have to say they could flat do it. I came, I heard, I saw - I was conquered.

Needless to say, after hearing the Downbeats once, I had to go some more. Like Lays Potato chips, you can't eat just one. I went with Billy Wayne to several Downbeat dances. I remember one was in downtown Grenada and another was in a high school gym in Belzoni where the Downbeats battled the Rolling Stones (not the ones from England - this was before their time). Not since hearing the Red Tops in 1956 had I heard another band anywhere close to the Downbeats.

Members of the Downbeats that I heard in 1959 & 1960 are as follows: Buddy Flowers (piano, arranger, and leader), Billy Wayne Herbert (lead guitar), Ed Forsythe (drums), Tommy Gray (bass), Jim Slocum (saxophone), Tommy Christopher (saxophone), Leon DeLoach (trumpet), and Bobby Jones (singer and trombone). Jim Slocum came to the Grenada VFW and played sax with me and my band (Mack Allen Smith & The Flames) several times in 1959 & 1960.

After Billy Wayne Herbert graduated in 1961 and left for the Navy, his brother Durwood Herbert graduated from high school and started attending Ole Miss in the fall of 1961. Like Billy Wayne, Durwood was honored to become a member of the Downbeats. He played drums. I don't know if they were the only brothers to play with the Downbeats since I don't have a list of all 33 members, but I suspect they were. Billy Wayne and Durwood are highlighted in chapters six and seven respectively.

The Downbeats recorded two singles in 1960 for Ardent Records in Memphis, Tennessee, where they were billed Ole Miss Downbeats. They were the first band to record for Ardent. The Ole Miss Downbeats' singles are as follows:

Ardent 101 - Hucklebuck/Slewfoot

Ardent 103- Geraldine/Mr. Crump

Sometime after the Downbeats recorded for Ardent, John Fry closed his studio. He started up again in 1966 and has been going strong ever since. In 2006 he had a forty year celebration (1966-2006) with tee shirts and all. Based on artists listed on the back of the Ardent tee shirt, about everyone has recorded there. Some of the artists that have recorded at Ardent from 1966 to the present time are: The Fabulous Thunderbirds, Led Zepplin, 3 Doors Down, Cheap Trick, ZZ Top, Bob Dylan, Stevie Ray Vaughan, Box Tops, Lynard Skynard, B. B. King, Isaac Hayes, Leon Russell, Tanya Tucker, Waylon Jennings, the Allmon Brothers, and Travis Tritt, just to name a few.

Regarding the Downbeats, they are not remembered as much for their recordings as they are for the great band they were. With the great horn section made better with those Buddy Flowers arrangements and Billy Wayne Herbert knocking the walls down with Bo Diddley, the Downbeats' legacy lives on, not only in Mississippi but throughout the mid-south, in the hearts of all who were fortunate enough to hear them. I'm proud to say I'm one of the fortunate ones who heard them.

By the time we are all gone, the Downbeats' legacy will be so ingrained into southern musical history that I believe they will live forever. Not bad for a band that was started in Winona, Mississippi, by a few country boys who started out playing for $25.00 per gig.

Chapter 10
Red McGregor

Red McGregor was born March 1, 1931, in Carrollton, Mississippi. He died February 1, 2000, in Carrollton and is buried in Evergreen Cemetery near North Carrollton.

Red graduated from J. Z. George High School at North Carrollton in 1951. After graduating from high school, Red served in the Army during the Korean War. He was engaged in combat as a member of the Army Tank Division.

I met Red McGregor while I was in grammar school and, although, he was several years older than I was, he became my best friend. After school in the fall I couldn't wait to get out of school and head for the pasture in front of Red's house where we played football. Red was on the J. Z. George High School football team where he played end and was famous for the end around. Since Red was a star at J. Z. George, his function at the pasture was to referee the game and oversee the activities.

Beside football, Red used to sit on his porch and play rhythm guitar while he sang Hank Williams and other country songs. I spent many hours on Red's porch just listening and, I suppose, taking mental notes for future reference.

During my childhood days and throughout life, Red McGregor was not only my best friend, he was one of my heroes. The number one hero in my life was, of course, my daddy. He and Red were also good friends.

As discussed in Chapter 3, I re-formed the Flames after returning from the Marines in January 1959. Red was a member of the original 1959 Mack Allen Smith & The Flames. Red played rhythm guitar and took care of the rest of us. Specifically, Red didn't drink, and he never went to sleep in a moving vehicle. Therefore, he usually drove the band home. When I insisted on driving, Red watched me like a hawk watching a chicken because I drank too much and, sometimes, saw things in the road that weren't really there. Once I saw a man run across the road between me and a truck I was meeting. I slammed on the brakes and slid about fifty yards, throwing bodies all over the place, and Red was shouting, "What the hell are you doing?" I said, "Red, didn't you see that man run between me and that truck?" For a few seconds there was silence, then Red said, "Pull this van over on the shoulder and get your ass from behind that steering wheel, and don't ever plan on driving again."

Red played rhythm guitar on the 1959 session at Sun Records' studio in Memphis, and he played on both sides of my first two singles in 1962 that were recorded at Hi Recording Studio in Memphis and released on Vee Eight Records. For details see the Appendix.

After the Vee Eight records in 1962, Red left the band. He was several years older than I was and, I believe, he was much wiser. I guess Red got tired of coming home in the wee hours of the morning, as well as other things that go along with playing in the honky-tonks. I hated to see him leave the band, but I understood.

When I returned from the Marines in 1959 and re-formed the Flames, Red was working for Supreme Electronics in Greenwood, Mississippi. After Supreme, he worked for the Winona Times newspaper in Winona, Mississippi. Red later became a corrections officer for the State of Mississippi, and when he reached retirement age he retired and started drawing his state retirement.

Over the years Red McGregor was a big supporter of education for children. In fact, one of his crowning achievements, that he was extremely proud of, was being one of the founders of Carroll Academy in Carrollton, Mississippi.

I stayed in touch with Red over the years and was honored to be an honorary pall bearer at his funeral.

In conclusion I say: "Red McGregor, I salute you. Thanks for fighting in Korea, and supporting us for many years at home. You were a class act like none I've ever known. Thank you for being my very best friend."

Chapter 11
Jim Rorie

Jim Rorie was born January 28, 1939, at New Albany, Mississippi. He graduated from Amory High School at Amory, Mississippi, in 1956.

My connection to Jim Rorie is through my first cousin, Billy Wayne Herbert. He and Billy Wayne were friends and partners in the Memphis music scene for 37 years (1970 until Billy's death in 2007). Jim and Billy Wayne were partners in Song City Music Publishing Company which owned publishing on two songs I wrote and recorded at Lyn-Lou Studio in Memphis in 1970.

Jim grew up in Amory, Mississippi, which is just a hop, skip, and a jump from New Albany where he was born. After graduating from high school in 1956, Jim spent a few months in Los Angeles, and four years in Chicago before moving to Memphis in 1960.

In 1963, Jim went to work for Delta Airlines at the Memphis airport where he worked for 30 years. He still kept on the fringes of Memphis music, occasionally doing a gig with friends. Jim also joined friends Billy Wayne Herbert and Maurice McGehee in forming Block 6 Recording and Song City Publishing Company. They also owned the Cotton Records label. The Block 6 group worked out of Lyn-Lou Recording Studio at 1518 Chelsea Avenue, which they leased from Larry Rogers.

Jim managed popular singer James Govan for a couple of years and enjoyed some writing success in 1975 when Jerry Reed recorded "Rooster Jones," a song co-written by Jim and Billy Wayne Herbert.

After the Jerry Reed recording in 1975, Block 6 closed and Jim formed Jim Rorie Music, a BMI affiliate that is still in operation today. Jim has continued to write, often with his friend, Jerry Ward. In 1981, Don McMinn recorded Jim's song, "The Blue Light Christmas Tree." Like a lot of other wannabes, Jim couldn't break the Nashville barrier so in 1994, he formed his own record label, JIRO Records and started recording his own songs. Jim also returned to performing, often appearing at clubs and festivals across the country.

In 2007, Scana Records, a Swedish record label, released a CD with Jim singing 12 songs on which he was writer or co-writer. The songs were recorded at the Billy Herbert Studio in Hernando, Mississippi, and Billy Wayne Herbert played all the instruments on these recordings. The CD entitled "One More For the Ditch" has received air play throughout Europe, Australia, and New Zealand (17 foreign countries altogether).

Jim has six CDs for sale on his website: www.jimrorie.com. He is currently working on a new CD of Memphis songs.

HISTORY OF THE AIRPORT LOUNGE

Since Jim Rorie was instrumental in the birth of the infamous Airport Lounge in Memphis, I felt compelled to present his story. Jim's story as given to me by him in writing is presented as follows:

"Bill Norton was the manager of the Tropical Club where Willie Mitchell played in the early 1960s and he and I became friends. He came by my apartment one night in 1964 and some of my musician friends and I were practicing. He listened for a while and said, "You guys ought to come down to the club and play some night." I said, "What club?"

He and Leo Peiraccini who owned the Tropical Club were opening up a new lounge and cafeteria on Winchester down from the airport. It was to be called the B & L Cafeteria and Lounge. The area had just voted in alcohol, and it would be the first club in the area to sell beer. I told him to let us practice for a week or two and we might do that. I was in charge of the Delta Airlines picnic that we held each year at Ellendale Park, and we always had a large crowd in attendance. Delta also had a stewardess base in Memphis then, and we had 75 or 100 good looking young ladies in our entourage. I planned our debut at the new club for the evening after the picnic and set it up with Bill. At 7:00 o'clock that night, we shut down the beer truck at the picnic and told everyone that we were playing at the B & L Lounge on Winchester at 9:00. It was like the Pied Piper leading the flock of mice; everybody showed up. Norton was ringing the cash register and grinning from ear to ear. He thought that he had discovered the Memphis version of the Beatles. He asked us to come back the next Friday and Saturday night, and we filled the place again. Two weeks later, they closed the cafeteria portion and made it part of the lounge. They put an airplane on the roof and renamed the place The Airport Lounge. It remained so until the airport expansion leveled the whole block 30 years later."

Jim Rorie and his band, which was formed in 1963 as Daddy Rube and the Renegades, were the house band at the Airport Lounge their first year in operation. During the lounge's 30 years of operation, many guest musicians and singers graced their stage, and they will long be remembered as one of the top watering holes in Memphis, Tennessee, if not the entire state and nation.

To leave this chapter without mentioning some of the stars that Jim Rorie has been associated with would be a huge injustice. The list of stars presented here is not all inclusive, but rather from pictures of Jim and various stars shown in the liner notes of his Sweden CD, "One More For the Ditch." They are as follows: Carl Perkins, Jerry Lee Lewis, Charlie Pride, Merle Travis, and Vince Gill.

Where Jim Rorie grew up in Amory, Mississippi, is just a short distance from Tupelo where Elvis Presley was born and spent his early years. Jim may not be a household name around the world like Elvis, but for an ole country boy from Amory, Mississippi, he has sure rubbed elbows with a lot of big stars. It's kinda like the old country song, "I Did the Best I Could With What I Had." Jim Rorie has done that and then some, if that's possible.

Chapter 12
Jerry Jaye

Jerry Jaye was born October 19, 1937, in Manila, Arkansas. I have heard that when Jerry was born he was singing "Hello Josephine." Reportedly, Jerry has denied this allegation or, at least, claims he can't remember.

The first time I heard the name Jerry Jaye was when a radio disc jockey was introducing "Hello Josephine." Jerry had recorded the song at Roland James Sonic Studio in Memphis for $13.00, and the record was first released "Hello Josephine" on Jaye's own Connie Label (named after his daughter). Joe Cuoghi re-released the record on his Hi label in February 1967 with its correct title, "My Girl Josephine." As they say, the rest is history. "My Girl Josephine" cracked the billboard charts in April 1967, eventually peaking at number 29.

I first met Jerry Jaye in May, 1971, when I booked him at my club (Mack Allen Smith's Town & Country Night Club) in Greenwood, Mississippi. Band members at that time were as follows: Jerry Jaye (guitar and singer), Bobby Neal (lead guitar), Ben Jacks (steel guitar), Jerry Ward (bass), and Roger Fry (drums). Bobby Neal will be highlighted in the following chapter.

I booked Jerry a number of times at my club, and several times we had a battle of the bands. Jerry is a great singer and musician and we always had a packed house whenever he was there. My band (Mack Allen Smith and The Flames) also battled Jerry Jaye and his band (The Jaywalkers) several times at the Greenwood Moose Lodge.

Regarding Jerry's recording career, he was never able to capture the magic again like he did when he recorded that Fats Domino song ("Hello Josephine," aka "My Girl Josephine"). He even tried another Fats Domino song, "Let the Four Winds Blow"; however, lightning just wouldn't strike twice and, subsequently, follow-ups failed to sell. In 1975 Larry Rogers produced a Jerry Jaye album for Hi Records at the Lyn-Lou Studio in Memphis entitled "Honky Tonk Women Love Redneck Men."

According to Colin Escott, a noted writer and music critic, "Honky Tonk Women Love Redneck Men," was Jaye's finest work- a superlative collection released on the wrong label roughly ten years too soon." Regarding "Hello Josephine," Mr. Escott stated: "At the very least, Jerry Jaye cut the last hit record that cost $13.00 to record."

Jerry and wife, Darlene Battles, who is a fine singer and composer in her own right, played their first overseas show in Sweden in 1995. This was followed the same year by a series of shows in the U.K. In 1999, the couple returned to Sweden for another successful tour. This time Jerry went into the recording studio and laid down a track with Scandinavian rocker Teddy Hill.

Jerry and Darlene currently live in Gulfport, Mississippi. They have been on the Mississippi gulf coast for 30 years. I recently talked to Jerry and learned that he didn't have his own band anymore but was playing steel guitar with five different bands.

I have heard Jerry Jaye sing, play sax, and play steel guitar. I suppose he can play anything. Most people are lucky if they get a job playing in one band, but Jerry plays steel guitar with five different bands. When you think about it, that's really remarkable. In fact, those two words could be used to describe Jerry Jaye - <u>REALLY REMARKABLE</u>.

In 2007, Larry Rogers recorded a ten-song CD on Jerry at his studio in Nashville. As Larry stated in the liner notes, the same magic that Jerry brought to the studio in Memphis is still with him. Naturally, this CD includes Jerry's million seller, "Hello Josephine." According to Jerry, these ten songs can be downloaded from the internet.

For more information write:

Lyn-Lou Records
P. O. Box 50381
Nashville, TN 37205
1-800-327-4927

The CD is dedicated to Bobby Neal, Jerry's original lead guitar player, who died in the Ricky Nelson plane crash December 31, 1985.

Chapter 13
Bobby Neal

Bobby Neal was born July 19, 1947, in Parkin, Arkansas. He died December 31, 1985, in the Ricky Nelson plane crash. Bobby is buried in Dogwood Cemetery at Blytheville, Arkansas.

As noted in the preceding chapter (12), Bobby Neal was the lead guitar player in Jerry Jaye's band when I booked him at my club (Mack Allen Smith's Town & Country Night Club) in Greenwood, Mississippi, in May 1971. We later played a number of battles of the bands and I have to say Bobby Neal was the best lead guitar man I ever shared a stage with. Further, I believe he was as good as any I ever heard and that includes James Burton. With Neal and Burton I'll call it a draw. That's my opinion, for whatever it's worth.

In my memoir, *Looking Back One Last Time*, I said that Bobby Neal was the best I ever heard, so I guess I'm hedging a bit now. That's the way it is though - you get older and things change, including your mind. Nonetheless, Bobby may have been the best; if not, he was as good as the best. Billy Wayne Herbert was good with boogie and blues, but Bobby Neal was good with everything, whether it was boogie, blues, jazz, country, or whatever. In fact, I heard Billy Wayne Herbert make the statement that Bobby Neal was his hero. You don't become Billy Wayne Herbert's hero unless you are the creme of the crop. Enough said.

Bobby Neal was a great picker and a great person. I consider myself fortunate to have known him. I hired Bobby to play guitar for one of my recording sessions in Memphis in 1975 at Lyn-Lou Studio, and I will always cherish those recordings because Bobby was playing on them.

In Memphis, Bobby was in great demand as a session player. In one of Jerry Jaye's CD liner notes, the writer stated that Jerry's 1975 recording of the "Honky Tonk Women Love Redneck Men" album Bobby Neal took most of the solos. Later, Bobby joined Ricky Nelson's touring band. He perished in the DC-3 crash that claimed the lives of Ricky Nelson, his fiancee, and the entire band.

Jerry Jaye believes this was to be Bobby's last gig with Ricky Nelson and that he had intended to concentrate on doing sessions and writing with Ronnie Scaife. This would have been a great partnership. Ronnie has written songs for Alabama, Randy Travis, and a host of other big stars. If Bobby Neal and Ronnie Scaife had become a song writing team, they may have become the greatest of all time. At least they would have been highly successful and cranked out hundreds of hit records.

Like many others, Bobby died way too young, and he is sorely missed by all who knew him. His guitar licks will live on. Praise the Lord.

Chapter 14
Ellis Hopper

Ellis Hopper was born June 25, 1935, in Cleveland, Mississippi. He died December 2, 1991, in Greenwood, Mississippi, and is buried in Mt. Moriah Cemetery in Calhoun County, Mississippi, near the town of Bruce.

As discussed in Chapter 3, Ellis Hopper played lead guitar in a group formed in 1956 called The Carroll County Rock & Roll Boys. The name was later changed to Mack Allen Smith & The Flames. When he first started, it was me (rhythm guitar, lead singer), Billy Wayne Herbert (rhythm guitar), and Ellis Hopper (lead guitar). This doesn't sound like much of a band, but all we did to begin with was the Elvis stuff and Ellis Hopper had those Scotty Moore guitar licks down pat. For those who remember, Elvis's first few records on Sun only had Elvis singing and playing rhythm, Bill Black playing bull bass, and Scotty Moore playing lead guitar. This was also his touring band.

Don't get me wrong, I don't want to even think about comparing The Carroll County Rock & Roll Boys to Elvis, Bill, and Scotty. They were originators, and we were the imitators. I know I could never come close to Elvis' singing. He was the best of all time and always will be. Nonetheless, Ellis Hopper was as close to Scotty Moore as you could get on lead guitar. I might add that after a while we also did other Rock-A-Billy songs by Gene Vincent, Charlie Feathers, Warren Smith, and Roy Orbison to name a few.

The highlight for the band was getting to perform at a ballpark in Greenwood with Warren Smith, Sonny Burgess, and Charlie Feathers. Ellis Hopper was the one that got us this booking and hired Joe Gary to help us out on drums. As mentioned in Chapter 3, Bob Neal talked to me about coming to Memphis for an audition at Sun Records, and Ellis Hopper tried his best to get me to postpone college and give it a try in Memphis.

I have often wondered if I made a mistake by not listening to Ellis and following his advice. As it turned out, I only went to college one semester, failed everything I was taking, then quit and joined the Marines. How stupid can you get? Looking back now it's a no-brainer. I should have listened to Ellis Hopper. But, like they say, hindsight is twenty-twenty.

After Ellis quit the band in 1956, I didn't see him again until 1961. I was looking for someone to replace Keith Worrell on lead guitar since Keith was leaving for college. Ellis had moved from Carrollton back to Cleveland several years before, but I was successful in locating him. He played a few gigs with us, but the magic was no longer there. Music had changed, and I suppose we had all changed as well. It was no longer just Rock-A-Billy. For whatever the reasons, it just didn't work anymore, and we both knew it. Therefore, we parted trails again.

It was almost 30 years before I saw Ellis Hopper again. He opened a jewelry repair store in Greenwood around 1990, and we renewed our friendship to some extent. We never took the stage together again, but Ellis kept a box guitar in his store so, naturally, we did "That's All Right Mama" and a few more old Elvis Rock-A-Billy songs for old time's sake.

I attended Ellis' funeral in Greenwood on December 2, 1991, and rode in the hearse with Bill Lord to the cemetery near Bruce, Mississippi. At the grave site, two girls from the church Ellis attended played guitar and sang "I'll Fly Away." Everyone joined in the singing, including me.

Bill Lord said I was the only one to sing "In the Morning" after the second "I'll Fly Away". I always thought that was the way the song went - "I'll Fly Away, Oh Glory - I'll Fly Away In the Morning, When I Die, Hallelujah By and By - I'll Fly Away."

Whatever the case may be, I'm glad Ellis and I renewed our friendship, and I'm glad I was there for his final send-off.

Chapter 15
Sanford Horton

Sanford Horton was born December 25, 1944, in Grenada, Mississippi. He graduated from Rundle High School in Grenada, Mississippi, in 1963. After high school, Sanford attended Mississippi State University (MSU) where he received a Bachelor's Degree in Industrial Engineering in 1968 and a Master's Degree in Business Administration in 1969.

After graduating from MSU in 1969, Sanford was drafted into the Army where he served until 1971. His service included a one-year tour of duty in Vietnam. When he returned from Vietnam and was discharged in 1971, Sanford stated that he took one year off to indulge in wine, women, and song, but not necessarily in that order.

When Sanford finished his year of catching up somewhat on the good things he missed while in Vietnam, he decided he needed some more education. Therefore, he enrolled in law school at the University of Mississippi (Ole Miss) in Oxford, Mississippi, where he received a law degree in 1975. Sanford is without a doubt the most educated person I have ever shared the stage with.

In 1975 after receiving his law degree, Sanford went to work for the State of Mississippi as an attorney for the Board of Health. He served 30 years before retiring in 2005. For most of the time with the state, his title was Assistant Attorney General.

Irrespective of his education and successful day job, Sanford has always been a good ole boy, and he has always managed to play his bass as much as he wanted to. Sanford played bass with me (Mack Allen Smith & The Flames) for two and one-half years (mid 1974 through the end of 1976) and I must say the music was great.

Before playing bass with me, Sanford played with the Southern Five. After playing with me, he again played with the Southern Five. Then he played with the El Dorado band. Sanford said he actually started out playing with Jessie Yates before he played with the Southern Five.

A list of musicians with Southern Five and El Dorado bands are as follows: Sanford Horton (bass), Bill Daly (drums), W. C. Taylor (lead guitar), Albert Morrison (sax), Steve McGregory (piano), Alan Purdy (singer), Jimmy Purdy (singer), Bridge Downs (lead guitar), Robert Box (lead guitar), Mike Jacks (guitar), Larry McClellan (drums), Lisa Purdy (singer), Earl Bishop (lead guitar), Obie Atkins (lead guitar), and Doug Thomas (drums).

In addition to the above mentioned bands, Sanford later played bass with Jamie Isanhood. This group backed Ace Cannon for two years at the Las Vegas casino in Greenville, Mississippi, after which Sanford played bass with the Bobby Lloyd band.

Sanford Horton made my day when he told me that the highlights of his career in music were getting to play bass with Mack Allen Smith and Ace Cannon. I can understand the Ace Cannon part. He also said that when he was in high school he heard on the radio that Warren Smith would be at the Grenada VFW with Mack Allen Smith and The Flames. Sanford said he was too young for his parents' approval, but considered slipping off. He said he knew he couldn't get into the VFW at his age, so he gave up on the idea of slipping away from his parents. He could probably have gotten into the Grenada VFW easier than he could have slipped off from his parents.

Sanford still plays bass occasionally and even played with me a couple of times recently. However, his main gig now is karaoke. As of this writing (10/20/09), Sanford has been doing karaoke for ten years. According to reports I have received from various sources, Sanford Horton is the undisputed king of karaoke in Mississippi. For those in the know, karaoke with Sanford is a household name.

Sanford played bass with me on ten songs that were released by Ace Records in Jackson, Mississippi. One song (King of Rock & Roll) is perhaps more popular overseas than any I've recorded. Some articles have proclaimed it the best, and I'm sure Sanford will agree. HA! Just kidding, but it is a real rockin' mother as Jerry Lee might say. Finally, let me say this: If you need to know anything about people in the music business just call Sanford. If he doesn't know the answer, nobody will.

Chapter 16
David Lee Cox

David Lee Cox was born December 23, 1940, in Winona, Mississippi. He died in December 2000 while living south of Jackson, Mississippi, near Florence.

As noted in Chapter 3, I met David Lee Cox in 1959 shortly after I returned from the Marines in January. David Lee and his band from Winona, Mississippi, played a variety show at J. Z. George gym in North Carrollton, Mississippi. My group (Mack Allen Smith & The Flames) was also on the show. We talked David Lee into joining the Flames, and he became a member of what I call the original 1959 Flames.

David Lee played piano on the 1959 Sun recordings where I sang, "Sandy Lee," "Kansas City," "Mean Woman Blues," and "Young Dreams". On this session, David Lee also sang a song he wrote entitled "I Got A Fever".

David Lee played with us through the end of 1960. He had moved to Jackson a couple of months earlier, and the travel to our gigs in North Mississippi was getting too much for his body and pocket book. The last gig he played with the Flames was a dance at the National Guard Armory in Columbus, Mississippi. This was in December 1960 after Warren Smith had started performing with us. Needless to say, I will never forget that gig.

When David Lee left the band, it really hurt. He sang Jerry Lee Lewis songs and others, and he could play the Jerry Lee Lewis stuff note for note. He was good, and he was hard to replace.

For more than 30 years David Lee made a living playing music all over the world. When not on the road, David Lee worked with Wright Music Company in Jackson, Mississippi, as an instrument repair specialist.

I figured when David Lee left the Flames after 1960 we would never be in a band together again. However, in 1983 we were back on stage together again. We played together from January 1983 to October 20, 1984, at which time I hung up my Rock-A-Billy shoes and retired from the honky-tonks. As discussed in Chapter 3, it seemed only fitting that my honky-tonk career end with David Lee Cox, who had been a member of the original 1959 band, being with me at the end, along with his son, Junior, on drums, who wasn't even born in 1959. In addition, icing on the cake was having Laney O'Briant, who also played with me for a while in 1959, playing lead guitar for me when I finished my singing career in the honky-tonks.

I am aware of at least one album that David Lee and his son, David Lee Cox, Jr., recorded while playing on the road. The album entitled "The Double Dave" was recorded at Audio Arts Unlimited in Rapid City, South Dakota. I have a copy of the album which I assume was given to me by David Lee, although he didn't sign it. Perhaps he thought his signature wasn't worth much. If so, he was wrong.

The album includes eight songs. According to the liner notes, five tunes appearing on this album are original tunes written by David Lee Cox, Sr. And David Lee Cox, Jr.

A tribute to David Lee Cox, Sr. by his children appeared in the Jackson newspaper (The Clarion Ledger) after his death. The tribute is as follows:

"At age 59, Dave is now in the loving hands of the Lord. Everyone who had the pleasure of knowing him will miss him. He had 3 girls and 2 boys who will dearly miss him. Dave Lee was a musician with a variety of talent. He was raised in the Baptist Church singing gospel music. His favorite religious song was "Amazing Grace". In his early years, he was the movie projector control man at the movie theater. He began tuning pianos and later repairing all types of music instruments. He could repair horns that vehicles ran over and they would look brand new. During this period, he was playing the organ on the week-ends for various gatherings. He was such a good musician, he went on the road all over the world, along with one of his sons who started playing the drums at age 12. He was more than a musician; he was an entertainer and wanted to make everyone happy. He could impersonate Ray Charles, Willie Nelson, Elvis, and even Wolfman Jack. His life was surrounded by music and now he is singing with the angels in heaven. We love You!"

All I can add to this is "AMEN."

Chapter 17
Jamie Isonhood

Jamie Isonhood was born July 4, 1944, in Yazoo County, Mississippi. He graduated from Anding High School in Bentonia, Mississippi, in 1961. He currently lives in Yazoo City, Mississippi.

Jamie discovered at the age of five that he could play the piano. While in high school, he played at Slick Fulcher's Nightclub, which was about two miles from his grandparents' house where he lived. His grandparents thought he and Pete Ketchum, a best friend with a car, were at the Midnight Picture Show in Yazoo City.

Also, while in high school, Jamie played parties and dances with Jessie Yates and The Rhythm Aces. In addition, he played some gigs with Mack Allen Smith and The Flames in early 1961 after David Lee Cox left The Flames and moved to Jackson.

Besides the honky-tonks, Jamie played in local churches on Sundays and some nights when they weren't officially open.

Shortly after finishing high school in 1961, Jamie Isonhood moved to Memphis. In Memphis he played at parties, clubs, and studios. Then, he was hired as a studio musician with the legendary Roland James at Sonic Recording Studio. The staff band at Sonic also included the great guitar player Travis Wammack and Prentiss McPhail on bass. Prentiss McPhail played with me (Mack Allen Smith and The Flames) in the honky-tonks for several months during the seventies.

Jamie told me that he and Travis Wammack became lifetime friends. They recorded in the studio during the week, and many weekends were spent playing clubs and stage shows with recording artists like Matt Lucas, Bobby Lee Trammel, and Ace Cannon.

After the sixties and seventies in Memphis, Jamie worked out of Las Vegas and Portland, Oregon. From these two locations Jamie played throughout the western United States and Canada.

In the eighties Jamie returned to his roots in Yazoo City, Mississippi. He now lives in Yazoo City with his wife Angela and their three children. Jamie makes his living playing piano and singing at many venues including festivals, clubs, sessions, cruises, and private parties. Jamie even played several gigs with me this year (2009), and I'm looking forward to doing it some more in the future.

Jamie and Travis Wammack were out of touch for a number of years, but in 2007 they were reunited on Jamie's CD "I Played My Blues in Memphis". This CD was recorded at Sam Phillips' studio in Memphis with Roland James, producer and engineer. Jamie wrote the title song, "I Played My Blues in Memphis". The rest of the tracks go from Warren Smith to Randy Newman to Jimmy Reed to Johnny Ace and more.

The musicians on this session are as follows: Jamie Isonhood (vocals and piano), Travis Wammack (lead guitar), Duff Durrough (lead guitar), Donnie Gullett (bass), Sanford Horton (bass), Terry Moxley (drums), Carty McMullan (organ), and Leonard

McIntosh (saxophone). The liner notes list Prentiss McPhail as a special studio guest. I suppose that means Prentiss was drinking coffee, listening, and killing time. HA!

Back on the serious side, the liner notes also contain a statement from Matt Lucas that is worth including in its entirety. The Matt Lucas statement is as follows: "Well over 40 years ago I was putting a band together of studio musicians to go on tour with me. Before I did that, the great guitar genius Travis Wammack introduced me to Jamie Isonhood and after he played on some sessions of mine at Sonic Studios in Memphis I knew I had to have this unique rockin' singer, piano player in my band. I think he was only 18 years old and loaded with fire and excitement in his playing and vocals. On this new CD he's teamed up with a couple of legends of Memphis music, Roland James and TravisWammack, along with great bass man, Donnie Gullet, and Terry Moxey on drums that played with my old friend, Charlie Rich. I seldom listen to radio anymore as they try to pass off music that is supposed to be real Rock-A-Billy/Rock & Roll/Country, but the people I hear can't wash Jamie's bathtub. As Sam Phillips used to say when he had faith in an act - "That boy's got it." Jamie's still got it and it shows on this CD. Crank it up and I think you will agree. It's great music that you don't get to hear anymore."

This year (2009) Jamie released a gospel CD entitled "Testifying." The title song (Testifying) was written by Jamie. This is a great gospel CD that is different from any I've ever heard. Perhaps one reason I'm partial to this CD is because Jamie recorded one of my songs: "I Made a Deal With Jesus." In my opinion this would be a great CD even without my song, but it's better with it. My opinion, for what's it worth - thank you.

Besides the above two CDs Jamie had a CD released in 2008 entitled "I Just Do It When It's Good." This is a 14-song CD which includes 10 studio tracks and 4 live tracks. The 10 studio tracks were recorded at Terminal Recording Studio in Ridgeland, Mississippi. Terminal Recording Studio won a Grammy award for recording the soundtrack of Brother Where Art Thou, The Williams Brothers, and more.

Jamie Isonhood is in such demand throughout the Delta and beyond that he actually has to turn down lots of bookings. For the most part, he does a one-man show, but can put together a first rate band whenever one is needed. You can do that when you are the best around. If Sam Phillips was still alive, and you asked him about Jamie Isonhood, he would probably say: "That boy's got it."

Chapter 18
Jessie Yates

Jessie Yates was born December 11, 1939, at Kosciusko, Mississippi. He graduated from high school at West, Mississippi, in 1957. Jessie died June 21, 2009, while living in Batesville, Mississippi. He is buried in Chapel Hill Cemetery at Pope, Mississippi.

The first time I saw Jessie Yates was in 1956 at Holmes Junior College in Goodman, Mississippi. He was playing rhythm guitar and singing while Laney O'Briant from West, Mississippi, played lead guitar. Jessie was a senior in high school, and I was a freshman at Holmes Junior College. I also sang several Elvis songs on this variety show with Ellis Hopper on lead guitar and Billy Wayne Herbert on rhythm guitar.

The last time I saw Jessie Yates was May 23, 2009, at Carroll County Market in Carrollton, Mississippi. Less than a month later he was dead. We (Mack Allen Smith & The Flames) played two 45 minute sets with a 30 minute break in between, so we had some time to visit with Jessie and his son, Jessie Jr. They also brought their wives, Rose and Jamie, and several other people to this gig. Susie James was there, so she took some pictures of the band along with Jessie, which she got into the Greenwood newspaper with a nice article. I'm really thankful for this reunion with Jessie before he died.

Over the years Jessie played three tours of duty with me and my band (Mack Allen Smith & The Flames). He played with me for several months in 1959 and two periods during the seventies.

Jessie played organ with me on 20 songs cut at Statue Recording Studio in Tupelo, Mississippi, in 1972. These songs were released on Delta Sound Records as a double album entitled "Saturday Night With Mack Allen Smith & The Flames". The songs were released again on a CD in 2004 entitled "The Tupelo Session".

My most memorable association with Jessie Yates is, without doubt, July 1979. Martin Hawkins from England had booked me on a two-week tour of England and Jessie went with me to sing harmony. I'm glad he did because Jessie was a real asset on that 1979 tour.

Alan Cackett from a local paper, *The Kent Evening Post*, wrote about our first gig at Greenways, a large club about 30 miles from London. A small part of his review is as follows: "Being his first gig in the country, Mack Allen Smith was noticeably nervous to begin with, but with his right-hand man, Jessie Yates, on harmony-vocal giving him encouragement, he settled down to a highly commendable set."

I remember Jessie saying after the show, "Damn, Mack Allen, I never saw you so nervous."

I told Jessie, "Thanks, man, for pulling me through."

The show at Greenways, as well as the whole tour, went over really well. The Roger Humphries Band was fantastic, and Jessie Yates was a big help with his harmony singing and his encouragement. Jessie really saved me on that gig. I don't believe I could have made it without him.

Besides playing on 20 of my recordings, Jessie recorded six songs with him doing the lead singing that resulted in three singles. Pertinent information is presented as follows:

1. "Long Tall Texan/Together Again": recorded at Statue Studio in Tupelo, Mississippi.
2. "Send Me a Letter/All the Praises": recorded at Hardy Station in Grenada, Mississippi.
3. "Stagger Lee/Swingin'": recorded at Riverside Recording Studio in Greenwood, Mississippi.

Obituaries in Kosciusko and Batesville show Jessie's day jobs as mechanic and trucking. I talked to Jessie Junior, and he confirmed my knowledge that Jessie also worked in the timber business with his father for 15 years. In addition, he owned a body shop in Batesville for several years, and was service manager at auto and body shops for ten years.

The above mentioned obituaries also noted that Jessie was a musician for 60 years and was nicknamed "The King of Honky-tonks." The obituaries further stated that he was well known all over the state for his love of music and for packing dance halls and keeping them on the floor until the early hours of the morning. Further, the Batesville obituary stated that: "Jessie was known for his love of people, cars, family, and laughter. If you were his friend you were part of his family."

Since Jessie Yates came to hear me sing at Carroll County Market less than a month before he died, I hope that meant he considered me his friend. One thing for sure - I considered him my friend.

I can't close this chapter without returning to my first gig in England, specifically, my conversation with Jessie after the show.

From Jessie Yates: "Damn, Mack Allen, I never saw you so nervous."

From Mack Allen Smith: "Thanks, man, for pulling me through."

Chapter 19
Laney O'Briant

Laney O'Briant was born May 10, 1940, at West, Mississippi. He attended West High School until they merged with Durant the year before Laney graduated. He graduated from Durant High School at Durant, Mississippi, in 1959.

After graduating from Durant High School in 1959, Laney played with me and the Flames for a few months. We had two lead guitars (Laney and James Keith Worrell). Then, Laney and Jessie Yates left my band before the end of 1959 and formed the Rhythm Aces. Laney and Jessie played together for about three years (through 1962).

When the Rhythm Aces broke up Laney played several years during the sixties with The Ivories. They were a first rate band which included: Laney O'Briant (lead guitar), Jimmy Smith (singer and piano), Johnny Baker (trumpet), Jimmy Belk (bass), Doug Steen (sax), and Norman Freeland (drums).

Laney told me that he started playing lead guitar in 1954 with Jessie Yates and has played ever since without a period of inactivity. As of this writing (November 2009) Laney has been playing lead guitar for over 55 years. He also plays fiddle, banjo, and mandolin. According to Laney's wife, Kathryn, he can play anything that has strings on it.

Before retiring in May 2003 from American General, Laney's day jobs included 14 years in local factories and 30 years in the insurance business.

In 1973 Laney O'Briant started playing with me and the Flames again and played with us until I hung up my Rock-A-Billy shoes and stopped playing in the honky-tonks on October 20, 1984 (my 46th birthday). During the seventies and early eighties Laney played with me on 15 studio recordings that wound up on four singles and six albums, five of which were overseas releases. In addition, Laney played on 38 songs that were recorded live at the County Music Palace in Vaiden, Mississippi, on October 31, 1981. These recordings were released on CD in 2005 entitled "Live on Halloween".

After my retirement from the honky-tonks in October 1984, Laney played with several groups before we got back together in October 2002. Some of these groups and/or musicians are as follows: David Lee Cox Band (1984-1985), Black River Band (1985-1992), Ronnie Stone & Prime Cut (1993-1997), and Bill Walker, Randy Williamson, etc. (1998-2002).

As noted in Chapter 3 (Mack Allen Smith and The Flames), I came out of my 18 year retirement in October 2002 for a performance at the old school house in Black Hawk, Mississippi. Laney played lead guitar with me at this "just doing it for fun" gig and has been playing with me ever since. Laney is not living on borrowed time like I am, but he's getting close. Nonetheless, if Laney's fingers keep working I believe he will keep pickin' and grinnin' for years to come. I just hope I can hang in there with him for a while.

Chapter 20
James Keith Worrell

James Keith Worrell was born March 16, 1942, in Kosciukso (Attala County), Mississippi. James Keith died February 26, 2001, in Greenwood, Mississippi. He is buried in Moore Cemetery behind Mt. Pisgah Baptist Church in Carroll County, Mississippi, near Teoc.

James Keith's family moved to Carroll County, Mississippi, when he was five years old. He attended Valley School where his father was superintendent and his mother a teacher. James Keith graduated from Valley High School in 1961.

In January 1959 when I completed my tour of duty with the Marines and returned to Carrollton, Mississippi, it was only a few days before I heard about this fantastic guitar player who was a junior at Valley High School. Red McGregor came to see me and asked if I planned to form another band. Red said he would like to play rhythm guitar with me and suggested that I consider James Keith Worrell, this high school junior, as our lead guitar player. I remember saying, "He can't be that good if he's only a junior in high school." Red, said, "Just listen to him." I did go to James Keith's house at Valley and listened to him, and I have to say I was wrong about what a high school junior could do on lead guitar. He was so good I wanted to get down on my knees and beg him to join my band. Since he was so young, I was ready to beg his parents to let him be my lead guitar player. To make a long story short, so to speak, he joined my band with his parents' approval. Mr. & Mrs. Worrell went to all our gigs, and Mr. Worrell sat at the door whenever we played for 60% of the door so that we wouldn't get screwed. Or, to say it nicer, so we would get 60% of what was collected.

As noted in Chapter 3, James Keith was one of the original 1959 Flames, along with me (lead singer), Red McGregor (rhythm guitar), David Lee Cox (piano), and Durwood Herbert (drums.)

James Keith played on our 1959 recordings at Sun Records in Memphis, and I'm proud that after 50 years the master tape is now in my possession. I can now hear James Keith play his 1959 licks whenever I want to. This goes for the rest of the original 1959 Flames, plus Billy Wayne Herbert.

For all of 1959 and 1960, and until James Keith left for college in 1961, he was the lead guitar player for Mack Allen Smith and The Flames. For this period of time, he was a perfect fit because he could play everything people were hearing on the radio. This is probably the most up-to-date group I was ever associated with, mainly because James Keith listened to the radio more than the rest of us and he learned the lead guitar parts note for note. Therefore, when we practiced James Keith was the teacher.

When James Keith graduated from Valley High School in 1961 and left for college, he took his guitar and amp with him. Needless to say, he continued playing for many years. Some of the bands that he played with included The Casuals, Jessie Yates, and Grover Duke. During periods when he was not with a band he would go sit-in with some group he knew if the urge to play hit him. I'm happy to say that James Keith came and sat in with me and the Flames a number of times over the years.

In 1981 James Keith was learning to play steel guitar, so he called and asked me if he could come sit in on the steel guitar. Of course, I was happy to have him sit-in on anything. I am particularly glad that this gig happened because we recorded the gig and it resulted in a double CD with 38 songs entitled, "Live On Halloween" October 31, 1981. Now I can not only hear his 1959 lead guitar licks on the 1959 Sun Recordings, I can hear him play steel guitar on my October 31, 1981, gig at the Country Music Palace in Vaiden, Mississippi.

Regarding James Keith's day jobs, he had a highly successful career in radio and engineering. After high school he attended Ole Miss, Holmes Junior College, and Mississippi Delta Junior College. At Holmes he received an Associates degree, and at Mississippi Delta he received a degree in electronics. He used his degree in and knowledge of electronics to launch a thirty-plus year career as a radio engineer.

In 1965 James Keith joined Dixie Broadcasting as chief engineer. According to his wife, Alice, he built radio stations in Mississippi and Arkansas, including WSWG in Greenwood, Mississippi. This brought to mind something most folks don't know. Specifically, James Keith Worrell built a radio station in his bedroom at Valley when he was in high school. He used to tell me to put my radio dial on a certain number and drive down the road with my radio on. Then he would talk on the radio and play me a song. If there was anyone around smarter than James Keith Worrell, I never met them.

I saw James Keith three weeks before he died, and he mentioned the fact that he and I were the last two left from the original 1959 band. We joked about how we weren't feeling so good either. Now, I'm the only one left.

Chapter 21
Arthur Browning

Arthur Browning was born June 16, 1944, at Greenwood Leflore Hospital in Greenwood, Mississippi. The Browning family lived in Carroll County, Mississippi. Arthur graduated from J. Z. George High School at North Carrollton, Mississippi, in 1962.

As discussed in Chapter 3, when Keith Worrell left for college in the fall of 1961, we tried out a couple of guitar pickers before selecting Arthur Browning to replace Keith Worrell on lead guitar. Arthur was a senior at J. Z. George High School when he joined the Flames as lead guitar player. In retrospect, I have to say that Arthur Browning was a good choice - the right man at the right time.

Arthur played lead guitar on my first four recordings in 1962 which became my first two singles for Vee Eight Records. For details see the Appendix. One of the songs, "Hobo Man", which I wrote, has become a collector's item overseas. In my opinion, one of the reasons for this is the full, almost indescribable guitar work of Arthur Browning.

In 1962 after recording our first two singles for Vee Eight Records, Arthur left the band to attend X-ray school. After completing his course work, he worked 23 years as an x-ray technician for hospitals in Nashville, Tennessee, Memphis, Tennessee, and Huntsville, Alabama. In addition, Arthur worked 11 years at Redstone Arsenal in Huntsville, Alabama, where he was a building inspector for the federal government.

Arthur moved back to Carroll County, Mississippi, in 1994. He started picking John Hurt songs on the guitar, and today he plays John Hurt songs as close to the way John played them as you can get. To do them any better, you would have to be John Hurt. Arthur has also become one of John Hurt's biggest fans, and he has done more than anyone I know to keep John Hurt's memory and his music alive.

Since 2001, Arthur has been curator of the John Hurt Museum in Carroll County, Mississippi, near Teoc. Since becoming curator, thousands of people from all over the world have come to see the John Hurt Museum and hear Arthur Browning play those John Hurt songs on one of John's old guitars that is on display at the museum. One of the visitors from Scotland has written a book about John Hurt which was released in 2010.

If Arthur Browning has his way, the memory and music of John Hurt will live forever. Further, because of Arthur Browning, "Hobo Man" might just hang around for a while, too.

Chapter 22
Hardin B. Browning

Hardin Browning was born December 29, 1945, at Greenwood Leflore Hospital in Greenwood, Mississippi. He and Arthur are brothers. The Browning family lived in Carroll County, Mississippi. Hardin graduated from J. Z. George High School at North Carrollton, Mississippi, in 1964.

As discussed in Chapter 3, the original 1959 Flames began breaking up in 1961. Our piano player, David Lee Cox, moved to Jackson and was replaced by Hardin Browning. Like his brother, Arthur on guitar, Hardin was a good choice - the right man at the right time. He played with me and the Flames throughout most of the sixties and was the piano player on over twenty of my recordings. For details see the Appendix. According to Arthur, Hardin played with me from age 15 to age 22.

After leaving the Flames, Hardin played solo at lounges (with an acoustic guitar) through 1972. Then in 1973, he formed a band called "Williams Landing." This group consisted of Hardin Browning (guitar and vocals), Barry Smith (bass and vocals), and Benny Herring (drums and vocals).

Other groups that Hardin played with after leaving the Flames included the Kasuals and Magnolia Blue. He played with the Kasuals for six months in 1975, then joined them again in 1981 and played several years. More about the Kasuals will be presented in Chapter 23; more about Magnolia Blue will be presented in Chapter 24.

Besides playing and singing, Hardin had day jobs in radio where he was a very successful D.J. for over 30 years. He worked several stations including three and one-half years at a large station in Louisville, Kentucky (www.79WAKY.com). Hardin started at WLEF in Greenwood in 1965 where he worked three years. Then he worked one year at WDDT in Greenville and two years at WWUN in Jackson. After returning from Kentucky, Hardin worked over twenty years at WSWG in Greenwood. About half of this time was for Hardin Browning Productions which recorded commercials for various TV and radio stations. Even though Hardin is now retired, his voice is still being heard daily on TV and radio commercials throughout Mississippi and surrounding states.

From his radio days in Kentucky, Hardin got to know a lot of big name stars as follows: Exile, Arthur Conley, Rufus Thomas, Don McLean, Tommy James and the Shondells, Jethro Tull, Janis Joplin, Junior Walker and the All Stars, Bill Cosby, The Fifth Dimension, John Denver, Muddy Waters, Lightin' Hopkins, James Brown, and Dick Clark of American Bandstand fame. Hardin introduced Dick Clark at the Kentucky State Fair.

In addition, Hardin recalled an instance when he was involved in a guitar pullin' at a motel room one morning about 3:00 AM with Roger Miller, The Girls Next Door, and The Average White Band. I must admit that I've never heard of a 3:00AM guitar pullin' in a motel room; however, I will take Hardin's word for it.

Hardin ended his e-mail to me with a statement that I really liked, so I decided to include it as written by Hardin. He said, "I will say that my seven years playing all over the southeast with Mack Allen Smith & The Flames was some of the most fun I had playing music." Thank you, Hardin, for this flattering comment. I had fun, too, and wish we could turn back the clock and do it again.

Chapter 23
The Casuals / The Kasuals

Since several members of the Casuals played with me and my band (Mack Allen Smith & The Flames) over the years, and since Hardin Browning was one of them, I decided to assign this Chapter 23 which follows Hardin's chapter (22). Actually, there is no good reason for making this chapter 23; however, I see no good reason for not making it Chapter 23 either.

Having said that, I will now present information on the Kasuals as provided to me by Hardin Browning.

According to Hardin, he and Tony Browning formed a group in 1975 with the following members: Hardin Browning (guitar), Tony Browning (bass), and Kelly Hall (drums). They called the group The Kasuals because Tony had previously played with a group with the same name, and they figured this name recognition would be good for bookings. Later, they added Kelly's brother (Ray Hall) on organ.

When the band formed in 1967 the name was the Casuals, but later changed it to Kasuals thinking this had more class.

The 1975 Kasuals played six nights a week at King's Restaurant & Lounge in Greenwood, Mississippi, for about one year. Sometime during this period Ray and Kelly left the band, so Hardin and Tony hired John Evans from Belzoni, Mississippi, on keyboards and Mike Dill from Greenville, Mississippi, on drums. In 1976 Hardin left the band and didn't play for a while.

Hardin stated that in 1981 he and Tony re-formed the Kasuals with the following members: Hardin Browning (lead guitar and piano), Tony Browning (bass), Keith Worrell (lead guitar), and David Browning (drums). This band played several years and were in great demand throughout north Mississippi.

Based on information received from Tony Browning, the first band of Kasuals called Casuals was formed in 1967 with the following members: Tony Browning (bass), George Vernon (drums), Doug Steen (sax), and Keith Worrell (lead guitar). Tony said that in 1969 Charlie Watts joined the band as singer and on keyboards, and Buddy Millett joined the group on drums replacing George Vernon. He stated that Ray Hall later joined them on keyboards and Hardin Browning also joined the group later.

One group called the Casuals consisted of Tony Browning (bass), Benny Herring (drums), Keith Worrell (lead guitar), and Hardin Browning (keyboards). Arthur Browning gave me a newspaper ad of this group playing at the Holiday Inn in Greenwood. The date was not known.

Since this band formed, disbanded, and then re-formed several times over the years it would be an understatement to say that their history is somewhat confusing. Nonetheless, the musicians who played with the Casuals/Kasuals were first rate and their legacy is enduring.

I was also told that Jerry Waugh from Winona once played with a group of Casuals. Jerry was a great singer and harmonica player who later moved to the gulf coast.

Chapter 24
Magnolia Blue

In an effort to obtain a substantially accurate history of Magnolia Blue, I talked to Kenny Loftin (member of the original band), and Hardin Browning (member of the band 17 years later).

When I talked to Kenny Loftin in January 2010 he stated that he was 15 years old when the band was formed. He further stated that since he is now 55, it has been 40 years. Kenny subtracted 40 years from 2010 and concluded that the band was formed around 1970. Good old Carroll County arithmetic.

Kenny said that the first name given the band was the Keynotes. He doesn't remember the year they changed their name to Magnolia Blue. Members of the original band are as follows: Van Simpson (vocals, guitar, and harmonica), Kenny Loftin (lead guitar), Ronnie Collins (drums), and Larry Parker (bass).

During the 70s Magnolia Blue played some of the same clubs we did (Greenwood Moose Lodge, Cleveland American Legion, Country Music Palace in Vaiden, and King's Lounge in Greenwood). We had several battles of the bands, and they were always worthy opponents.

Based on information from Hardin Browning, Magnolia Blue made additions in 1987 that took them to a higher level. The 1987 band included the following members: Van Simpson (lead singer, guitar, and harmonica), Kenny Loftin (lead guitar), Mike Sullivan (lead guitar and slide guitar), Hardin Browning (synthesizers), Tony Browning (bass), and David Browning (drums).

Magnolia Blue was now a big outfit. They were comprised of a six-piece band with a light man (Bill Jordan), sound man (Randy Kirby), and a road crew of two (Danny Elmore and Walter Tullos). A total of ten people.

This new and updated group of talented musicians did shows with a large number of hit country, top 40, and blues artists. Some of the stars that Magnolia Blue appeared on stage with are as follows: Merle Kilgore, Leon Ashley, Margo Smith, Percy Sledge, B. B. King, Keith Whitley, John Anderson, Earl Thomas Conley, Mickey Gilly, Steve Warner, Shelly West, David Frizell, Ace Cannon, Billy Joe Royal, and Delbert McClinton.

Since I retired from the honky-tonks in 1984, I never got to hear the 1987 band but wish I had. Knowing the great musicians in that band they had to be one of the best bands around.

Van Simpson, who was lead singer and harmonica player from their start in 1970 until their finish in the 90s, was, in my opinion, one of the best singers to ever come down the pike. Van is now deceased, but he is not forgotten. Nor is Magnolia Blue.

Chapter 25
Murry Moorman

Murry Moorman was born January 24, 1942, at Teoc (Carroll County), Mississippi. The Moorman family moved to Greenwood in 1946 where Murry attended school at Davis Elementary and W. C. Williams.

As noted in Chapter 21, in 1962 after recording our first two singles for Vee Eight Records, Arthur Browning left the band to attend X-ray school, and Murry Moorman became our lead guitar player. Murry played with me and the Flames for over ten years. After joining the band he was my lead guitar man on all songs recorded by me and the Flames through the rest of the sixties. He also played on the 20 song album I recorded at Tupelo in 1972. For complete details see the Appendix.

I have heard that Murry Moorman is the best fisherman in Mississippi, but I have no firsthand knowledge to support this claim. However, if Murry is half as good at fishing as he is at picking a guitar, then he may be the best fisherman in the whole wide world. I firmly stand behind the statement I made in Chapter 3 that my sixties band ('63-'69) was the best butt-kicking band I was ever associated with. Without Murry Moorman this would probably not have been the case.

Today, Murry is still playing. He plays regularly with a fine gospel group and has played with me a few times since I came out of retirement in 2002. He is just as good now as he was in the sixties. I have to say that guitar pickers in this part of the country with talent equal to Murry Moorman are few and far between. And, in my opinion, there ain't none.

Chapter 26
Tony Browning

Tony Browning was born June 20, 1947, in Grenada, Mississippi. He graduated from Greenwood High School in 1965, after which he attended college at Mississippi Delta Community College at Moorhead, Mississippi, and Delta State University at Cleveland, Mississippi.

When Tony joined me and my band (Mack Allen Smith & The Flames) in 1980 he was already a well-established bass player who was considered one of the best around. He played with me through 1982 and was the bass player on 38 songs we recorded live on October 31, 1981, at the Country Music Palace in Vaiden, Mississippi. These 38 songs were released in 2006 on a CD entitled "Live On Halloween." I believe Tony was in his prime when we recorded these songs as evidenced by some of the best bass playing I've ever heard.

Before playing with me and the Flames, Tony played with the Continentals, The Kasuals (or Casuals), and Magnolia Blue. These bands are highlighted in other chapters under the band's name. For quick reference see the index.

Regarding day jobs that Tony had over the years, I am aware that he worked for TV and radio stations in the area for a number of years. He sold advertising and spent some time as an announcer. He ended his day job career in automobile sales where he worked as a salesman and manager for 25 years.

In 2009 Tony suffered a heart attack and stroke. He received by-pass surgery and is now retired. I wish Tony and his family the best and hope everyone will remember them in your prayers.

Chapter 27
Steve McGregory

Steve McGregory was born August 27, 1953, in Marks (Quitman County) Mississippi. His parents, Hubert Alvis McGregory and Vester Odell Smith McGregory, later moved to Panola County near Batesville with their nine children, of which Steve was the youngest. Steve attended school at South Panola which is famous for their championship football teams.

Steve played piano with me and my band (Mack Allen Smith & The Flames) for 2-1/2 years (mid 1974 through the end of 1976). Members of this band, which started in the summer of 1974, are as follows: Mack Allen Smith (lead singer), Laney O'Briant (lead guitar); Sanford Horton (bass), Gary Lee Worsham (drums), and Steve McGregory (piano).

In 1975 we recorded "King of Rock and Roll" and "Lonely Street" at Ace Recording Studio in Jackson, Mississippi. These two songs were released on Ace Records in 1975 and "King of Rock and Roll" has gained much recognition overseas because of Steve's fantastic piano ride. In addition, Ace Records released a 17-song LP in 1977 with Steve playing on nine of the tracks. See the Appendix for details.

Regarding Steve's day job, his primary one was with the Corp of Engineers where he worked 26 years before retiring in 1998. Since his retirement, Steve has kept busy with his music. He lives on a five-acre spread in Panola County near Batesville where he has a nice house and a recording studio. Steve has done some outstanding recording in his studio, including a 15-song CD on the legendary Ace Cannon. The CD entitled "Back to the Beginning" features songs that, at the beginning, were called Rock-A-Billy. Not only did Steve engineer this session, he played guitar and keyboards. His son (Danny McGregory) also did some keyboard work. In my opinion, Steve captured the extraordinary talent of the greatest sax player on earth - Ace Cannon. Ace is highlighted in Chapter 28.

Besides recording in his own studio, Steve has recorded in Nashville since retiring from his day job. One project in Nashville resulted in a gospel CD entitled "In the Master's Hands" by the group Souls for Christ, of which Steve is a member. In fact, Souls for Christ is a family gospel trio comprised of Scotty Aldridge (Steve's son-in-law on lead and harmony vocals), Delise McGregory Brown (Steve's daughter on lead and harmony vocals, and Steve McGregory (instrumentation and harmony vocals). The Souls for Christ CD was released in 2005 by Lamon Records of Charlotte, North Carolina. Lamon Records has offices throughout the United States and around the world. This has brought Steve and his group much recognition in recent years.

Steve was kind enough to prepare and present me with a typed mini-memoir recapping the life and times of Steve McGregory. This recap is presented as follows:

Born August 27th, 1953, Marks (Quitman County), Mississippi, parents Hubert Alvis McGregory and Vester Odell Smith McGregory.

Youngest of nine children. Started playing guitar at the age of nine. First introduction to musical instrument was a guitar given to me by my brother Jimmy Dale. This was a True tone acoustic guitar bought from the local Western Auto Store in Batesville, Mississippi. When my brother first got the guitar I really wanted to play with it, but to no avail. He would not let me put my hands on it. He later implanted it with various colored fake rhinestones that were driven into the outer edges all the way around the front of the guitar. I think he was trying to look like Porter Waggoner or one of those fancy country music stars we had seen on the Grand Ole Opera on TV. He played on the guitar for a while; I don't remember him ever learning anything other than strumming the open strings and singing along. So, finally, he just gave up on his musical journey and gave the guitar to me. Well, I was in hog heaven (if there is such a place). I had no idea how to tune it or even how it worked. I just knew that when you plucked those strings it made a sound that I liked. I had no one in the immediate family that knew how to play; as a matter of fact, I didn't know anyone who played except those guys I had seen on TV on Saturday afternoons. As I beat and banged on that old guitar finally one day I accidentally played the first three notes of a tune. I realized that I had just played the first three notes of an all time favorite song called "The Wildwood Flower." Those three little notes changed my life forever. I knew then just learning this very small portion of that song that nothing was impossible, there were no limits. I might add that I played those three little notes on one string only. I had not ventured to using more than one string at a time. So, as I learned a few things on that guitar, man, it was really getting interesting. So, within a year or so I had learned enough chords to play several three chord songs. It just seemed at that time nothing was impossible when it came to learning to play music.

I kept on working on guitar but at the age of about twelve for some reason, and I don't remember why, I had gotten interested in piano. My dad and I went to a place where this blind guy tuned and sold pianos. My dad bought this old upright from the man for one hundred dollars. When we got it home, I would usually practice about two hours a day. Well, that seemed to be the instrument I loved the best.

Piano is my favorite instrument and that's where I feel most at home when I sit down to play. Throughout the years I have learned to play several other instruments such as fiddle, banjo, mandolin, harmonica, bass guitar, and dobro. I have had the opportunity to play and record with some outstanding singers and musicians in my life such as Ace Cannon, Mack Allen Smith, The Southern Five, Percy Sledge, Jerry Wallace, This Mississippi River Bottom Band, Paul Burleson, Stella Parton, The Fire House Gang, and countless others.

Music is and always will be a real blessing in my life. Now my son, daughters, grandsons, and granddaughters are all playing and singing. And what a blessing that is!!!

Many blessings to you all.

Your friend,
Steve McGregory

Thank you, Steve, for the great piano work you did for me and my band during the 70s. Also, thanks for your continued support with the work you are doing in the studio for me from time to time in recording songs I've written. I hope to keep writing songs, and hope you will record my demos.
Your friend
Mack Allen Smith

Chapter 28
Ace Cannon

Ace Cannon was born May 5, 1934, in Grenada, Mississippi. For the past 20 plus years he has lived in Calhoun City, Mississippi, and they have claimed him as their own. As you enter the city limits of Calhoun City, there is a sign that reads, "Calhoun City-home of Ace Cannon-the greatest sax player in the world."

The fact that Ace Cannon is Chapter 28 should be proof enough that the order of chapters has nothing to do with which person or group is better known. If I started with the best known, then the second best known, etc., Ace Cannon would be Chapter one.

I had been hearing Ace Cannon on the radio for over ten years before I finally got to meet and hear him live in May 1971 at my club outside Greenwood, Mississippi. My club (Mack Allen Smith's Town & Country Night Club) was packed, and Ace knocked everyone's socks off, including mine. He had a great back-up band, and his sax playing was the best I had ever heard. I might add that I haven't heard anyone since that even came close to Ace Cannon.

I booked Ace several more times at Town & Country and we even played a couple of those battles of the bands. Regarding the battles, I'm claiming a draw. I won the singing and Ace won the sax playing.

Ace started his career in Memphis, Tennessee, in the 1950s playing on many Sun Record hits. I read a quote from Sam Phillips where he said, "Ace Cannon is the greatest saxophone player who ever lived, but then he came out of the same stables as Carl Perkins, Elvis, Jerry Lee, Bill Justice, etc."

In 1959 Ace started playing with the Bill Black Combo. He traveled on all concert dates and played the lead saxophone on all the original recordings. They appeared on The Ed Sullivan Show, The Merv Griffin Show, Dick Clark's American Bandstand, and the Buddy Dean show in Baltimore, Maryland, to name a few.

In 1962 Ace started recording under his own name. He recorded the instrumental smash "Tuff" which sold over a million records and, like they say, the rest is history. Ace has recorded 67 albums and 46 singles. His recordings include "Blue Eyes Crying In the Rain,' million selling TV albums such as "Golden Classics," "The Entertainer," and a duet with trumpeter legend, Al Hirt. The duet resulted in a historic album of country classics that could be one of the biggest TV albums in history.

In 1986 Ace performed on the Class of '55 Album with Jerry Lee Lewis, Carl Perkins, Johnny Cash, and Roy Orbison. This led to Ace and Carl Perkins performing together for the entire year of 1986. They played shows all over the U.S., and a tour of Norway, Sweden, and Denmark, and the World's Fair in Vancouver, British Columbia. During the early 1980s my band and I shared the stage with Ace again at The Delta Queen and Country Music Palace in Vaiden, Mississippi. My band backed up Ace at these gigs and did a great job.

Ace Cannon, often called The Godfather of Sax, is considered a musical genius as far away as the Caribbean where more than 23,000 people showed up for two sold-out shows at The Spectakula Forum and Queen's Park in the tiny port of Spain, Trinidad, Tobago, and British Guyana, South America, Hamilton, and Bermuda.

Throughout the 1990s Ace continued to be in great demand. He recorded two CDs for WIRL records in Barbados entitled "Music For Lovers," and "Sweet Dreams." They were also distributed in the U. S. with tremendous response.

In 1997, Scotty Moore and D. J. Fontana, two of the original Elvis Presley band, recorded an album entitled "All the King's Men," which consisted of eleven songs by various artists including the Bill Black Combo. Of the eleven songs, The Bill Black Combo selection was nominated for a Grammy award. This was an exciting honor for Ace, as this was a group he started his career with 40 years before.

As I write this chapter (January 2010) Ace is still in demand, and his sax playing is as good as ever. Even at age 75, he's still the greatest sax player in the world. From 1997 to the present time, Ace Cannon and Carl Griffin (Ace's manager and drummer) have recorded and co-produced 10 albums for RMD Music, Inc.

Ace Cannon has been inducted into the Smithsonian Rock and Soul Hall of Fame, the International Rock-A-Billy Hall of Fame, and the Memphis Music Hall of Fame. On December 9, 2008, Ace was inducted into the Mississippi Musicians Hall of Fame.

While on tour, Mayor Bobby Dyer of Lexington, Tennessee, presented Ace with the keys to the city following a recent concert there. Ace was also presented with the coveted Legislative Award from the State of Tennessee (House Resolution No. 217). This resolution praised his six decades of contributions to the music industry and enumerated his many achievements and concluded with the following:

"Whereas, artists of Mr. Cannon's caliber do not often walk among us, and this body wishes to pay tribute to this extraordinary musician, entertainer, and human being; Now, therefore, Be It Resolved by the House of Representatives of the One Hundred Fifth General Assembly of the State of Tennessee, that we hereby honor the inimitable Ace Cannon, "The Godfather of the Saxophone," upon a long and varied career that is truly unparalleled in artistry and achievement."

On May 30, 2009, Ace was presented the coveted Mississippi Legislative Award for his long career and contributions to the music industry. This award was presented by Rep. Jim Beckett.

Information for the Ace Cannon chapter was obtained in part from my personal experience of sharing a stage with Ace on a number of occasions during the 1970s and 1980s. Other sources of information came from recent interviews with Ace and three musicians that played with Ace during the 1990s. These three musicians are Sanford Horton (bass), Jamie Isonhood (piano), and Steve McGregory (piano). As previously noted in other chapters, Jamie played several months with me in the early 1960s and Sanford and Steve played 2-1/2 years with me during the 1970s. The other source was the Internet: http://www.acecannon.com/bio.html.

To have known and shared a stage with Ace Cannon is really a dream come true. Like Elvis, Ace is one of a kind. Imitators may come and go, but Ace Cannon will remain "The Godfather of the Saxophone - the greatest saxophone player who ever lived on planet Earth."

Chapter 29
Dominic Fratesi

Dominic Fratesi was born June 18, 1924, near Leland (Washington County), Mississippi. He died August 23, 2000, in Greenwood (Leflore County), Mississippi. Dominic is buried at Odd Fellows Cemetery in Greenwood.

Dominic attended school in Leland, after which he served in the Marine Corp. After completing his tour of duty in the Marines, Dominic settled in Greenwood around the early 1950s where he spent the rest of his life.

During the 1950s Dominic worked for Malouf Music. He placed and serviced jukeboxes and pinball machines at various locations in Greenwood and surrounding towns and counties. Then, around 1960 he and Raymond Rustom formed Dixie Amusement Center. For the remainder of his life Dominic Fratesi was self-employed.

I first started seeing Dominic and his brother Orlando (Lan) in 1959 when we played at the VFW in Greenwood. Later, when we played at the Greenwood Moose Lodge they were always there. Lan was a Moose member and was elected governor of the lodge. Of course, Dominic had his machines in the Moose and VFW, as well as hundreds of other locations.

In 1962 Dominic approached me about recording for his Vee Eight record label. I knew that Dominic had jukeboxes with records on them, but I didn't know he was in the recording business. He told me that he couldn't play and he couldn't sing but had always loved music and wanted to own a record label. Bill Biggs, a record salesman from Memphis, had helped Dominic set up Vee Eight and was serving as his producer.

When we got to Hi Recording Studio in Memphis for our first session in 1962 we learned that Hershel Wiggington had replaced Bill Biggs as producer. Hershel also had a vocal backup group that sang with us on several future recordings. Hershel's group was later the backup group on Hee-Haw in Nashville and sang on numerous Nashville recordings.

My band and I had recorded several songs at Sun Records in Memphis in 1959 but didn't get a release. Therefore, if Dominic Fratesi hadn't come along we may not have ever had a record release. I believe there are some other singers and bands that could make the same claim.

We recorded four songs at Hi Studio in 1962 which became two Vee Eight singles. Then Dominic switched us to his newly formed Statue label. We recorded eight songs (four singles) for Statue. All but one of these recordings were recorded at Fame Recording Studio in Muscle Shoals, Alabama. The other ("Skeleton Fight") was recorded at Hi in Memphis. For complete details see the Appendix.

For a person who couldn't play or sing, Dominic Fratesi was quite successful in the record business. The Mack Allen Smith records all started off slow then tapered off; however, he did better with a couple of other artists. Specifically, he put out "Little Band of Gold" on Jimmy Gilreath which he leased to Joy Records in New York City and wound up with a song on the national charts. After that he released "Road Runner" on The Gants which he leased to Liberty Records in Los Angeles, California, and wound up with another song on the national charts.

I'm thankful to Dominic Fratesi for the confidence he placed in me and my singing. I just wish I had recorded "Little Band of Gold" and "Road Runner." But, then again, I couldn't have sung them like Jimmy Gilreath or The Gants, so I would have probably turned out with two more songs that started off slow then tapered off like the rest of my records.

Chapter 30
Jamie Winters

Jamie Winters was born July 13, 1946, at Charleston (Tallahatchie County), Mississippi. He graduated from East Tallahatchie High School in 1964.

I first met Jamie Winters in March 2004 at the old school house in Blackhawk, Mississippi. Susie James had written a story about Jamie in the Greenwood newspaper with his picture on the front page. Susie wrote that this was a welcome home from Iraq where Jamie had served 16 months and was the oldest soldier in his unit to fight in the Iraq war. The front page picture showed Jamie with a guitar on stage somewhere playing and singing.

I wasn't singing at Black Hawk the night Jamie appeared in March 2004 and had never gone before unless I was singing. However, this time I had to go see this old man with a guitar who had fought for us in Iraq. After all, he was only eight years younger than me. I met Jamie that night, and he told me his favorite artist as a teenager was Mack Allen Smith. I couldn't believe what I was hearing. After that night in March 2004 Jamie started playing rhythm guitar with me and he has continued to be a member of my band. He is also a great bass player and plays bass with me when my brother Barry is absent.

Jamie provided me with some pertinent information about him and his family which is presented as follows (in order presented):

- Started playing guitar at six years of age;
- Favorite artist as a teenager - Mack Allen Smith;
- Started recording as a musician in 1969;
- Married Yvonne Newton October 19, 1966;
- Has two children, Stephen and Vicki, and six grandchildren;
- Joined the military August 16, 1965, and served to 1971;
- Joined the military again in 1987;
- Served in Iraq in 2003 and 2004;
- 2004-2008 served at Camp Shelby near Hattiesburg, Mississippi, training
- troops deploying to Iraq
- Retired from the military July 31, 2008
- Now works for the State of Misisisppi, but plans to retire April 30, 2010;
- Highlight of musical career - finally getting to meet and play with Mack Allen Smith.

I hope Jamie will continue to be a member of my band until I hang up my Rock-A-Billy shoes. Not because of all the good things he has said about me, but because he is one of the best human beings I've known. He is also one of the best musicians I've known.

He said he used to hear my records on radio stations in Greenwood and "Skeleton Fight" was his favorite song. With all the great records and artists around back then, to choose me as his favorite artist is the ultimate compliment. Without a doubt, this is the greatest compliment I have ever received.

Chapter 31
Stephen Winters

Stephen Winters was born January 4, 1970, at Charleston, Mississippi. He graduated from Charleston High School in 1988. After high school, Stephen attended Northwest Community College at Senatobia, Mississippi, where he graduated in 1990 with a major in General Business. He then attended Delta State University at Cleveland, Mississippi, where he graduated in 1993 with a Bachelor of Business Administration degree and a major in Computer Information Systems.

When I came out of my eighteen year retirement in October 2002 I had to sing without a drummer at my Black Hawk performance. None of the groups at Black Hawk were using drums, but I knew this wouldn't work for me. After 30 years in the honky-tonks I had gotten used to a good drum beat behind me and didn't want to sing without a good drummer. The Rock-A-Billy and old rock and roll stuff I did just wouldn't work without one.

For a while Michael Bole helped whenever he could and he was real good. However, he played with another band and couldn't always make it. I tried a couple of other drummers who put us in a bind by not showing up for a gig after saying they would play. Laney O'Briant wanted to give one of them another chance, but I went with the old: "Fool me once, shame on you; fool me twice, shame on me." I didn't want any shame on me; I just wanted a good, dependable drummer.

To make a long story short, I was about ready to go back into retirement again when Jamie Winters introduced me to his son Stephen. Jamie stated that he didn't want to brag on Stephen too much because he was prejudiced but believed I would like his drumming. Man, did I ever. Stephen started playing with me in June 2005, and as of this writing (February 2010), he is still with me. If Stephen ever quits then I'm gonna retire again for good. I believe Stephen is the best drummer around these parts and it has been a real pleasure having him in the band. I might add that his musical talent is not limited to just drums. He can play almost anything you put in front of him.

Stephen married Lynn Simmons on September 21, 1990, and they have four children (Audrey, Stephen Jr., James, and Carolyn). Regarding Stephen's day jobs, he has worked primarily with computers since graduating from DSU in 1993. He worked for a couple of banks as a computer operator, and since 2005 Stephen has worked for Advanced Distributor Products (ADP), in Grenada, Mississippi, as a business systems analyst.

As for Stephen's musical history, it is quite impressive to say the least. After playing for months on his mother's pots and pans with spoons, his parents bought him a set of drums at age five. Within a few months he was playing on stage and he hasn't stopped since. Stephen started playing at church but soon added country and old rock-n-roll which he performed at school houses and community centers. Today, when

Stephen is not playing drums with me, he plays steel guitar with the Slaton Family gospel group.

Besides live performances, Stephen has done lots of studio work. In fact, he recorded a CD at his home studio with him playing all the instruments (guitar, bass, drums, steel guitar, piano, etc.). To say that Stephen Winters has talent would be an understatement. He is unbelievable.

Chapter 32
Bob Timmers

    Bob Timmers was born March 8, 1941, in Appleton, Wisconsin. He attended high school at Menasha, Wisconsin, where he graduated in 1959.
    From an early age Bob loved Rock-A-Billy so no one was surprised when he created the Internet's Rock-A-Billy Hall of Fame (rockabillyhall.com). The Rock-A-Billy Hall of Fame was born March 21, 1997.
    Bob gave me a short listing in rockabillyhall.com in 1997 which consisted of a paragraph from page 154 of Martin Hawkins book (Sun Records). In getting started, I suppose Bob was including people regardless of their position on the totem pole. HA! The paragraph from Martin Hawkins is as follows:
    "Mack Allen Smith-born Carrollton, Mississippi, 1938. Learned some guitar from Mississippi John Hurt. Recorded for Sun with his band, The Flames, in 1959. The tape including "Sandy Lee" and "Mean Woman Blues" left Sun with producer Ernie Barton before it could be released. Smith later made excellent recordings for Vee Eight, Statue, Delta Sound, and other local Mississippi labels. He has kept the Delta sound alive to the present and has fine country rock albums issued on Ace and Delta Sound (U.S.) and on Redneck, Checkmate and Charley (U.K.)."
    Jimmy Harrell, a previous Sun artist now living in Florida, called me in 2000 and asked me to send Bob Timmers additional information so Bob could expand my listing. Jimmy Harrell is the brother-in-law of a former sax player of mine, Sonny Strohm. After sending the info, I received a Rock-A-Billy Hall of Fame certificate August 1, 2000. It is in a frame on the wall over my desk. I have been told that Jimmy Harrell is now my sponsor. So, to Jimmy I say thank you. Also, thanks to Martin Hawkins. Without Martin I suppose I would never have been listed at rockabillyhall.com, and, without Jimmy, I wouldn't have received an expansion of my listings and a certificate. To be honest, I have never felt like a Hall of Famer; however, I'm proud of this honor.
    Getting back to Bob Timmers, I want to say straight away, as they say in England, that I am very impressed and grateful for his contribution to Rock-A-Billy and his many accomplishments. I sent Bob a letter with a questionnaire in August 2009 requesting information for my book and he promptly replied with the pertinent information needed. I know Bob is extremely busy, and I want to say thank you, Bob, for your prompt reply.
    Bob stated that in high school his classmates couldn't understand why he was always excited about Warren Smith, Billy Lee Riley, Johnny Horton, and all those cats. Who was he talking about? Could they actually be cooler than Pat Boone?
    While in high school Bob joined a group (as an upright bassist) called The Jitterbugs with two classmates, Dave Pozkinski (drums) and an excellent guitarist, Ricky Leigh Smolinksi. This group also included a sax and an accordion. They played cover songs of only two artists: Elvis and Bill Haley. The Jitterbugs did many school

parties, worked as a tag-along band to local disc jockeys' record hops and performed on-stage during intermission at the local theater in Neenan, Wisconsin.

When Gene Vincent broke on the scene Bob bought everything Gene put out and focused on playing lead guitar. He started a spinoff group from The Jitterbugs. In his junior year, Bob joined "Jerry Williams & The Rockets," the top rock band in Wisconsin. Bob went back to bass, electric this time. Later, the lead guitar man, Jerry Starr, left to play with Wanda Jackson and Bob went back to playing lead guitar. He played with the Rockets several years. Bob's favorite guitarist was (and still is) Johnny Meeks of Gene Vincent's Blue Caps.

During the sixties Bob worked with many rock bands in Wisconsin, Northern Illinois, and Upper Michigan. One of the highlights was in 1965 when Bob brought an English singer to Wisconsin and spent the better part of a year doing British invasion music with a real Brit: Lord Beverey Moss.

During the 1970s and 1980s Bob spent most of his time with family and the family's publishing business, but still kept one ear tuned to his roots....Rock-A-Billy, early rock, and traditional country music.

Upon visiting the Rock & Roll Hall of Fame in Cleveland, Bob was disappointed to see displays that just didn't fit the mold of early rock and Rock-A-Billy. He went on line to the Rock-A-Billy discussion group and suggested that someone form a real "Rock-A-Billy Hall of Fame" on line to keep costs down and exposure up. Bob volunteered to give it a try and, with the help of JoeWaigel, the "Rock-A-Billy Hall of Fame" was born March 21, 1997, as previously mentioned.

He had the Rock-A-Billy Hall of Fame name and logo registered and trademarked with the federal government so no one else would be able to use (or mis-use) it.

Bob moved from Wisconsin to the Nashville, Tennessee, area June 5, 2000, and set up the Rock-A-Billy Hall of Fame at Burns Station Sound, 211 College Street in Burns, Tennessee 37029.

The building contains an excellent vintage recording studio, owned by Gordon D. Stinson.

Bob Timmers has played on recordings in Wisconsin; Lincoln, NE; Nashville, TN; Burns, TN; and Memphis (Sam Phillips International and Sun Records) and others. For complete discography see rockabillyhall.com/Bob Timmers. This site also lists over thirty stars that Bob has been on stage with.

Of special note is the fact that Bob Timmers has had the privilege of recording with three of the top original drummers who created rock 'n roll: D. J. Fontana (Elvis), Dickey Harrell (Gene Vincent), and W. S. Holland (Carl Perkins and Johnny Cash).

Bob Timmers has four children: Scott, Becky, Steve, and Ric. In addition, Bob has five grandchildren: Arianne, Ben, Cody, Ryan, and Marsia. Today he devotes much of his time to the website trying to keep the Rock-A-Billy Hall of Fame going and promoting the music.

Chapter 33
Martin Hawkins

Martin Hawkins currently lives in Southern England. He was born in England in 1949.

I first met Martin in 1975 at Ace Records in Jackson, Mississippi. Based on liner notes that Martin recently wrote for a CD of mine released in 2010 in the Netherlands, it was in April 1975 when we met. He said that I was 36 years old and he was 25. Therefore, since I was born in October 1938, I added 11 years to that and predicted that Martin was born in 1949. I believe 1949 is substantially correct.

When I met Martin at Ace Recording Studio in Jackson, Mississippi, I had just signed with Johnny Vincent, owner of Ace, and we were recording a couple of songs for a single release on Ace Records. At the time we met, Martin Hawkins was a collector of rock-a-billy records and a music writer. He was on his annual month-long trip around the USA, looking for records to buy and singers and musicians to interview. He approached me about letting him take some of my studio recordings and see if he could get me some releases overseas. We signed a contract and I sent him a bunch of my recordings.

My contract with Martin Hawkins resulted in one single and three albums in England and one album in Holland (see Appendix for details). Martin also got several of my recordings on compilation albums with other rock-a-billy artists. Martin was a writer for music magazines in America and overseas, and he wrote a number of articles trying to promote my career.

Besides the recordings and articles, Martin booked me on a two-week tour in England in July 1979. Roger Humphries and his Cherry Pickers, a group from Kent, England, backed me up. They were very good. As discussed in Chapter 18, Jessie Yates went with me and sang harmony. We performed at several clubs, as well as an annual outdoor concert which was attended by over ten thousand people. In the previously mentioned liner notes, Martin made the following statement about my singing on that 1979 tour of England: "Mack Allen sang rockers, ballads, old country, new country, the works. His voice sounded astoundingly good, everyone said so."

It wasn't in the cards for me to be a big star; however, Martin Hawkins did all he could to make it happen. For all his time and efforts on my behalf, I will forever be grateful.

Martin Hawkins co-authored with Colin Escott two books - *Sun Records and the Birth of Rock 'N' Roll*, and *Good Rockin Tonight*. In addition, Martin wrote *A Shot In the Dark: Making Records in Nashville, 1945-1955*. This book was published in 2006 by Vanderbilt University Press and the Country Music Foundation Press. The publishers made the following statement about him: "Martin Hawkins is one of the finest researchers in the whole realm of American vernacular music." They further stated, "He is a historian by nature, a career manager in the British health service, and a nocturnal writer of books, articles, and CD booklets. He writes about the people who recorded and promoted regional and roots music in the days before rock & roll. He is married with two grown-up children, lives in Southern England, and probably plays too much golf and watches too much football."

What else is there to say except: Martin, I'm glad our paths crossed in 1975 at Ace Records in Jackson, Mississippi.

Chapter 34
Larry Rogers

Larry Rogers was born in Corinth, Mississippi. The family later moved to Tennessee. Larry graduated from Central High School at Savannah, Tennessee, in 1961. After high school, he attended the University of Mississippi (Ole Miss) at Oxford, Mississippi. Larry graduated from Ole Miss in 1965 with a Bachelor of Music degree.

After graduating from Ole Miss, Larry joined Bill Black at Lyn-Lou Studio in Memphis. This team only lasted a few months because Bill Black died in October 1965; however, this short time with Bill Black gave Larry a good base that has served him well ever since. Larry told me that he would always be grateful for the opportunity Bill Black gave him to work in the studio and learn the ins and outs of recording.

I had the privilege of working in the studio with Larry from early 1967 to August 1969 when I moved back to Greenwood. Jim Bickerstaff opened the studio at 1518 Chelsea Avenue with Larry and Jim talked me into moving to Memphis.

About six months into 1967, Jim Bickerstaff moved to Arizona. According to Jim, he had to move to Arizona because of his wife's health. Before he left, Jim talked me into buying his half of the recording studio, so I borrowed some money and became partners with Larry Rogers. What this partnership encompasses was this: I owned the lease on the building and Larry owned the equipment. I paid the rent, and we split the utility bills. We split all money received from renting out the studio. As far as trying to cut a record, we were each free to do our own thing.

To make a long story short, Larry knew how to cut a good record and I didn't. Therefore, I wound up back in Greenwood, Mississippi, where I am as poor as ever, while Larry Rogers wound up in Nashville, Tennessee, where he owns three recording studios and is reportedly a multi-millionaire.

Even though I moved back to Greenwood in 1969, I continued recording at Lyn-Lou throughout the 1970s (see Appendix for details). I'm glad I got to know and work with Larry, and I am proud of his many achievements.

A brief summary of Larry's work and achievements, as obtained from internet research, is presented as follows: "Larry Rogers appears along with Sam Phillips, Scotty Moore, Alan Reynolds, and Isaac Hayes on the Honor Roll of Memphis Music in the Memphis Hall of Fame as one of the legendary producers that made rock, soul, and country music history during Memphis, Tennessee's musical heyday.

"He produced hit after hit for Billy Swan, Rick Nelson, Mel McDaniel, and Charley McLain at his world renowned Memphis recording studio, Lyn-Lou, a legend into itself. Larry also founded Partners and Partnership Music, two highly successful music publishing companies recently acquired from Larry and partner, Pat Brewer, by Polygram.

"In the early eighties Larry worked in Nashville with Jerry Kennedy at Mercury Recording Studios, Jim Malloy at Mega Records, and was part of one of the most extraordinary country music A&R teams of all time at CBS Records during Billy Sherrill's tenure.

"Larry Rogers opened his first studio in Nashville - Studio 19 - in 1984. Studio 19's almost instantaneous success led to the opening of his second Nashville studio - Studio 20 - which again became one of Nashville's most popular recording studios. Studio 20's success begot yet a third studio, this one, unnamed, with an unlisted telephone number and hidden in what appears to be a garage in the middle of one of Nashville's prominent residential neighborhoods, has become a popular recording destination for many of country music's biggest stars who prefer great sound quality mixed with the ultimate in privacy.

"Larry Rogers is much more than a legendary record producer and successful studio owner. He's also a mentor and business advisor to a legion of artists and countless songwriters who he has set on their paths to successful recording and writing careers. He prides himself in his ability to recognize talented people at a very early stage in their career and direct the development of their talent to the fullest realization of every aspect of its potential."

In reading all of the above accolades, I caught myself thinking that I was reading about the Pope. HA! I just want to say that I'm happy I got to know Larry and work with him in the studio before he got so rich and famous.

Chapter 35
The Continentals

According to Tony Browning, The Continentals were formed in 1965 and played together until sometime in 1967. Tony stated that band members were as follows: Tony Browning (bass), Doug Steen (sax), George Vernon (drums), Buddy Keys (lead singer), and Freddie Matthews (lead singer and rhythm guitar).

During the period they were together, The Continentals recorded two songs ("No Other Love" and "Someone") at Fane Studio in Muscle Shoals, Alabama. I released the two songs as a single on one of my record labels (Cynthia Records). In addition, the two songs were published on my BMI Publishing Company (Mack Smith Music). I really appreciated them letting me release their record and publishing their songs.

In 2009 Psychedelic States, a record company from Littleton, Colorado, released a 29-song CD entitled Mississippi "In the 60s". Number 26 on the CD is "No Other Love" by The Continentals. It appears that even though they were only together for a short period, their legacy will continue for years to come.

As I write this chapter (2/28/10), I believe all but one of the band members still live in Mississippi. Doug Steen lives in Crossett, Arkansas, Tony Browning lives in Greenwood, Mississippi, George Vernon lives in Carroll County, Mississippi, and Buddy Keys and Freddie Matthews live around Indianola, Mississippi. Freddie Matthews lived in Texas over 20 years, but has been back in the Delta several years teaching school around Cleveland. He is also singing with a band (Country Jack and the Silver Eagle Band) which is very popular now throughout the Delta and hill country.

Doug Steen played sax on my first single, "I Got My Mojo Working". He also played with other groups over the years and has always been in demand and remembered as a great sax player.

Tony Browning was highlighted in Chapter 26. He played with a number of great groups including Mack Allen Smith and The Flames. Tony had a heart attack and stroke last year (2009), but I talked to him recently and he said he was doing fine. I sure hope so.

As for George Vernon, I see him fairly often walking around Wal-Mart or sitting on a bench. George told me he is retired and says he walks one mile each day inside the Wal-Mart store.

I haven't talked to Buddy Keys in years, but as far as I know, he is well. I know he was singing with The Cracker Jacks a few years ago.

The Continentals were comprised of a group of five musicians and singers that fit in nicely with what was happening in the mid-sixties.

Chapter 36
The Reets

Dick Stevens and I formed a record label in 1967 for the sole purpose of releasing a record on The Reets. The record label (DIMAC) came from our first names (Dick and Mack). Clever, huh. HA! The songs we recorded and released were "Why Can't Time Stand Still" and "When You Brought Me You". The band members were as follows: Jimmy Pambiacci (vocals), Alston Meeks (lead guitar), Teddy Buckley (bass), Rick McQuirter (rhythm guitar), and Don Turnipseed (drums).

At the time of these recordings (early 1967), I was living in Memphis and trying to get something going at Lyn-Lou Studio (1518 Chelsea Avenue). Dick was at Delta State, and he called me about this great group, The Reets, who were DSU students. I had heard of The Reets but had never heard them play. Anyway, Dick brought them to Memphis and we hired studio owner (Larry Rogers) to engineer and produce the record. What resulted from this session were two fine recordings that Dick and I both believed had lots of potential. We pressed 1,000 records.

We got air play on some Mississippi stations, but were never able to get air play in Memphis. I had hoped we could break the record in Memphis then lease it to a major label like Dominic Fratesi had done with Jimmy Gilreath ("Little Band of Gold") and the Gants ("Road Runner"), but we just couldn't make it happen.

Psychedelic States from Littleton, Colorado, which was discussed in Chapter 35, released The Reets recording "When You Brought Me You" on their 2009 CD entitled Mississippi in the 60s. As with The Continentals, this should help ensure their legacy for years to come. However, even without a record, their fame was so wide spread they will long be remembered as one of the top bands in the sixties.

The Reets (1966-1969) were comprised of Delta State University students. Guitarist Alson Meeks has been quoted as saying that The Reets came along at a good time. Specifically, he noted that by 1967 the most popular groups like The Downbeats, Joe Frank and the Knights, and Andy Anderson and the Rolling Stones had broken up, thereby leaving a huge void to be filled. Without a doubt, The Reets were instrumental in helping fill this void.

The Reets were so good they did great on the frat house circuit - not only at Delta State but throughout Mississippi, Louisiana, Arkansas, Tennessee, and Alabama. They stayed booked. In 1969, after all the members had finished school at Delta State, the band broke up. But, as written in the book, *A History Of Garage & Frat Bands*, The Reets joined all those great groups before them as one of the best groups of the time.

Chapter 37
Curb Service / Johnny Jennings

Curb Service has been a popular fixture in the Mississippi Delta and surrounding areas for over thirty years. The original band was formed in 1978. Original members were: Johnny Jennings (rhythm guitar and singer), Johnny Freeman (lead guitar), Joe Seawright (bass), and John Elliott (drums). Shortly after forming, Fish Michie was added on piano.

Since I know Johnny Jennings better than the rest, and since he provided me with some information, I will present a little Johnny Jennings' history as follows:

Johnny was born September 30, 1947, in a hospital at Clarksdale, Mississippi. The Jenkins family lived at Tutwiler, Mississippi. Johnny graduated from West Tallahatchie High School in 1966. After high school, Johnny tried to find a college he really liked. During this quest, he attended Northwest Junior College, Mississippi Delta Community College, Ole Miss, Mississippi State, and Delta State. Johnny says he liked them all about the same. As some of you know, Johnny is a politician.

In addition to college, Johnny served in the Army before settling in Greenwood. He has lived in Greenwood since 1973. His day jobs in Greenwood are as follows: *Greenwood Commonwealth* (1973-1986) and City Council (currently as of 2010 in fifth four-year term). Johnny has also worked in real estate and owns a photography business. He has done photography work over 40 years. Johnny took the pictures at my 50th high school reunion and I might add, he did a great job.

I first heard Curb Service at the first annual River to the Rails event in 2006. They were everything I had heard they were and then some. Based on what I had heard about them, their signature song was "Rockin' Robin" and they had stolen the show from many name artists at the local Civic Center with this one song. I requested "Rockin" Robin" and they played it for me. Now, I know what the fuss is all about. They are a fantastic group. Everything they play is good, not just "Rockin' Robin." But, their rendition of "Rockin' Robin" is about the best I ever heard.

Current members of Curb Service are as follows: Johnny Jennings (rhythm guitar and singer), Johnny Freeman (lead guitar), Joe Seawright (bass), Harrison Smith (drums), Duff Durrough (lead guitar), and Charles Hall (piano).

The Curvettes were added as singers on New Year's Eve, 2006. They are: Vickie Morgan, Cathy Jennings, and Connie Black. Johnny Jennings stated that adding the Curvettes has really boosted Curb Service stock. According to Johnny, they not only book for a lot more money now, they also get a lot more bookings.

Chapter 38
Lawrence (Buddy) Millett

Buddy Millett was born September 12, 1935, at Ferriday, Louisiana. The family later moved to Yazoo City, Mississippi, where Buddy attended school. He died April 4, 2009, near Wolfe City, Texas. Buddy is buried at Restland Cemetery in Dallas, Texas.

As noted in Chapter 3, when Durwood Herbert left for college in 1961, I hired Buddy Millett to play drums. Buddy had never played drums before but told me he would buy a set of drums and learn if I would give him a chance. I was desperate and hired him. Buddy learned fast, and before long he could hang in there with the best around. He played with me and The Flames for eight years and was the drummer on most of our record releases during the 1960s. For details see the Appendix.

During the eight years Buddy played with us, his day job was at Baldwin Piano Company where he was supervisor of the finishing department. After 1969, Buddy played with The Casuals/Kasuals for a while, then he accepted a day job in Dallas, Texas, in the same line of work as at Baldwin Piano, but for more money. Buddy told me that when he moved to Dallas in the early 1970s, he sold his drums and never played again.

After coming out of my eighteen year retirement, Buddy came from Texas to hear us on two occasions (once at Carmack and once at the Carrollton Community House). I asked him to set in on drums at both gigs but he wouldn't do it; said he didn't remember which end of the sticks to hold. Unlike some folks, when Buddy quit, he quit. However, I must say this: when Buddy Millett played with Mack Allen Smith & The Flames, he was solid as a rock. And, as stated in Chapter 3, the sixties band ('63-'69) was the best butt-kicking band I was ever associated with.

Chapter 39
Lawrence Stacy

Lawrence Stacy was born in 1945 at Ruleville, Mississippi. He attended Ruleville High School then Delta State University at Cleveland, Mississippi, where he received a Bachelor of Business degree in 1967. Lawrence died August 1993 while living in Dallas, Texas.

Toward the end of 1969 our drummer since 1961 (Buddy Millett) left the band, but thanks to Lawrence Stacy we never missed a beat. In fact, the drums were featured more now than they had been since Durwood Herbert. Specifically, both Durwood and Lawrence took long solos on "Bo Diddley." The solos were from 15 to 30 minutes depending on crowd reaction. The other band members would leave the stage and sit in the audience during these solos, then return one at a time until all were back on stage playing at the song's conclusion. I have to say that Lawrence Stacy truly mastered the "Bo Diddley" solo.

Lawrence Stacy played drums with us for five years, then he got a federal job in Houston, Texas, in 1974. Lawrence later transferred back to Mississippi and played drums with me again (1977-1979). After Lawrence's second tour of duty with Mack Allen Smith and The Flames, he quit playing and sold his drums. Lawrence was moving up the federal ladder. He moved to New Orleans as assistant director and then to Dallas, Texas, as district director.

Before going to work for the federal government, Lawrence worked for the State Unemployment Office, and owned a grocery store and two restaurants (cafes).

Lawrence played on a 20-song album that we recorded in 1972 and on one side of a single we recorded for Ace Records in 1977. See Appendix.

Lawrence Stacy was an insulin dependent diabetic, and he died way too young. His day jobs brought much success and I know he did the right thing when he quit drumming to concentrate on his career. He was a great drummer and I appreciate the years he spent playing with me and The Flames.

Chapter 40
Gary Lee Worsham

Gary Lee Worsham was born October 18, 1950, at Grenada, Mississippi. He graduated from Grenada High School in 1968. After high school, Gary Lee attended Delta State University at Cleveland, Mississippi, where he graduated in 1972. Since graduating from Delta State in 1972, Gary Lee has been in banking. As of this writing (March 2010), Gary Lee is city president with Regions Bank in Grenada, Mississippi.

As discussed in Chapter 3, Gary Lee played drums with me for two and one-half years (summer of 1974 through the end of 1976). Gary Lee played with me on ten songs that were released by Ace Records in Jackson, Mississippi. Four of the songs were recorded at Ace Studio in Jackson and six more were recorded at Lyn-Lou Studio in Memphis, Tennessee. See Appendix for details.

Gary Lee hung up his drumsticks many years ago; however, he has a son (Charlie) who is a professional musician. I heard Charlie with his band, King Billy, at Carroll County Market in 2008. If I ever heard a better band or a picker better than Charlie then it was a long time ago. One picker (Bobby Neal) comes to mind - at least on guitar. Charlie is a singer, songwriter, and session player in Nashville, Tennessee, and I predict much success for him in years to come.

Mr. and Mrs. Gary Lee Worsham are extremely proud of their son, Charlie, because many parents don't have children as talented as Charlie. When Gary Lee played drums with me during the mid-seventies, he wasn't bad either. In fact, he was one of the best around.

Chapter 41
Johnny Vincent

Johnny Vincent (1927 - February 2000) was born in Hattiesburg, Mississippi and died in Jackson, Mississippi.

Johnny moved to Jackson in the late 1940s where he opened a record shop. He started the Champion Records label in the early fifties. Then, Johnny was A&R man for Speciality Records where he worked with artists like John Lee Hooker and Earl King. In 1954, he left Speciality to form his now famous Ace Records.

As noted in Chapter 3, I signed a contract with Johnny Vincent in 1975 to record for Ace Records. This resulted in four record releases on Ace, one in 1975, one in 1976, and one in 1977, and an album in 1979.

Most everyone agrees that Sam Phillips, with Elvis, Jerry Lee Lewis, and a huge roster of other stars, did more in the 1950s than anyone in the world to change the course of music. Nonetheless, Johnny Vincent with his records in the 1950s of "Sea Cruise" by Frankie Ford, "Just A Dream" by Jimmy Clanton, "Rockin' Pneumonia and a Boogie Woogie Flu" by Huey Piano Smith, and a bunch of other great records, was certainly a major contributor in shaping music for future generations. In my opinion, Johnny Vincent would have to be rated second behind Sam Phillips.

I consider it an honor to have known Johnny Vincent and be listed on his roster of Ace recording artists. And, the fact that we became good friends is priceless.

Chapter 42
Quinton Claunch

Quinton Claunch was born December 3, 1921, in Tishomingo County, Mississippi, where he grew up with his parents and two sisters.

I first met Quinton Claunch in 1979 at Ace Recording Studio in Jackson, Mississippi. He approached me about recording a song he had written entitled "Natural Gas." He said that Johnny Vincent had played some of my recordings for him and he thought my voice was the right one for his song. To make a long story short, we recorded "Natural Gas" at Lyn-Lou Studio in Memphis in 1979, after which he released it on QMC Records.

After not seeing Quinton for almost 30 years, we got together again for a session in Memphis where I re-recorded "Natural Gas" and another song he had written entitled "The Politician's Song." These two songs, plus ten other songs by other artists (i.e. Gene Simmons, Billy Lee Riley, Ivory Joe Hunter, and more) were released in 2009 on Soul Trax Records. The CD is available on the internet.

I heard a lot about Quinton Claunch for years before I met him and wish our work together had been longer and not so far in between. As I write this chapter (March 2010), Quinton is 88 years young and, as they say, he ain't no spring chicken anymore. For that matter, I ain't either. I am happy that we got back together after all those years, and I appreciate the brief period I was able to record for a legend in the music business.

Some Quinton Claunch history is presented as follows:

Quinton's father bought him a guitar when he was 13 years old and a neighbor taught him basic chords and procedures. In 1942 the family moved to Muscle Shoals, Alabama, where he teamed up with vocalist Edgar Clayton. Soon, they had their own radio show on local station WLAY. After one year the manager of a new station in Florence, Alabama (WJOI), persuaded Quinton to organize a full band and do a daily show on his station. Before long, the program was so popular that a flour company sponsor bought time on 15 additional radio stations in Tennessee, Alabama, and Mississippi to carry the programs.

Due to the increased popularity, the flour company (Blue Seal Flour) furnished them with a new automobile, fancy uniforms, and a salary so they could go on the road and promote their product. Appropriately, they named the band The Blue Seal Pals. This arrangement was so successful the company purchased time on the premier radio station, WSM in Nashville, Tennessee, for a weekly Saturday morning program. The Blue Seal Pals wound up working with many great country acts such as Minnie Pearl, Rod Brasfield, Cowboy Copas, Jimmy Work, and others. In 1947, the band broke up as most of the members had gotten married and went their separate ways.

Quinton and his wife moved to Memphis in 1948, and he got a day job with a wholesale distributor of heating and air conditioner supplies and equipment, sheet metal products, and building materials. Quinton said he needed a steady pay check to feed and clothe his family, but he still had music fever. He worked his day job on the road from Memphis throughout North Mississippi as far south as Jackson. Quinton recalls a good account in Greenwood, Jessie Quinn at Greenwood Roofing and Sheet Metal.

For a man with a day job, Quinton Claunch has accomplished a lot in the music business. He played guitar on a couple of Carl Perkins records at Sun Records and was hired by Sam Phillips to talent search and do pre-productions on some of the new artists he had signed.

In 1955 Quinton went to see Joe Guoghi, owner of Popular Tunes, about starting a record label. He was aware of Quinton's experience and thought it was a great idea, thus Hi Records was born. With Quinton aboard, Hi had several hits on the Bill Black Combo and another ("Haunted House") on Gene Simmons.

After Hi, Quinton moved to another new label, O. J. Records, to work on a project by the late Brother Dave Gardner. He came up with another winner called "White Silver Sands."

In 1964 Quinton formed Goldwax Records after which he signed James Carr, Roosevelt Jamison, and O. V. Wright. Other artists that were signed soon thereafter were The Ovations and Spencer Wiggins. During the 1960s Goldwax was considered one of the best soul labels in the world. As for James Carr, who can ever forget "Dark End of the Street," an all-time classic. Quinton produced fifty songs on James Carr during the Goldwax years, as well as three CDs during the 1990s. Quinton stated that many music publications have labeled James Carr as the world's greatest soul singer and, to his knowledge, no one has challenged this analogy. If Quinton Claunch is ever proclaimed the worlds' greatest producer of soul records, I doubt if anyone will challenge this analogy either.

Besides being a great producer and musician, Quinton is also a great song writer. His songs have been recorded by Ry Cooper, Percy Sledge, Little Milton, The Beatles, Ringo Starr (a former Beatle member), and numerous R&B and rock and roll artists. In addition, many country artists have recorded Quinton's songs. They include Jimmy Newman (Dot Records), Wanda Jackson (Capitol Records), Rita Robbins (RCA Records), Tammy Wynette (Epic Records), and Doug Bragg (Coral/Decca Records). Also, many local artists have recorded his songs for Memphis-based record labels.

Quinton is an amazing person. He has been retired from his day job for twenty years, but as long as the Lord will let him, he'll keep on writing and recording songs. That's the way it is when you've got the music fever.

Chapter 43
Pete Bartosch

Pete Bartosch was born March 17, 1946, at Corpus Christi, Texas. He graduated from H. B. Ray High School at Corpus Christi in 1965. After high school Pete attended Delmar College at Corpus Christi.

Pete played bass with my first cousin, Billy Wayne Herbert, in Texas and came to Memphis when Billy Wayne moved there in 1970. It has been my pleasure to hear Pete play bass a number of times since he moved from Corpus Christi, Texas, to Memphis, Tennessee. He also played with me on two songs that I recorded at Lyn-Lou Studio in Memphis in 1970. For details see the Appendix.

Some pertinent information about the life and times of Pete Bartosch as relayed to me by Pete himself is presented as follows:

Pete started playing bass and singing when he was five years old. He played with bands at the local Moose Lodge that were friends of his parents. At age six (first grade) Pete started singing in school choirs and continued through 12th grade. He also played in a couple of bands while in high school.

In 1967 Pete landed his first full time playing gig with The Gary Beck Trio. Then, in 1969 Pete joined what he calls the best band in Corpus Christ, Texas, The Revelation. This band was comprised of Billy Wayne Herbert (lead guitar and vocals), Ronnie Korner (drums), Pete Bartosch (bass), and Gary Beck (organ and piano).

Since moving to Memphis with Billy Wayne Herbert and Ronnie Korner in 1970, Pete has been quite busy. He has earned a reputation as one of the best bass players in Memphis.

Besides continuing to play with The Revelation, which later became Stone Blue, Pete worked all the major studios in Memphis (Hi, American, Sun, Sonic, Onyx, Lyn-Lou and Stax).

Other bands that Pete has played with include: The Ace Cannon Band, Bill Haney, and Tiny Bonds. Starting in 1983, Pete worked with Tiny Bonds for ten years. They played at Bad Bob's, Vapors, and Tiny Bonds own club. In 1995 Pete joined The Memphis Deftonz, a nine piece Mo-town, Blues Brothers type group (Memphis Music) with whom he still plays today.

With the exception of eight months in Nashville (1975) and nine months in Washington State (1981), Pete has lived in and around Memphis since moving there in 1970. As of this writing (March 2010), Pete is living in Barton, Mississippi, with Kathy, his wife of 36 years. They have one daughter who was born in August 1975.

I saw Pete at Billy Wayne Herbert's funeral in July 2007. This was the first time I had seen him in over 30 years. I haven't seen him since the funeral, but we have talked on the phone, and he was kind enough to send me the information I needed to write this chapter.

Perhaps sometimes in the future I can go hear some great Corpus Christi bass playing that Pete Bartosch brought to Memphis in 1970.

Chapter 44
Stone Blue
(1972 - 1980)

Billy Wayne Herbert moved to Memphis from Corpus Christi, Texas, in 1970. Two musicians came with him: Pete Bartosch (bass) and Ronnie Korner (drums). Besides working at the Lyn-Lou Studio, they played at the Airport Lounge. This group, which was called the Revelation, added Don Chandler on organ and James Govan as lead singer. Then, in 1972 they changed their name to Stone Blue.

During the eight years they were together, Stone Blue played the Airport Lounge, The Water Hole at Quality Inn on Brooks Road, The Underground Club, and September Place, to name a few. In 1973 I booked them at my club in Greenwood, Mississippi (Mack Allen Smith's Town & Country Night Club). We had a battle of bands and, as noted in Chapter 6, I think Stone Blue kicked our butts.

Stone Blue was considered undisputed champions of bands working the nightclub circuit in Memphis during their reign. I talked to Don Chandler not long ago and he mentioned the fact that there were always long lines at the Memphis clubs they played. And, if you didn't get there early you couldn't get in. I went to several of the Memphis clubs to hear Stone Blue during the 1970s and they were always packed.

A brief blurb of where they are now and what they are doing is as follows:

<u>Billy Wayne Herbert (lead guitar)</u> - As noted in Chapter 6, Billy Wayne died July 4, 2007. From the time Stone Blue broke up until he died, Billy Wayne did a one-man show and owned a recording studio at his home near Hernando, Mississippi.

<u>Pete Bartosch (bass)</u> - Pete is highlighted in Chapter 43. He currently lives in Barton, Mississippi, and plays with a nine-piece band from Memphis.

<u>Ronnie Korner (drums)</u> - Ronnie now lives in Navasota, Texas, and works as a CPA in Houston. After Stone Blue he played for Bill Haney and a couple of other bands before going to college and getting a degree in accounting.

<u>Don Chandler (organ)</u> - Don now lives in Byhalia, Mississippi. For the past 20-plus years he has played at Rum Boogie on Beale Street in Memphis, Tennessee.

<u>James Govan (lead singer)</u> - James still lives in Memphis. For the past 20-plus years he has been the lead singer at Rum Boogie on Beale Street in Memphis, Tennessee. He and Don Chandler have been working together for a long time now. I hope it doesn't end before I get to Memphis and hear them.

Chapter 45
Ray Hall

Ray Hall was born December 22, 1947, at Senatobia, Mississippi. He attended high school at Hernando High and Greenwood High. He graduated from Greenwood High School at Greenwood, Mississippi, in 1966.

When I moved back to Greenwood from Memphis in August 1969 and went to work as a car salesman for Delta Chevrolet-Olds-Cadillac, I met Ray Hall for the first time. He was also an automobile salesman at Delta Chevrolet. While we worked together at Delta Chevrolet, I didn't know Ray was a musician, and he never told me that he was. I later learned that he was not only a musician, he had an impressive resume.

The following information on Ray Hall is based on several interviews with him and a written synopsis he presented to me:

The Ray Hall music story starts in the Memphis, Tennessee, area, where Ray was living when he got his first guitar and started playing at age 12. Ray's first Memphis gig was on the Larry Kennon Country Music Show which was broadcast on Saturday mornings. Other performances while living in the Memphis area are as follows:

1.) Played rhythm guitar at Vaughn Theater in Hernando, Mississippi, where he backed Bobby Lee Tramell, Eddie Bond, and a number of other stars.

2.) At age 13 Ray played at Eddie Bond's club in Memphis. According to Ray, he was so young they had to sneak him in to play.

3.) When Ray got older he turned to rock-'n-roll and played with a group called The Escapades, followed by a stint with C-L and the Backfires. Ray's tour with rock bands led to gigs at Memphis A-go-go clubs as well as senior proms and private parties.

When Ray was 15 his mother moved the family to Phillip, Mississippi, near Greenwood. The remainder of Ray's music history occurred in and around Greenwood. This included stints with the following groups: The Newtones, The Casuals/Kasuals, and later with gospel groups called The Open Hearts, Redeemed, and, finally, Perfect Heart who recorded two CDs.

When I returned from my 18-year retirement in October 2002, Ray Hall was playing bass with a gospel group, The Deltones, headed by Leman Gandy. Vicky Carlisle was the lead singer and, I must say, she has a great voice. My band and I (Mack Allen Smith and The Flames) subsequently played several shows with the Deltones at the Black Hawk school house, Carmack school house, and Carrollton Community House.

As I finish this chapter (4/14/10), Ray is playing bass with some pickup musicians at Black Hawk and at nursing homes. I hope he keeps on playing for years to come.

Chapter 46
Benny Rigby

Benny Rigby was born August 26, 1951, in Carmack (Attala County), Mississippi. He attended school (grades 1-8) at Carmack. Then, Benny went to Vaiden High School in Vaiden, Mississippi, where he graduated in 1970. After finishing high school, he attended Holmes Junior College in Goodman, Mississippi.

Shortly after coming out of my 18-year retirement in October 2002, I was on a show at the Black Hawk school house which also included Benny Rigby and his gospel group, His Majesty. I had heard about Benny for years from his music ministry in various churches, but had never heard him in person. Needless to say, I was impressed.

Since meeting Benny Rigby, he has played rhythm guitar and piano with me a number of times and now is the piano player with me and my band (Mack Allen Smith & The Flames). Occasionally, I have to excuse him to perform with his gospel group, but he makes most of my gigs. Besides shows with his gospel group, he also sings and plays with musicians at nursing homes and various benefits, as well as eating establishments in Winona and surrounding areas.

Benny was kind enough to provide me with a mini-memoir, which I am presenting verbatim as follows:

"I have always loved music even as a child but never had the opportunity to own a musical instrument until I was married in 1970. I bought a Gibson guitar from Self's Music in Kosciusko, Mississippi, and had no idea that one of the greatest guitar pickers around was teaching music there. So, I signed up to take a few lessons from the legendary Laney O'Briant. After learning a few chords on the guitar I bought a bass guitar and learned a few licks on it and went on to play bass with Lloyd Bailey backing Richard McLaughlin and the late James Gray. Lloyd Bailey was a big help in advancing me in what I had already learned.

"Later on, some of the other musicians and I formed a group called Country Crossroads. We sang mostly for benefits, festivals, and local events. In addition to me, the members included Keith Norris, David Durham, Kelly Hall, Toad Donahoo, and Lloyd Bailey. It was in the later part of the 80s when the Lord called me in the gospel music ministry. Linda Stafford, Judy Stanford, and I attended the same church and began singing together, and later formed the group We're Redeemed. Later Laverne Palmertree came on board to play keyboard; my two sons, Benjie and Brian, alternated playing drums, as did Kelly Hall. Ray Hall played bass, as did Timmy Slaten at one time.

"Later, when Linda and Judy retired, Marcia Dozier, Lisa Threat, and Tommy Armstrong joined the group with their vocals. We sang about 60 dates per year all around the Mississippi and Tennessee areas. We released two singles this time: "Mr. Timms" and "In the Master's Hands."

"We also won Mississippi Country Gospel Group of the year award in 1994. The song, "Mr. Timms," was nominated Country Gospel Song of the Year and came in second place. Our last date to sing together was at the First Baptist Church of Eupora in August 1997. After a couple of years off I, along with Martha Britt and Tyanne Newsome, formed the group His Majesty, which Martha and I are still a part of.

"I have had the pleasure of being music director at Community Baptist Church, Winona, Mississippi, Calvary Baptist Church, Greenwood, Mississippi, and North Winona Church, Winona, Mississippi, in the past 20 years.

"For the past few years I have had the pleasure of playing keyboards for Mack Allen Smith, along with Laney O'Briant, Barry Smith, Bill Walker, Jamie Winters, Stephen Winters, and also with Toad and the Good Ole Boys. The Lord has truly amazed me with the many opportunities that He has given me through music. As a young man I used to listen to Mack Allen Smith and his great band and thought how great it would be to have the talent to play with guys like that. I never dreamed I would be on stage with them some day. I thank all of you guys who have inspired me through your music ability and for giving me the opportunity to play with the best!

"I would like to thank my wife, Sheila, for supporting my love for music.

"Thanks to Mack Allen for giving me the opportunity to share a little about my musical experiences."

Chapter 47
George Thomas

George Thomas was born March 13, 1956, in Goodman, Mississippi. George attended high school at East Holmes Academy in West, Mississippi. He graduated from high school in 1974. After high school, George attended Holmes Junior College in Goodman, Mississippi, where he graduated in 1976.

George started playing drums with me and my band (Mack Allen Smith & The Flames) in 1978 and played with us through the end of 1982. During his tenure with The Flames, George played on one single, "Memphis, You Ain't Nothing But the Best," which was recorded in 1981 at Lyn-Lou Studio in Memphis and released by Grape Records. This recording was also released on a 16-song album by Charly Records of London, England, in 1981. In addition, George played drums on the 38-song double CD entitled "Live On Halloween". This CD was recorded live on October 31, 1981, at the Country Music Palace in Vaiden, Mississippi. Without a doubt, this was our best live recording ever. The band was the tightest ever, and listening to George's work on the drums is all the evidence I need to proclaim him one of the best drummers to ever play with The Flames.

Some of George's other music gigs are presented as follows:

From 1971-1976 George played with The Losers, which were later named Deep South. Members were George Thomas, Bruce Aldridge, Earl Aldridge, Alvin Green, Chuck Estes, Roy Irby, and Eddie Michaels.

In 1977 George played with a band whose members were George Thomas, Bobby Philyaw, David Philyaw, Bobby Alexander, and Van Simpson. George didn't remember the name of this band.

- In 1978 George played a while with Magnolia Blue whose members were George Thomas, Van Simpson, Kenny Loftin, Larry Parker, Eddie Michaels, and Mike Sullivan.
- 1978-1983 - As previously noted, George started playing with Mack Allen Smith & The Flames in 1978 and played through 1982. Members were George Thomas (drums), Mack Allen Smith (lead singer), Laney O'Briant (lead guitar), Paul Melton (bass), Tony Browning (bass), Larry Acy (piano), and Chris Mims (piano).
- In 1984 George played with another no-name band - George Thomas, Charles Hall, Roxanne Hall, and Mike Sullivan.
- 1985-1997 - George didn't play much during this time because his job had him on call full time at radio stations. He did a few True Value Country Showdown contests, speciality gigs, and fill-ins.
- 1997-2000 - During this period George played with his teenage son, George Thomas, III, and his band, Time Squared. Members were George Thomas, George Thomas III, Sam Adcock, and Brian Fuentes. They recorded a couple of

CDs. His son now plays bass with The Crisis in Houston, Texas, for a living. George stated that they have been at it for a few years and are very good.
- 1999-2002 - George played in the church band at Rivercrest Fellowship in Jackson, Mississippi.
- 2006-2008 - George played at various blues jams in the Jackson, Mississippi, area. He also played with Jimmy Buffet's harmonica player, Fingers Taylor.
- 2008 - current - Playing with Madison Station Band in Jackson, Mississippi: George Thomas, Jay Robinson, Jessie Smith, and Robert Jackson. According to George, T-Bone Robert is the bass player for a number of famous blues artists from the Jackson, Mississippi, area.

Throughout his music career, George has been active in recording demos, shows, and originals for friends, bands, and himself with his home studio gear. He has also worked in a few regular studios.

George has a large collection of original recordings of himself and friends from the mid 1970's through the present. He hopes to release them on a CD one day soon. George stated that he recently ordered a 24-track recorder and plans to do more recording in the future.

Besides music, George is an avid licensed amateur (ham) radio operator. He enjoys using the airwaves to talk with friends all over the U.S. and around the world. George and a few friends do an amateur radio-related Internet TV show available at www.amateurlogic.tv.

George Thomas is married to Phyllis D. Thomas and they have four children: George III (age 27), Randi (age 17), Hannah (age 12), and Claire (age 11). George's parents are still living in Goodman, Mississippi.

Some information about George's day jobs over the years is presented as follows:
- August 1972 - June 1976: Engineer/announcer at WKOZ/WBKJ Radio in Kosciusko, Mississippi.
- May 1976-December 1980 - Service manager/buyer at Stereo City in Kosciusko, Mississippi.
- January 1981 - January 1983 and August 1983 - February 1985 - Assistant chief engineer at WABG-TV in Greenwood, Mississippi.
- From Feburary 1985 to February 1987 George was chief engineer with SFX broadcasting in Jackson, Missisisppi.
- From February 1997 to the present time (June 2010) George has served as president of Pristine Systems, Inc. They have offices in Los Angeles, CA, and Ridgeland, Mississippi.

Training that prepared George for his impressive day job career includes: Continental Electronics Transmitters in 1986, Sony Broadcasting Training in 1983, and Holmes Junior College Broadcasting Electronics Servicing (1974-1976).

George Thomas has accomplished much in his life, and I'm happy that he chose to play four years with me and The Flames. Whenever I want to hear a great drummer, I turn on my CD player and stick in "Live On Halloween". It just doesn't get any better than that.

Chapter 48
Richard McLaughlin

Richard McLaughlin was born May 22, 1935, in Shreveport, Louisiana. In 1952 Richard graduated from Winnsboro High School in Winnsboro, Louisiana. After high school Richard served four years in the U. S. Navy. In 1957 he married Kathleen Hood from Grenada, Mississippi, and they have lived in Grenada ever since.

I met Richard in 2003 when I purchased a sound system from his music store. Since then we have appeared on a number of shows together in North Mississippi. He plays rhythm guitar and sings. His specialty is Hank Williams. Richard has been a Hank Williams fan for many years and got to meet his idol in 1949. Hank played a show at a high school in Castor, Louisiana, and Richard said meeting Hank was one of the top highlights of his life. His number one highlight, of course, was when he married Kathleen Hood in 1957.

Richard has been singing since the early sixties and has been the leader of two country music bands, Richard McLaughlin & The Country Playboys and Richard McLaughlin & the Gray Rebels. He has appeared on stage with performers like Narvel Felts, Claude King, Hank Snow, Jr., The Kendalls, Billy Crash Craddock, and Ace Cannon. Richard has recorded two CDs.

I saw a bumper sticker once on a musicians guitar case that read, "Real musicians have day jobs." Well, Richard, like most of us, has had some day jobs. A few are as follows: nine years as a movie projector operator, 18 years as a potato chip salesman, and 23 years as a retailer of music supplies. Richard has also promoted a number of country music shows including the popular "Legends of Country Music."

I am glad that Richard and I met and became friends in our sunset years, and I am thankful for the brother-in-law price he gives me whenever he makes CD copies for me. At least, he tells me I'm getting the brother-in-law price, even though we are not brothers-in-law. Richard also gives me a good deal when I buy music equipment from his music store in Grenada. I recommend Mack's Music. On my next batch of CDs, I will expect a discount for this advertising. HA!

Chapter 49
Jenkins B. Ruscoe

Jenkins Ruscoe was born August 13, 1902. He died February 13, 1965, while living in North Carrollton, Mississippi. North Carrollton had been his home for many years. Jenkins is buried in Evergreen Cemetery at North Carrollton. For most of his adult life, his day job was with the C&G Railroad in Greenwood, Mississippi.

Unlike most musicians I have known, Jenkins didn't start his singing career until he was middle aged. Reportedly, he started his band in the 1940s when he was around 40 years old. As for me, I was about worn out by the time I reached 40.

If anyone could be considered the Godfather of Country Music in North Mississippi honky-tonks, it would have to be Jenkins Ruscoe. Before Jenkins, it was mostly acoustic instruments in old country homes with no electricity. Jenkins took it to another level with his band which featured electric instruments and singing through a PA system at honky-tonks that were just springing up with electricity and indoor plumbing.

Many band members and/or musicians in bands that were formed in the 1950s actually got their starts playing in Jenkins Ruscoe's band. People like Grover Duke, Kenny Minyard, Eddie Lee Alderman, and a host of others started out playing with Jenkins.

Shortly after moving to Carrollton, Mississippi, in 1947, I started hearing about Jenkins Ruscoe and his band playing at the 82 Club on Highway 82. Daddy had opened a grocery store in Carrollton in 1947 and I often heard customers talking about going dancing where Jenkins played. I was too young to go to the honky-tonks, but when I heard that Jenkins was coming to the Carrollton Community House, I begged daddy to let me go listen. He agreed, but I couldn't go inside. I would have to stand outside and listen. I found out later that, in those days, people drank whiskey in the Community House just like they did at the 82 Club and other honky-tonks in the area.

I must say that hearing Jenkins Ruscoe in 1947 when I was just nine years old made a lasting impression on me. Who could ever forget "That Old Rain is Cold and Slowly Falling," and who could ever forget Plute Johnson playing that auto sax. In those days I don't remember other bands having a sax, and it really set Jenkins and his band apart from the competition.

In 1959 my band and I (Mack Allen Smith & The Flames) finally got to do a show with Jenkins Ruscoe and his band. It was a street dance in Greenwood, Mississippi. Hearing Jenkins sing "That Old Rain is Cold and Slowly Falling" up close, and sharing a stage with Plute Johnson, is something I'll never forget.

Although times were changing, Jenkins Ruscoe played into the 1960s. As previously noted, he died February 13, 1965. Nonetheless, I believe Jenkins left a lasting legacy in this part of the country.

Chapter 50
Grover Neal Duke

Grover Duke was born May 5, 1924, in Carroll County, Mississippi. He died March 16, 1982, while residing in Carroll County near Teoc. Grover is buried at Mt. Pisgah Cemetery in Carroll County near Teoc.

When I was fifteen years old, Sonny and Pauline Noland took me to the VFW Club in Grenada, Mississippi. Sonny and Pauline were renting the upstairs at our house in Carrollton, so daddy let me go to hear the music. Daddy didn't know I would participate in anything except listening to music; however, as they say, this was my first taste of sin. Besides listening to music, I drank some Old Crow for the first time. Now - back to Grove Duke.

Grover Duke and the Delta Rhythm Boys were playing that night and, I must say, they made a lifelong impression upon me. The Delta Rhythm Boys consisted of the following: Grover Duke (lead guitar and singer), Kenny Minyard (bass), Alton Cheek (lead guitar), Eddie Lee Alderman (steel guitar), and Billy Marcus (drums and singer). A couple of years later (1956) when I was a senior at J. Z. George High School in North Carrollton, Mississippi, I heard Grover Duke again at the Community House in Carrollton. I will never forget Billy Marcus jumping up from the drums, grabbing the microphone, and singing "Lawdy Miss Clawdy." He brought the house down.

After finishing high school in 1956, I got to share a stage with Grover Duke at the Greenwood VFW. There was a radio show there on Saturday afternoons and Grover often sat in with me and my little band on lead guitar. We needed all the help we could get, and Grover was the best lead guitar player around these parts. In the fall of 1956, I left for college and then the Marines, so I didn't see Grover Duke again until 1959.

In January 1959, I returned to Carrollton from the Marines, and the first music I heard after returning was Grover Duke at the Carrollton Community House. Before the music started, Grover told me he had a surprise for me. When he got on stage, he picked up a saxophone and started playing it like he had been doing it all his life. The last time I had seen Grover was 1956 and he was playing lead guitar. Now, here he was in 1959 playing sax like a real professional.

Information about Grover Duke and his career, which was written by his widow, Sue J. Duke, and included in a book entitled *Carroll County, Mississippi - History and Families* is presented with Sue Duke's permission as follows:

"Grover's career in music began with his playing mandolin at the age of six. He progressed on to guitar, often playing "second" to the fiddling of his parents, the late W. E. (Will) and Dora Halsey Jackson Duke, at home and for community dances in private homes as was the custom in those days. Grover also played guitar with Mississippi John Hurt, Willie Narmour, and Shell Smith. Later, he played lead guitar with Jenkins Ruscoe at local nightspots such as the 82 Club, which was located in

Carroll County on Highway 82 between Carrollton and Winona. They also played VFWs and other clubs in North Mississippi.

"Grover Duke was nearly 40 years old before attempting to play saxophone. Reportedly, his mother told him that she knew he had played a tune on every instrument he ever put his hands on, but didn't believe he'd ever get one out of that thing. After learning the sax, Grover started playing a style of music which leaned toward the standards. At a time when music was changing so rapidly, he stayed with the same thing. His music was timeless, and his sound was so unique that people all over the state got to know it and would travel a long way to hear him.

"For a number of years after starting to play sax, Grover was the leader of Grover Duke and the Cavaliers. They were in great demand performing dance music at dance halls, nightspots, and country clubs. Grover and the Cavaliers also played at the world famous Peabody in Memphis, Tennessee.

"Following the dissolution of the Cavaliers, the mellow sound of Grover Duke remained in demand so Grover performed as Grover Duke's Combo until his untimely death. During his musical career, Grover cut two single records and one album.

"Grover Duke worked 30 years for the Illinois Central Gulf Railroad. It has been observed by many that he was just as good a railroad employee as he was a musician. If this is true, then he was an excellent employee. Apparently, he didn't let his sax playing interfere with his day job, and he didn't let his day job interfere with his sax playing.

"To sum it all up, Grover Neal Duke, who never had a music lesson in his life, was a fabulous musician. He was an accomplished guitarist, saxophonist, and keyboard player. Grover was a natural entertainer who possessed a great musical talent bordering on genius.

"Grover Neal Duke, the person, is remembered for his gregarious personality, his kind and generous spirit, his joyful mood, and his ability to lift people up and make them laugh. In short, he loved and was loved by all who knew him."

Chapter 51
Two Sons of Grover Duke

If ever there were two chips off the old block, it would have to be Grover Neal Duke, Jr. and Roby Ward Duke. Pertinent information follows:

<u>Grover Neal Duke, Jr.</u>

Neal was born in 1952. He is an accomplished musician who followed in his dad's footsteps. Neal has carried the sound of Mississippi blues and old standards he learned from his dad from Tucson, Arizona, to Orlando, Florida, as he performed dance music in local country clubs. As a young man, he also performed gospel music throughout the Mississippi Delta.

Grove Neal Duke, Jr. married Deborah Kaye Bowman of Ruleville, Mississippi. They have three children: Grove Neal Duke, III, Leslie Kate Duke, and Joshua Roby Duke. Like Neal, his three children are chips off the old block. They are all talented musicians and are carrying on the Duke legacy.

<u>Roby Ward Duke</u>

Roby was born in 1956. He died in 2010 at Seattle, Washington. He is buried at Mt. Pisgah in Carroll County, Mississippi, near Teoc.

In 1977 Roby left Mississippi to follow his dream. He enrolled in the seminary in Louisiana after answering God's call on his life to serve as a contemporary Christian artist. Roby incorporated the inherited talents from his mother and father to compose music and write lyrics. His songs primarily relate to what God has done for him. He has six albums that are sold internationally and has received Grammy nominations for producing records on artists such as Denice Williams.

Roby has performed all over the world. Japan, Italy, France, and England are a few of the countries in which he has performed concerts, as well as from coast to coast in the United States.

Besides playing, singing, and writing music, Roby carried his talent into the technological field with his "Symphony of Voices Rom." This CD rom received the Keyboard Magazine award for best product of the year. This is the highest industry technical award that is given. Roby's CD-Rom was used in the movies Titanic, Good Will Hunting, Matrix, and about 20 other major films. It was also used on the Sting CD.

Roby married Wendi Leigh Hunter in 1978. This union produced one son, Brantly Joseph Duke. Brantly inherited the Duke musical talent and performed many concerts with his dad before Roby's untimely death.

A special thanks to Barbara Sheppard who wrote about Grover Neal Duke, Jr. and Roby Ward Duke in the book *Carroll County Mississippi-History and Families*. Her writings made this chapter in my book possible.

Chapter 52
James (Jimmy) William Gilbreath

Jimmy Gilreath was born November 14, 1936. He died September 7, 2003. According to the internet's free encyclopedia Wikipedia, Jimmy was born in the Una community (Clay County), Mississippi, near Prairie which is in Monroe County. When I first met him in 1961, he was living in the Trebloc community which is in the county near Houston, Mississippi. Both Trebloc and Houston are in Chickasaw County.

In 1972 Jimmy Gilreath married Kay Long. They lived on a farm at Saltillo, Mississippi, where Jimmy died in a tractor accident September 7, 2003. He is buried in Lee Memorial Park near Tupelo. Jimmy and Kay had no children.

I first met Jimmy Gilreath in 1961 at the VFW Club in Grenada, Mississippi. My band and I went to hear this great singer we had been hearing about. We had been playing the VFW every other Saturday since 1959, and the club had just hired Jimmy and band to play the other Saturday. What we heard was the best singer we had ever heard. And, I might add, I haven't heard his equal since.

Jimmy and I became good friends and did numerous shows together at nightclubs in Greenwood, Grenada, and throughout the Delta. We both also recorded for Vee-Eight and Statue Records which was owned by Dominic Fratesi of Greenwood, Mississippi.

In addition, I recorded two songs that were written by Jimmy: "The Skeleton Fight" in 1964 and "Big Silver Tears" in 1966. For complete details see the Appendix.

Pertinent information regarding the recording and song writing career of Jimmy Gilreath is presented as follows:

Jimmy's first songs, "I Need It" and "Time Hasn't Helped," were released in 1962 on Dominic Fratesi's Vee-Eight Records. Then, in 1963, lightning struck when Jimmy recorded "Little Band of Gold." Dominic Fratesi released this song on his Statue Records, and after getting good airplay in Memphis he sold the rights to Joy Records in New York City. As they say, the rest is history. "Little Band of Gold" reached #21 on the U. S. pop charts and #19 on the R&B charts. It hit #19 on the U.K. singles chart.

Besides Jimmy's recording of "Little Band of Gold," his song was recorded by several other artists. Some of these artists are: Bill Anderson, Boots Randolph, Sonny James, Tennessee Guitars, and Vince Hill.

Joy Records released three other singles on Jimmy Gilreath: The first was "Lollipops, Lace, and Lipstick," backed with "Mean Ole River;" the second was "Keep Her Out of Sight," backed with "Blue is My Color;" and the last was "Your Day is Coming," backed with "Pearls, Gold, and Silver." These singles were unsuccessful and in 1965 Joy Records ceased operations. At this time, Jimmy decided to concentrate on song writing rather than recording records.

In 1967, Jimmy Hughes released a single written by Jimmy Gilreath entitled "Why Not Tonight," which peaked at #5 on the R&B charts.

After the 1960s, Jimmy Gilreath mostly hung around his farm and John Mihelic's studio in Tupelo where he did some writing. Jimmy told me in later years that most of his time was spent on his farm in Saltillo where he fed catfish in his pond and watched the mailbox for royalty checks from "Little Band of Gold." What a great singer and songwriter! Jimmy Gilreath, I'm glad I knew you.

Chapter 53
John Mihelic & the Nite-Liters

As noted in the previous chapter, I first met Jimmy Gilreath in 1961 at the VFW Club in Grenada, Mississippi, where he and his band were playing. His band, known as The Nite-Liters, was the perfect band to compliment Jimmy's great singing. Members of the original Nite-Liters are as follows: John Mihelic (trumpet and band leader), Jimmy Gilreath (lead singer), Jerry Hood (lead guitar), Wayne Brown (piano), Hershel Hood (drums), Gerald Little (bass), and Gary Page (saxophone).

I talked to Jerry Hood recently (August 2010), and he stated that The Nite-Liters group was formed in 1960. Then he said, "Well, it may have been 1959." From my conversation with Jerry, I have concluded that he doesn't remember for sure; therefore, I'm saying it was either the last half of 1959 or the first half of 1960. How's that for brilliant deduction? HA!

Regardless of when the group was formed, they were one of the best nightclub bands to ever come down the pike. Like my band and me (Mack Allen Smith & The Flames), The Nite-Liters mostly played the night club circuit in North Mississippi. We had many battles of bands with The Nite-Liters at the Moose Lodge in Greenwood, Mississippi, during the 1960s. To this day, I still have people mention those great battles.

Besides the Greenwood Moose Lodge, The Nite-Liters also played other clubs that my band and I played, like the VFW in Grenada, Mississippi, and the American Legion in Cleveland, Mississippi. In addition, John Mihalic came and played trumpet with my band and me at my club (Mack Allen Smith's Town & Country Night Club) in Greenwood in 1971. Since John Mihelic lived in Tupelo, The Nite-Liters played many gigs in that area. John also played trumpet on a couple of my early records (one recorded in Memphis and the other in Muscle Shoals, Alabama). For details see the Appendix.

John Mihelic was engineer/producer on a 20-song double album that The Flames and I recorded at Statue Recording Studio in 1972. Statue Recording Studio, which was owned by John Mihelic and Dominic Fratesi, was located in Tupelo, Mississippi. For details on this session see the Appendix.

Regarding The Nite-Liters recording career, they first recorded an instrumental entitled "Nervous" in 1962 which was released on Dominic Fratesi's Vee Eight label located in Greenwood, Mississippi. This recording, composed by Jerry Hood, the band's lead guitar player, featured the trumpet player and leader of the band, John Mihelic. Later "Nervous" was released by Verve Records of Los Angeles, California.

The Nite-Liters also backed Jimmy Gilreath on his first single in 1962 ("I Need It" & "Time Hasn't Helped") for Vee Eight Records, and his big hit, "Little Band of Gold" in 1963 which was released by Dominic Fratesi on Statue Records and then sold to Joy Records in New York. The B-side was "I'll Walk With You".

Chapter 54
Willie Narmour & Shell Smith

I'm way too young to have known and shared a stage with Willie Narmour and Shell Smith during their pickin' and grinnin' days; however, Shell Smith is a cousin of mine, so I'll use that as a reason for assigning them a chapter in my book. Even if Mr. Shell wasn't a cousin of mine, I'd still highlight them with a chapter because Narmour and Smith are responsible for putting Carroll County, Mississippi on the map. I know others have contributed in that regard but, in my opinion (for what it's worth), Willie Narmour and Shell Smith are the main reasons for Carroll County's widespread popularity, notoriety, or whatever you want to call it. They definitely had the "it" factor. As Terry Herbert said, "I don't know what the "it" factor is, but I know when someone has it." Narmour and Smith had it.

Pertinent information is presented as follows:

<u>William (Willie) Thomas Narmour</u>

Willie Narmour was born March 22, 1889. At Ackerman (Choctaw County), Mississippi. He died March 26, 1961, in Carroll County, Mississippi. Mr. Narmour is buried at Mt. Pisgah Cemetery in Carroll County near Teoc. The Narmours moved to Carroll County when Willie was seven years old. Willie remained in Carroll County until his death at age 72. He was survived by his wife (Velma), his sons (Coleman and Charles), and daughter (Hazel).

Not only was Willie Narmour considered the best fiddler in Carroll County and surrounding areas, he became known world-wide for his recording of "Carroll County Blues," which was released on Okeh Records of New York in 1929. Willie Narmour and Shell Smith wrote and recorded "Carroll County Blues" with Smith playing rhythm guitar while Narmour played the fiddle.

<u>Shellie (Shell) Walton Smith</u>

Shell Smith was born November 26, 1895, in Carroll County, Mississippi. He died August 28, 1968, in Carroll County and is buried in Carroll County at Moore/Mt. Pisgah Cemetery behind Mt. Pisgah Baptist Church near Teoc. Mr. Smith married Lillian Kirby and they had five children- Ray, Evelyn, Bernard, Sonny, and Shirley.

Besides playing rhythm guitar, Shell Smith also played fiddle. While Shell is best known for his guitar backup on the Narmour and Smith records, he played fiddle on one recording entitled "Rose Waltz". This song was recorded July 30, 1934, in Atlanta, Georgia. On this session Willie Narmour played rhythm guitar on "Rose Waltz." Sixteen songs were recorded at this session, with Narmour playing fiddle on the other fifteen.

<u>Narmour and Smith</u>

Willie Narmour and Shell Smith played and recorded together from 1928 to 1934. Other than recording, they played mostly in Carroll and surrounding counties. Willie and Shell played many country dances in this small area. They only traveled long distances for their recording sessions in Memphis, Tennessee, in 1928, New York in 1929, Atlanta, Georgia in 1929 and 1934, and San Antonio, Texas in 1930.

A discography of the Narmour and Smith recordings is presented as follows:

<u>Memphis, Tennessee - February 15, 1928</u>
"Captain George, Has Your Money Come?"
"Whistling Coon"
"The Sunny Waltz"
"Who's Been Giving You Corn?"
"Heel and Toe Polka"
"Little Star"

<u>Atlanta, Georgia - March 11, 1929</u>
"Charleston #1"
"Kiss Me Waltz"
"Gallop To Georgia"
"Midnight Waltz"
"Carroll County Blues"
"Someone I Love"

<u>New York, N.Y. - September 23-25, 1929</u>
"Charleston #2"
"Carroll County Blues #2"
"Avalon Blues"
"Winona Echoes"
"The Medicine Show Acts 1-6"
"Dry Gin Rag"
"Mississippi Waves Waltz"
"Sweet Milk and Peaches"

<u>San Antonio, Texas - June 6-7, 1930</u>
"Take Me As I Am"
"Texas Breakdown"
"Limber Neck Blues"
"Jake Leg Rag"
"Carroll County Blues #3"
"Avalon Quick Step"
"Bouquets of June Waltz"
"Where the Southern Crosses the Dog"
"Texas Shuffle"
"Tequila Hop Blues"
"Mississippi Breakdown"

<u>Atlanta, Georgia - July 30, 1934</u>
"The New Charleston-Part 1"
"The New Charleston-Part 2"
"The New Charleston-Part 3"

"The New Carroll County Blues-Part 1"
"The New Carroll County Blues-Part 2"
"The New Carroll County Blues-Part 3"
"Midnight Waltz"
"Someone I Love"
"Gallop To Georgia"
"Kiss Me"
"The Dry Gin Rag"
"Mississippi Waves Waltz"
"The Rose Waltz"
"Winona Echoes Waltz"
"Sweet Milk and Peaches"
"Avalon Blues"

After their recording career ended in 1934, Willie and Shell parted trails. Willie continued playing in public, but with other guitarists. One site where Willie played was the Alice Cafe in Greenwood, Mississippi, where he reportedly played for admirers until the late 1950s.

To say that the fiddle/guitar duo of Willie Narmour and Shell Smith was good would be an understatement. They were the best ever.

Chapter 55
John Hurt

John Hurt was born March 3, 1892, in Carroll County, Mississippi. He died November 2, 1966, while living in Grenada, Mississippi. John is buried at St. James Cemetery in Carroll County, Mississippi, near Avalon.

My uncle (Archie Herbert) and John Hurt got together many times at the bus shop where Uncle Archie was maintenance and shop manager. I had the privilege of attending several of these sessions and was blown away by John's guitar pickin.' Uncle Archie learned some John Hurt guitar licks, and I always liked his playing best when he used those licks. In addition, John came to our store in Carrollton several times where he tuned my Gene Autry guitar that I got for my 10th birthday. Then, we would go to the alley behind the store where John would pick and sing the blues for me, my brother (Barry), my first cousin (Billy Wayne Herbert), and anyone else who came along and wanted to listen. We didn't know at the time about his previous recordings. This was around 1949, and John never mentioned anything about his recordings.

John Hurt got his chance to record in 1928 after being referred to the recording company, Okeh Records, by Willie Narmour and Shell Smith. There were two sessions, the first in Memphis and the second in New York City. Shortly thereafter, he dropped out of sight.

In the early 1960s, John Hurt was rediscovered by blues enthusiast Tom Hoskins, and John has been kicking butt ever since. He may no longer be with us, but his music is all over the world. I have several of his CDs and listen to them often. One of the CDs was recorded for the Library of Congress in 1963 and released on Flyright Records in England. There are 20 songs on this CD. Another CD is on Columbia/Okeh and it contains the complete 1928 Okea recordings. I also have a 21-song CD that was recorded in concert April 5, 1965, at Oberlin College. The students went crazy. They really loved that old Avalon, Mississippi blues man.

John Hurt has too many songs on CD for me to list them all, even if I had all the CDs. According to Arthur Browning, curator at the John Hurt Museum, John Hurt recorded 171 songs throughout his lifetime.

As mentioned in the previous chapter, Willie Narmour and Shell Smith are responsible for putting Carroll County, Mississippi, on the map. After gettin' put on the map, John Hurt stepped in to make certain Carroll County stayed there. With John's unequaled talent recorded on 171 CDs distributed all over the world, Carroll County will remain on the map and John Hurt will never die.

Chapter 56
Samuel Caruthers (Doc) Herbert

Well, it's Herbert time again. This time it's my third cousin, Doc Herbert. I'm not good at figuring this cousin stuff, but Doc explained it to me. He said, "Your mama and my daddy were first cousins, so that means you and my daddy were second cousins, and you and I are third cousins." Doc said it, so I believe it.

Doc Herbert was born June 29, 1933, in the Calvary community of Carroll County, Mississippi. He now lives in Grenada, Mississippi. Doc attended high school for one year at J. Z. George High School in North Carrollton, Mississippi, then he transferred to Grenada High School in Grenada, Mississippi, where he completed his education.

Since coming out of my 18-year retirement in 2002, my band and I have appeared on a bunch of shows with Doc and his band at the old school house at Black Hawk, Mississippi. The first few times we appeared together, Doc was playing fiddle with Good Times Express. Since then, we have appeared with Doc a number of times, and he was playing fiddle with The Duck Hillbillies.

When Doc was six years old, his daddy, Jim Herbert, bought and old used guitar and fiddle. Doc started out playing guitar at age six, but when he was 11 years old, he switched to fiddle. Since then, the fiddle has been his instrument of choice, and he is considered to be one of the best around. I'm not a fiddle expert or diehard fiddle fan, but even I can recognize the fact that Doc Herbert is a durn good fiddle player.

Even though the fiddle became Doc's instrument of choice, he continued playing guitar over the years. In fact, he recorded a 21-song CD entitled "Doc Herbert and His Guitar." I recommend this CD highly. Doc strums the guitar and sings, and it is truly a classic that should be in everyone's cabinet. Besides singing and strumming the rhythm guitar, Doc wrote three of the songs on this CD ("Living My Life Alone," "I Will Never Change Your Name," and "I Just Can't Forget You"). If you are interested in Doc's CD, just write Doc Herbert, 621 Scenic Drive, Grenada, Mississippi, 38901, or call (662) 226-4262.

Over the years Doc played fiddle with Eddie Lee Alderman and my uncles (Jimmie Herbert and Archie Herbert). However, the three bands he mentioned as his steady gig bands were his Army band, Good Times Express, and The Duck Hillbillies. Members of these bands are presented as follows:

<u>Doc's Army Band</u> - Glen Glover (guitar), Doc Herbert (fiddle), Ray Cummings (guitar), Bob Barnett (bass), and Al Hauggy (guitar). Doc was in the Army for two years (1954 & 1955).

<u>Good Times Express</u> - Shirley Carroll (bass), Charles Carroll (guitar), Doc Proctor (mandolin), Neil Wrenn (guitar & singer), Jimmy Hamilton (guitar), and Doc Herbert (fiddle).

<u>The Duck Hillbillies</u> - The original band formed April 28, 1956, were Doc Herbert (fiddle), George Timbs (rhythm guitar & singer), and Curley Rainey (fiddle and backup

singer). Other Duck Hillbillies are Dusty Rainie (guitar); Ricky Windham (banjo), James Winters (guitar), and Mike Lovelace (bass). The Duck Hillbillies has been Doc's main music home as he has been a member of that group for over fifty years.

Doc's main day job over the years was at a manufacturing plant in Grenada where he worked 43 years before retiring in 1999. During his tenure the plant changed their name from McGuay to Heatcraft. Since retiring, Doc had heart surgery in 2001, and this year (2010) he had surgery on a carotid artery in his neck.

Nonetheless, he keeps on sawing that fiddle. I hope he keeps on doing it for as long as he wants to. Here's to you, cuz. Just keep on keeping on.

Chapter 57
William M. (Bill) Walker

Bill Walker was born April 22, 1939, at Hesterville, Mississippi, which is situated in Attala County. Bill attended Kosciusko High School in Kosciusko, Mississippi, where he graduated in 1957. After high school, Bill attended Jackson Barber College in Jackson, Mississippi. He graduated in 1961, after which he set up shop in Kosciusko.

I first met Bill in 1966 at the Moose Lodge in Greenwood, Mississippi. Bill, his wife Linda, and a bunch of their friends from Kosciusko started coming to hear us every Saturday that we played there. During this period of time, we played the Greenwood Moose Lodge more than we played anywhere else. In May 1971, I opened my own club (Mack Allen Smith's Town & Country Night Club) on Highway 49 South in Greenwood. Bill Walker and the Kosciusko bunch followed us to my club and supported us while we were there (1971-1976).

Bill's friends from Kosciusko soon informed me that Bill could sing and play the guitar, so I started getting him to sing a couple of songs whenever they came to hear us.

When I retired from the honky-tonks in 1984 and hung up my Rock-A-Billy shoes for 18 year, I lost contact with Bill Walker and the Kosciusko bunch. However, when I came out of my 18-year retirement in 2002, Bill and I got back together. We were both out of the honky-tonk business and had no intention of returning to it. In fact, Bill had been doing gospel for a number of years.

Since putting my Rock-A-Billy shoes back on in 2002, Bill Walker has played rhythm guitar with me at the old Black Hawk school house, the old Carmack school house, the Carrollton Community House, and various nursing homes in Kosciusko and Vaiden. Additionally, I look forward to singing for the annual fish fry in Kosciusko at the home where Bill's daughter lives with a number of other special needs residents. This gig is a real blessing for me and the band.

Regarding Bill's day job, he was a barber in Kosciusko for 36 years. Due to health problems, it became difficult for Bill to stand on his feet all day, so he retired in 1995. I have been told by a number of people that Bill Walker was the best barber in Kosciusko and the surrounding area.

Bill provided me with a mini-memoir which is presented as follows:

"As a small boy growing up, I was fascinated with the guitar. I taught myself to play on a borrowed guitar. My dad was a great influence on my drive to play. I must admit he was a better than average fiddle, harmonica, and juice harp player. He taught me at an early age how to play the straws on the fiddle. It was a thrill to do that (haven't tried it lately). My dad, at an early age, played and probably swapped ideas with Lanny O'Briant's dad. They were raised in Holmes County close together.

"As a young lad I could not wait to own my own guitar. I would spend hour after hour building my own guitar, but I could never get the darn thing tuned. My dream came true at the age of 14. My uncle, who lived in Memphis, came and carried me back home with him. He took me to Sears Roebuck Store and let me pick out the guitar I wanted. Boy, was I ever excited! I played that thing until my fingers could stand it no more.

"At the age of 18, I entered the United States Coast Guard and was sent to serve on the *C. G. Cutter Yakutat WAVP 380* docked in New Bedford, Massachusetts. While serving there, I met David Ray from Curtis Bay, Maryland, who was a lead guitar player. Boy, could he play that thing! He taught me licks I still use today. We spent a lot of time entertaining our shipmates while we were at sea. My interest really went to a new high. The guitar opened so many new doors for me. I traded chords to the ship's barber for some knowledge in the barbering profession, which led me to my chosen career of today.

"My guitar playing and barbering career introduced me to so many people of interest such as Lanny O'Briant, who has been such an encourager for me. How could I forget the Townsend Brothers (Ralph, Carl, and Cliff) who invited me to be a rhythm guitar player with their band?

"Another highlight of my music background was getting to know and be on stage with Nashville song writer, Carl Jackson, as part of the Big K Jamboree.

"I continue to play the guitar as often as I can. I never get tired of learning and trying to improve, and I always accept invitations to play at senior citizen and nursing home functions. I thank God for the talent He gave me and the many hours I spend praising Him while playing and singing.

"My playing took a big hit when early this year (2009) I was diagnosed with early stages of Parkinson disease; but I refuse to give it up. I will continue to play as long as God keeps the drive within me alive.

"I am so honored that Mack Allen invited me to be a part of this book."

Chapter 58
Don Clayton Chandler

Don Chandler was born October 22, 1945, at Huntingdon, Tennessee. He attended East High School in Memphis, Tennessee, where he graduated in 1963. After high school, Don attended college one year at Evangel College in Springfield, Missouri. Don served in the Air Force from June 1964 to June 1968.

As discussed in Chapter 44, which highlights Stone Blue, Don played keyboards with Stone Blue for eight years (1972-1980). Besides hearing Stone Blue a number of times at various Memphis clubs, I booked them in 1973 at my club in Greenwood, Mississippi. Also, Don Chandler played on a session with me in 1972 at Lyn-Lou Studios in Memphis. The song he played on ("Don't Be Cruel") was released on Delta Sound Records.

Based on information Don presented me, his birth was not your everyday normal birth. Specifically, Don was born on a gravel road about one-half mile from the sale barn on Highway 70 at Huntingdon, Tennessee. The doctor left an hour before Don was born to deliver another baby about five miles away. When the doctor got back three hours later, he was tired, his horse was tired, the three midwives (aunts) who delivered Don were tired, but Don wasn't tired at all. He was ready to boogie. Don has been boogieing ever since, and for the past 25 years he and his band have been boogieing at a club on Beale Street in Memphis called Rum Boogie.

The Chandler family moved to Memphis, Tennessee, before Don was a year old. His dad bought a lot and built them a house. He would lay seven concrete blocks each morning before leaving for work. According to Don, it took about a year, but he finally got it built. I always wondered where Don got all his energy and drive. Now I know - he got it from his dad. What a great man he must have been.

Don's mother saved up $500 and bought Don his first piano in 1949. The Chandlers didn't get a TV until Don got his driver's license, so he entertained himself, as well as family and friends. From the time he was five years old until he was twelve years old, Don's mother carried him to different churches where he would play solos. The people loved it, and so did Don.

Even though Don started playing in churches and still loves gospel music, he gradually formed a band and started playing for dances. Don says that he loved playing dance gigs because some even paid you money.

During Don's four years in the Air Force (1964-1968), he was stationed in Panama City, Florida, where he played in a band called The Embers. They played all over northern Florida.

After returning to Memphis in August 1968, Don Chandler has established himself as one of the top musicians on the Memphis scene. Besides Stone Blue, Don has played gigs with The Mar-keys, Memphis horns (Don was original member), Pappy Hilburn (Playboys sax player), and Jerry Masters (bass player and producer of the

Hombres.) In addition, Don Chandler, Billy Wayne Herbert, and James Govan were the back-up band for Tony Joe White ("Poke Salad Annie") for two years. They also backed Chuck Berry at the Memphis Coliseum and played for Charlie Rich. They played for many recording sessions in Memphis, Tennessee, and Muscle Shoals, Alabama.

A partial list of other big stars that Don Chandler has played with is as follows: Charlie Pride, Johnny Russell, Ace Cannon, Greg Alman, Steve Ray Vaughn, Joe Walsh (The Eagles), Percy Sledge, and Bo Diddley.

As of this writing (September 2010), Don Chandler and James Govan are still together. They have been playing at Rum Boogie on Beale Street over 25 years and are still going strong. Currently, they are playing on Thursday, Friday, and Saturday nights. The band's name is Boogie Blues Band. They have recorded two live albums for sale at www.rumboogie.com.

If you are ever in Memphis on a Thursday, Friday, or Saturday night and want to hear a great band with the best keyboard player in town, then Rum Boogie is the place to go. Boogie Blues Band is the band, and Don Chandler is the man.

Chapter 59
James Govan

As of this writing (September 2010), James Govan and Don Chandler have been together for 35+ years (8 years with Stone Blue and over 25 years at Rum Boogie on Beale Street in Memphis, Tennessee). Therefore, it seemed only fitting to highlight James in Chapter 59 right after Don Chandler's Chapter 58.

James Govan was born September 2, 1949, at Charleston, Mississippi. The Govans moved to Memphis in 1952 when James was three years old. James attended Manassas High School in Memphis where he graduated in 1967.

As discussed in Chapter 44 (Stone Blue) and Chapter 58 (Don Chandler), I heard Stone Blue a number of times at various Memphis clubs, and I booked them in 1973 at my club in Greenwood, Mississippi. During the five years I ran Mack Allen Smith's Town & Country Nightclub in Greenwood (1971-1976), James Govan was the only black singer to ever sing there. I might add that he was probably the best singer to ever sing there. James was well received by all who heard him and, to this day, people still ask about that great black singer who appeared at my club in 1973.

Besides the two live albums mentioned in Chapter 58, which was recorded at Rum Boogie, James Govan had an album entitled "I'm In Need" that was released in 1996 by Charlie Records in England. This album was a number one hit in England. However, James never got a release here in the United States. According to Don Chandler, people from overseas come to Rum Boogie on a regular basis and get James Govan to sign their "I'm In Need" album.

Wikipedia, the internet's free encyclopedia, states that James Govan has become one of the favorite musicians on Beale Street. They further state that he is known for his cavernous baritone voice.

Other accolades from Wikipedia are as follows:
- The Boogie Blues Band at Rum Boogie has won the Best House Band on Beale Street three times by Beale Street Merchants Association and they have headlined BSMA awards for three awards ceremonies (2002-2004).
- James Govan and fellow musician, Don Chandler, both received a key to the City of Memphis for their contribution to the music scene on Beale Street. Such an honor has not been received by any other musician on historic Beale Street.
- James Govan has been a big hit at the Porretta Soul Festival in Italy where he performed from 1993 to 1997. This festival is a tribute to Otis Redding.

Don Chandler told me that the economy has affected the nightclub business like it has most everything else. Their band played six nights a week at Rum Boogie for many years but is now playing three nights. This downturn in the economy has caused Don to start working on a one-man band where he will play drums, bass, piano, strings, and harmonica all at once. Regardless, Don further stated that he will still need James

Govan because he is the main drawing card, and singers like James are few and far between. I second that emotion.

Chapter 60
Susie Jean James

Susie James was born September 7, 1948, at Greenwood Leflore Hospital in Greenwood, Mississippi. The James family residence was in Carroll County, Mississippi. Susie's parents were David Franklin James and Hattie Eugenia Freeman James. Other siblings were David Franklin James, Jr. And Donald Robert James. Susie graduated from J. Z. George High School at North Carrollton, Mississippi, in 1966 and from Mississippi State College for Women in 1970.

Susie is not a musician or a singer, but she has done more to promote musicians and singers in this area than anyone I know. Specifically, she writes for various newspapers and magazines and has written numerous articles promoting local artists.

Susie and I are both from Carroll County, but she was in the second grade when I was a senior, so I didn't know her back then. The first time I met Susie was in 1966 at the USDA Cotton Classing Office in Greenwood, Mississippi. She was working to make money for college, and I was trying to make a living for me and my family (wife and daughter at that time). A son came later (March 11, 1967). Anyway, we finished the 1966 cotton season and I didn't see her again for thirteen years.

Fast forward to 1979: Susie called me and asked if she could interview me for an article in *Jackson Magazine*. She said she had finished college in 1970 with a Bachelor of Arts degree and had chosen journalism as her lifetime career. Susie said she always loved to write, and I soon found out that she was really good at it. She came to one of my gigs at the American Legion in Cleveland, Mississippi, for the interview. She did the interview before we started playing then stayed for the entire four hour dance.

The article, which appeared in the February 1979 edition of *Jackson Magazine* was entitled "The Delta's Old Flame: Mack Allen Smith." After this 1979 gig I didn't see Susie again for over 20 years. I quit singing in the honky-tonks in 1984 and stayed retired for 18 years. Then, I started back in 2002.

When I started back singing at the old Black Hawk school in Black Hawk, Mississippi, in October 2002, Susie started showing up with her note pad, pen, and camera. Since then she has written a number of articles about my band and me for *The Greenwood Commonwealth*.

Besides promoting me and my band, she has promoted other musicians and singers in Greenwood, Carrollton, and surrounding areas. She has also promoted local business establishments and kept people informed regarding what local government in Carroll County is doing or not doing. I have to say that Susie James is a true friend and ambassador to Carroll County and its people. I hope she keeps writing for many more years.

Other pertinent information regarding the life and accomplishments of Susie James is presented as follows:

- As a high school senior, Susie was editor of *The George High Times*, which was the school newspaper.
- Majored in journalism and English at Mississippi State College for Women (MSCW) at Columbus, Mississippi.
- While as MSCW, Susie did still photos to promote a student production of "The Miracle Worker."
- Worked as a student intern for *The Greenwood Commonwealth* following her sophomore year at MSCW.
- As a college senior at MSCW, Susie became photography editor of the college newspaper, *The Spectator*. Also, contributed photos to the yearbook.
- Susie wrote and did photography for the college literary magazine, *The Dilettanti*. One of Susie's poems that was published in the 1970 *Dillettanti* and was later (2009) included in a retrospective collection introduced during the Eudora Welty Symposium that year.
- After graduation in 1970, Susie took a job as news editor of the Oxford, Mississippi, *Eagle*. During her eight year tenure at the *Eagle*, Susie won a string of press association awards for both photos and stories.
- After leaving the *Eagle* in 1978, Susie found employment with *The Delta Democrat-Times* in Greenville, Mississippi, where she worked until early 1984.
- After leaving *The Delta Democrat-Times* in 1984, Susie worked for *The Arkansas Democrat* in Little Rock, Arkansas.
- Susie returned to rural Carroll County, Mississippi, in September 1985. Finally back home in Carroll County, she started re-introducing herself to the county in which she was reared.
- Back home in Carroll County, Susie wrote a couple of plays, along with some novellas and revised a novel entitled *Media People* that she started years before while living in Greenville.
- For the most part, her work after coming home to Carroll County has been freelance writing and photography for *The Greenwood Commonwealth* and Jackson, Mississippi's, *The Clarion Ledger*. She has also produced copy and photos for the Carroll County *Conservative* and *The Winona Times*.

Regardless of what Susie has or hasn't done, in the final analysis, she is a fine writer. I just hope that someday she will get her novel, *Media People*, published, and it will be a best seller. No one deserves a best seller more than Susie James.

Chapter 61
Dennis James

Dennis James (no known kin to Susie) was born March 25, 1952, in Kennett, Missouri. Dennis attended Delta C-7 High School in Kennett where he graduated in 1970. Dennis later attended the Association of Evangelical Gospel Assemblies (AEGA) in Monroe, Louisiana. He graduated from AEGA on May 12, 1993.

I met Dennis James through my first cousin, Billy Wayne Herbert, in 1971 at Lyn-Lou Studio in Memphis. I had spent 1967, 1968, and into August of 1969 at Lyn-Lou trying to cut a hit record. Then, in August of 1969 I gave up and moved back to Greenwood, Mississippi. Most of the time I was in Memphis, I lived in the studio because I couldn't afford to rent an apartment. When Dennis moved to Memphis in 1971, at Billy Wayne's request, he also lived in the studio. I had continued coming to Memphis and cutting demos of my songs which resulted in me meeting Dennis James.

After my Memphis sessions at Lyn-Lou during the 1970s, I didn't see Dennis James again until July 2007 at Billy Wayne Herbert's funeral in Winona, Mississippi. Dennis said that since I was Billy's first cousin and had lived in Lyn-Lou Studio, and since he had later lived in Lyn-Lou Studio that must mean that we were cousins-in-law. Since Billy Wayne's funeral in 2007, Dennis and I have remained in touch.

As of this writing (September 27, 2010), Dennis has a 24-track recording studio in Kennett, Missouri. I have been told that Dennis stays busy in the studio. I hope I can make it to Kennett in the near future so I can check out his studio and perhaps cut something.

Dennis said that the time he spent at Lyn-Lou in Memphis taught him a lot about music and engineering. Dennis further stated that he owes it to Billy Wayne Herbert, Jim Rorie, Bob Tucker, and Larry Rogers. Even with modern technology, Dennis says he still uses the same basic principles he learned at Lyn-Lou in the 1970s.

Over a long and distinguished career, Dennis James stated that he has been privileged to work with and open shows for the following stars: Jerry Jaye, Ray Price, Carl Mann, Bill Black Combo, Narvel Felts, W. S. Holland Band, Stone Blue, David Patillo, B. B. King, Albert King, Terry Cobb, Terry Ray Bradley, Ronnie McDowell, Belamy Brothers, Kenny Dale, and Darlene Battles.

In the future, I hope Dennis James cuts a bunch of hits at his 24-track studio in Kennett, Missouri. After all, Dennis is the only person to become my cousin-in-law simply because we both lived at Lyn-Lou Studio in Memphis at different times.

Chapter 62
Albert Austin "Sonny" Burgess

Sonny Burgess was born May 28, 1931, on a farm near Newport, Arkansas. His parents were Albert and Esta Burgess. Besides Sonny, there were five others siblings (two brothers and three sisters). Sonny attended Newport High School at Newport, Arkansas, where he graduated in 1948.

If you were to ask Sonny Burgess who Mack Allen Smith is, he would probably say, "Mack Allen who?" But I sure know who Sonny Burgess is. In 1956 when I was seventeen and rapidly approaching the ripe old age of 18, I was the opening act for several Sun Record stars at a ball park in Greenwood, Mississippi. One of these stars was Sonny Burgess. Sonny is over seven years older than I am, but he had those teenage girls throwing conniption fits or something. I remember "Red Headed Woman" was real popular in this area back then. After the ball park concert, Sonny and his band (The Pacers) played for a couple of hours at the Greenwood VFW Club. I went to the VFW and listened to their entire performance. What a great entertainer he was and reportedly still is!

Information regarding the career of Sonny Burgess is presented as follows:

In the early 1950s, Sonny Burgess played in dance halls and bars around Newport, Arkansas. Members of the band were: Sonny Burgess, Kern Kennedy, Johnny Ray Hubbard, and Gerald Jackson. The band's name was Rocky Road Ramblers.

In 1954, following a stint in the U. S. Army (1951-1953), Sonny re-formed the band, calling them The Moonlighters after the Silver Moon Club in Newport, where they performed regularly.

After advice from record producer Sam Phillips, the group expanded and changed their name to The Pacers.

Sonny's first record for Sun was "We Wanna Boogie" and "Red Headed Woman." This single was recorded and released in 1956. Both songs were written by Sonny. The songs have been described as among the most raucous, energy-filled recordings released during the first flowering of rock and roll. The on-stage antics of Sonny Burgess and The Pacers have been similarly described.

Sonny Burgess disbanded his group in 1971, but later found a new audience in Europe. He was inducted into the Rock & Roll Hall of Fame of Europe in 1999. His current band, now called The Legendary Pacers, was a hit that same year at a rockabilly concert in Las Vegas, Nevada. In 2000 they recorded "Still Rockin' and Rollin'" which was voted best new album in Europe in the country and roots field. In 2002 the group was inducted into the Rockabilly Hall of Fame in Jackson, Tennessee.

In 2006, Sonny Burgess and The Legendary Pacers performed at the National Folk Festival in Richmond, Virginia, to large, enthusiastic audiences.

Sonny Burgess hosts a weekly radio program called "We Wanna Boogie" with co-host June Taylor. The program, named after his first record, airs Sunday nights from 5-7 PM Central time on 91.9 FM KASU in Jonesboro, Arkansas.

In 1956 Sonny Burgess married Joann Adams and they have two sons, Peyton and John. Between performances, Sonny and his wife live in Newport, Arkansas, where it all began many years ago.

Chapter 63
Charlie Feathers

Charlie Feathers was born June 12, 1932, in Holly Springs, Mississippi. He died August 29, 1998, of complications from a stroke-induced coma.

In the previous chapter, which highlighted Sonny Burgess, I wrote about the 1956 show in Greenwood, Mississippi, where I was the opening act for Sonny Burgess and other Sun Records stars. One of the other stars was Warren Smith, who was highlighted in Chapter 4. The other Sun star was Charlie Feathers.

After the show in 1956, I didn't see Charlie again until 1979. This meeting was at Ace Records studio in Jackson, Mississippi, where I had been recording several years for Johnny Vincent, the owner of Ace Records. Charlie was with Quinton Claunch from Memphis. Quinton and Johnny Vincent were good friends, and Quinton was talking to Johnny about releasing some of Charlie's old rock-a-billy songs on Ace Records.

In the early 1980s, Johnny did release several compilation albums which included Charlie Feathers' songs. In fact, I have one Ace album entitled "Greatest Rockabillies of the 50s," which includes one song by me and one by Charlie Feathers. My song was "King of Rock and Roll," and Charlie's song was "Love Never Treated Me Right." It was a great honor to be included on Ace albums with Charlie Feathers.

Besides the Ace albums, Charlie has been on a number of compilation albums overseas. I also have one compilation album from overseas that includes four of my recordings and one Charlie Feathers recording. My recordings were "Memphis," "Sick & Tired," You Better Move On," and "King of Rock and Rock." Charlie's song was "Love Never Treated Me Right." This compilation album was released on White Label Records in Rotterdam, Holland during the late 70s and early 80s.

I'm glad that I knew Charlie Feathers, and am proud and honored to have had some of my recordings included on compilation albums with him.

Information regarding the career of Charlie Feathers is presented as follows:

Charlie Feathers started out as a session musician at Sun Studios. His first single was on a small label started by Sam Phillips called Flip Records. The two songs ("I've Been Deceived" and "Peeping Eyes") were released on Flip (#503) in April 1955. His next single was on Sun Records (Sun #231). The two songs for this single were "Defrost Your Heart" and "Wedding Gown of White." The release date was January 1956.

After the Sun release, Charlie moved to Meteor Records where he recorded the most successful and best known song of his career. This signature song was "Tongue-Tied Jill." The flip side was "Get With It." It has been said that "Tongue-Tied Jill" pretty much defined his career. This single was released on Meteor Records (#5032) in June 1956. Reportedly, Charlie's theatrical, hiccup-styled, energetic rockabilly vocal style inspired a later generation of rock vocalists.

Charlie Feathers went on to record at least 29 singles and 14 albums from April 1955 through 1995. His son, Bubba Feathers, is featured playing lead guitar on the album "New Jungle Fever" in 1987 and "Honky Tonk Man" in 1988. These later albums of original songs penned by Feathers were released on the French label, New Rose Records.

If you are a rockabilly fan, then you are a Charlie Feathers fan. His contribution to the genre is enormous.

Chapter 64
Benny Barrentine

Benny Barrentine was born April 8, 1948, in Greenwood, Mississippi. He graduated from Greenwood High School in 1967. After high school, Benny served in the Army from September 1967 to September 1969. His service included a tour of duty in Vietnam.

As of this writing (10/6/10), I eat lunch several times a week at a local senior citizens joint here in Greenwood and have been doing so for over one year. You get two vegetables, plus meat, bread, and milk for fifty cents. Benny Barrentine also eats here, and I see him on a regular basis. I eat here because it is cheap and I don't have much money. Some others (no names mentioned) eat here because they are tight and the food is cheap. HA! I suppose this is why they are rich. HA!

When we complete our meal each day, I go home and rest or write, Johnny Brown goes to his car lot, and Benny Barrentine goes to the golf club to play golf. Benny is also a professional bass fisherman.

Besides golf and fishing, Benny is a fine musician. He provided me with information about his music career, and it is presented as follows:

Benny told me that for two years (1980-1982) he played keyboards and guitar with a band called Generations. Other band members were: Hal Pleasants (bass), Stacy Wren (drums), Doug Walker (lead guitar), and Allison Fraiser (vocals). They played at local watering holes, as well as civic events in Jackson, Greenville, Grenada, and Greenwood. All of these cities are in Mississippi, and, according to Benny, are noted for their good taste in music.

From 1982 to 1986 Benny played with the Levi Gentry Band. Members were: Levi Gentry (lead guitar and lead vocals), Benny Barrentine (keyboard and vocals), Mike Morgan (drums), Bill McGarrity (bass), and Hamp Gentry (rhythm guitar and vocals). They played at honky-tonks in Greenwood and Vaiden, Mississippi, plus a gig at the Greenwood Little Theater. In addition, they performed at the Civic Center in Greenwood with several other bands: Mike Ellis and The Hometown Bands, Blue South, The Casuals, and Magic Cowboy Band.

For ten years (1986-1996) Benny played keyboards and guitar with Wintergreen, one of the most popular honky-tonk bands in this area during this ten-year period. Besides playing at the Country Music Palace in Vaiden and Partners in Grenada, they had a gig at the Ramada Inn in Greenwood where they played five nights a week, three weeks a month for six years. During this run, Wintergreen built a huge fan base. Not only here, but also in other parts of the country. Besides Bennie, other members were: Jimmy Williams (lead vocal & guitar), Jerry Hughes (vocals & guitar), Paul Melton (bass), Billy Womble (drums), and Larry McClellon (drums). Other musicians who played with Wintergreen over the years were Robbie Browning, Mike Jacks, Allen Smith, Ken Cooper, and Steve Pearson.

Benny Barrentine is retired now and enjoying the good life which includes golf, bass fishing, and travel. Before retirement, his day jobs included six years as vocational teacher at Greenwood High School and owner/operator of a repair shop called Repairs Incorporated.

Chapter 65
Ernie Barton

In 1930 Ernie Barton was born in Tallahassee, Florida, as son of a sea captain. He was raised in Daytona Beach. Elvis Presley convinced Ernie that Memphis was the place to be, so he sold his home in Daytona Beach and built another one in the Memphis suburb of Frayser. He was hired by Sam Phillips in early 1957.

From the book by Hank Davis entitled *From the Vaults: The Original Sun Singles, Vol. 5*, Mr. David wrote that: "By all accounts, Ernie Barton virtually lived in the Sun studio between 1957 and 1960. He recorded as vocalist and session guitarist and even took over management of the studio for a while." Colin Escott and Martin Hawkins wrote a couple of books about Sun Records, and Mr. Escott in the liner notes for "That'll Flat Git It" wrote "Ernie Barton was a jack-of-all trades at Sun: producer, songwriter, musician, and featured artist."

After Sam Phillips fired Bill Justis and Jack Clement in 1959, Ernie Barton took over as in-house producer/arranger. He remained with Sun until some point in 1961. It was in 1959, while Ernie was in-house producer/manager, that The Flames and I got our chance to record at the famous Sun studio on Union Avenue in Memphis.

As written in Chapter 3, we recorded four songs for Ernie in 1959, but a release was not forthcoming. Nonetheless, this recording session was the most exciting of my career, and I couldn't write this book without an Ernie Barton chapter. I talked to Ernie one time after he left Sun. He moved to Little Rock and formed Barton Records. I asked about our 1959 Sun recordings and he said they were still at Sun.

We talked about my band and me coming to Little Rock for a session, but it never happened. I'm not sure what happened to Ernie Barton after I talked to him in 1961. One internet site I reviewed stated that: "Barton and his wife both ran afoul of Sam Phillips at some point in 1961. Ernie eventually moved on to Midland, Texas." This may be true; however, when I talked to him in 1961, he was in Little Rock running Barton Records. If he moved to Midland, Texas, in 1961, then Barton Records in Little Rock was a short-lived operation.

The internet site mentioned above states that Ernie Barton "has drifted into obscurity and may even have died. There is an entry in the Social Security Death Index for one Ernest W. Barton, born November 21, 1930, who died on May 1, 2001, in Montezuma, Colorado. But it's probably not our man." If that's not our man, and Ernie is still alive and reads this book, I just want to say thank you for that 1959 session at Sun Records Studio in Memphis, Tennessee. If Ernie has died, I'll tell him when I get to Heaven. Anyone who can make Mack Allen Smith and The Flames sound as good as he did at Sun Records in 1959 has just got to make it to Heaven.

Chapter 66
Jumpin' Gene Simmons

Jumpin' Gene Simmons was born July 10, 1937, in Tupelo, Mississippi. He died August 29, 2006, in his hometown after a long illness. Gene was a rockabilly singer and songwriter best known for his 1964 novelty single "Haunted House." KISS member Gene Simmons chose his stage name as a tribute to the singer.

During the early to mid-1970's, I booked Gene Simmons several times at my club (Mack Allen Smith's Town & Country Night Club) in Greenwood, Mississippi. By this time, "Haunted House" had become a standard, and Gene put on a fantastic performance. Needless to say, Gene Simmons always packed the house.

Besides playing at my club, Gene Simmons and Jamie Wood did backup vocals on 20 songs that my band and I recorded in 1972 at Statue Recording Studio in Tupelo, Mississippi. For details see the Appendix.

Information on Gene's career is presented as follows:

Gene Simmons began his recording career with Sun Records in 1958 while performing as an opening act for Elvis Presley. Sun Records only released one single from his recordings, and it never made the charts. However, because of Gene's sucessful career, Sun Records released a CD entitled "Drinking Wine:The Sun Years, Plus" in December 2006 with his 33-song collection.

The first and only Top 40 hit by Jumpin' Gene Simmons was "Haunted House" which was recorded and released by Hi Records in 1964. "Haunted House" peaked at Number 11 on the Billboard Hot 100 chart. This song represented one of Hi Record's early successes. The song was later covered by the Compton Brothers, Jerry Lee Lewis, and Hasil Adkins. In June 2001, Hi Records released a CD of Gene Simmons' recordings entitled "Haunted House: The Complete Jumpin' Gene Simmons."

Jumpin' Gene Simmons' last successful opus was "Indian Outlaw," which he co-wrote and was a hit for Tim McGraw in 1994.

When most people hear the name Gene Simmons, I suspect they think of the KISS member. But, when I hear the name Gene Simmons I think of "Haunted House." And, when I hear "Haunted House" I think of Gene Simmons. My band and I play "Haunted House" every time we play a gig, so as long as I'm singing, I'll be remembering Jumpin' Gene Simmons. In fact, he'll probably cross my mind from time to time even after I stop singing. That is if I ever stop. HA!

Chapter 67
Shylo

From the early 1970s to the mid-1980s, Shylo took North Mississippi by storm. I booked them at my club (Mack Allen Smith's Town & Country Night Club) during my five-year tenure (1971-1976). We did a number of battles of bands and after Town & Country closed, we did a number of battles at The Country Music Palace and The Delta Queen in Vaiden, Mississippi. The band was headquartered in Memphis, but they spent a lot of time kicking butt in Mississippi.

Members of Shylo during this period of time follows: Ronnie Scaife (lead guitar), Danny Hogan (bass), Butch Carter (piano), Perry York (drums), and Jerry Hays (rhythm guitar).

Besides the shows we did together, Shylo also played on some of my recordings at Lyn-Lou Studio in Memphis. I also recorded a song written by Ronnie Scaife and Danny Hogan entitled "Dog Tired of Catting Around." This band had talent to spare - no doubt about it.

When I started research for this book in June 2009, I tried to call the Shylo band members, but the numbers I had were no longer good numbers. All but Ronnie Scaife's had been disconnected, and I couldn't get through to him unless I knew the secret code. I guess Ronnie had gotten so big and important that he wouldn't talk to poor rednecks anymore. As of this writing (October 2010), I still haven't been able to talk to these cats. Therefore, basic information like dates of birth, where born, etc., is not included in this chapter.

Ronnie Scaife has been living in the Nashville area for around 25 years now and has written hit songs for stars like Alabama, Randy Travis, Jerry Jaye, and many more. In addition, Ronnie plays guitar on sessions at Nashville studios, and I've been told that his reputation as a session picker is impeccable.

In Memphis, Shylo was one of the top studio bands for over ten years. Colin Escott wrote in the liner notes of Jerry Jaye's "My Girl Josephine" CD that "the nucleus of the backing group was Shylo, who later recorded for Epic and Mercury." Being the nucleus of the backing group can be said about Shylo in regard to a large number of Memphis recordings - including mine.

During the writing of this book, I learned that Ronnie Scaife died on November 3, 2010, in Nashville. He was 63 years old.

Chapter 68
Ralph Douglas (Doug) Steen

Doug Steen was born September 6, 1940, at Kosciusko, Mississippi. Doug attended Kosciusko High School where he played saxophone in the high school band. He graduated from Kosciusko High School in 1959. After finishing high school, Doug attended Holmes Junior College in Goodman, Mississippi.

Besides playing in the high school band, Doug started playing in a combo while still in high school. This group was called The Blue Flames. Reportedly, they were very good and gained a nice fan base in Kosciusko and surrounding areas.

In 1959 and the early 1960s, Doug played several gigs with my band and me (Mack Allen Smith & The Flames). Then, in 1962 Doug played saxophone on my first record ("I Got My Mojo Working"). The sax ride he played on this recording is the best I've heard before or since.

Other bands that Doug Steen played saxophone with over the years include the following: Jessie Yates and The Rhythm Aces, The Ivories, The Continentals, and The Casuals.

Doug's day jobs have been primarily with manufacturers of musical instruments. He worked four years with Peavey in Meridian, Mississippi, which manufactured sound equipment, and three years as plant manager of a piano factory in Marion, North Carolina. His main day gig, however, was Baldwin Piano where he worked for 25 years (11 years in Greenwood, Mississippi, and 14 years in Conway, Arkansas).

Doug Steen married Wanda White from Crossett, Arkansas, in 1962. They have one son (Doug, Jr.) and two grandchildren (granddaughter Kayla and grandson Chase). Doug and Wanda live in Wanda's hometown, Crossett, Arkansas, where they have lived since 1989. Doug is retired now and no longer plays that good ole rock and roll like he used to, but he told me that the memories in his memory bank are vivid and hopes they remain for as long as he's still kickin.'

Doug told me on the phone today (10/20/10) that he has been having some heart problems. I just hope and pray that the Lord will heal him and let him stay with us for many more years.

"I Got My Mojo Working" is on CD now, and I listen to it quite often. If anyone ever has doubts about the greatness of Doug Steen's saxophone playing, then go listen to "I Got My Mojo Working" and you will doubt no more.

Chapter 69
The Red Tops
(1953 - 1974)

  I never shared a stage with The Red Tops nor did I personally know any of the band members. However, I did attend a Red Tops dance in 1956. Since The Red Tops achieved such phenomenal success as a dance band, and built a reputation unequaled before or since, I felt compelled to give them a chapter in my book.

  During the early to mid-1950s while I was in high school, there was nothing better than attending a Red Tops dance, but I never got to attend one then. However, while attending Holmes Junior College in the fall of 1956, I finally got the chance. I went to a Red Tops dance at the National Guard Armory in Greenwood, Mississippi. There were no tables or chairs, just wall to wall people. I can still see those red coats swaying from side to side while they played, and when Rufus McKay sung "Danny Boy" I was spellbound. No one danced while Rufus sang. Everyone faced the stage and marveled at this fantastic talent.

  A Blues Trail marker paying tribute to The Red Tops has been erected in Vicksburg, Mississippi.

  A brief history recap of The Red Tops is presented as follows:

- The group, part of a long line of dance bands in Vicksburg, started during World War II as the Rebops.
- Under the leadership of drummer Walter Osborne, the Rebops reorganized as The Red Tops in 1953. Their first performance was at the Sequoia Hills Club in Bovina, just east of Vicksburg, on June 20, 1953.
- The majority of The Red Tops' performances over the course of their history were for white audiences in Mississippi, Louisiana, Arkansas, and Tennessee.
- Besides places like the National Guard Armory in Greenwood, Mississippi, where I attended my Red Tops gig in 1956, other venues for Red Tops gigs included country clubs, ballrooms, high schools, colleges, and large auditoriums, to mention a few.
- In the early 1960s, saxophonist/bassist Andy Hardwick and vocalist Rufus McKay left The Red Tops and formed The Fabulous Corvettes, a band whose repertoire was more blues and R&B oriented than The Red Tops.
- The Red Tops stopped performing regularly in 1974 but have reunited on a number of special occasions.
- Multi-instrumentalist Andy Hardwick continued performing regularly as a jazz pianist, while Rufus McKay moved to Las Vegas and sang with The Ink Spots and other vocal groups before retiring to Vicksburg in 2000.

  The Red Tops blues trail marker in Vicksburg does not mention any recordings by The Red Tops, but I remember one entitled "Swanee River Rock" that got some air play in Mississippi. I know the song never made the Hot 100 Billboard charts, but if they had a Hot 100 for dance bands, The Red Tops would have been number one for over 20 years.

Chapter 70
The Gants

In 1963 my wife, Lois, and I purchased our first house on West Barton Avenue in Greenwood, Mississippi. Sometime after moving in, I started hearing about a teenage boy who lived down the street that could sing and play the guitar. Reportedly, all the girls loved him. Our daughter, Cindy, was only two years old at the time, so we didn't have to worry. HA! His name: Sid Herring; his group: The Gants.

Actually, the group was originally known as The Kingsmen (not to be confused with the "Louie, Louie" bunch). They got together in 1963 to play R&B covers and the kind of instrumental tunes popularized by The Ventures. The original band was: Sid Herring (lead vocals and guitar), Johnny Freeman (guitar), Vince Montgomery (bass guitar), and Don Wood (drums). Soon after forming and starting to play gigs, Johnny Freeman had to quit because his parents wouldn't let him play out-of-town gigs. He was replaced by Johnny Sanders. At this point, the band changed their name to The Gants after a popular brand of shirt with a button-down collar, which is also the French word for "glove."

In early 1965, The Gants were overheard by a U. S. tour coordinator for The Animals while playing in a hotel ballroom. They were chosen to open for The Animals Florida tour, and this gave them the exposure they needed to take it to another level.

In mid 1965, Dominic Fratesi took The Gants to Fame studio in Muscle Shoals, Alabama, for a two-song recording to release as a single on his Statue record label. By this time, I had already recorded eight songs (four singles) for Dominic and I was still starving.

Unlike my recordings for Dominic, The Gants' first recording was a hit. This first single was Bo Diddley's "Road Runner," backed with their own "My Baby Don't Care." Dominic leased the single to Liberty Records in Los Angeles, California, and "Road Runner" reached Number 46 on the U. S. pop charts. Dominic Fratesi invited me to attend their first session in Muscle Shoals in 1965, and I'm proud to say that I accepted his invitation. It was nice getting to witness the recording of a hit single. Perhaps I was a little jealous, but proud to be there nonetheless.

In the latter part of 1965, Liberty released The Gants' first album entitled "Road Runner." Other albums released by Liberty Records were "Gants Again" (1965) and "Gants Galore" (1966). Compilation albums were: "I Wonder" (1988), "Road Runner, the Best of The Gants" (2000), and "Introducing The Gants" (2005).

Singles by The Gants are as follows:
- "Road Runner/My Baby Don't Care" (1965)
- "What's Happening/Careless" (1965)
- "Crackin' Up/Dr. Feelgood" (1966)
- "I Want Your Lovin'/Spoonful of Sugar" (1966)
- "You Can't Blow Smoke Rings/Little Boy Sad" (1966)

- "Drifters Sunrise/Just As Good" (1967)
- "Greener Days/I Wonder" (1967)
- "Another Chance/Ain't Too Proud to Beg" (1969)

After the 1960s The Gants were history in regard to new records. Members had settled into careers (Johnny Sanders became a doctor, Vince Montgomery became a lawyer, and the rest were doing other day job stuff to make a living). However, in 2005, The Gants were performing together again with the following: Sid Herring, Don Wood, Johnny Sanders, Johnny Freeman, and on bass, Charles Hall, sitting in for Vince Montgomery, who died of natural causes in 2001 at his home in Clarksdale, Mississippi.

Besides getting to witness The Gants' first recording session where they recorded their hit record, "Road Runner," I attended a concert at the Greenwood Junior High School auditorium when "Road Runner" was on the national charts. The place was packed (standing room only), and The Gants put on a show that was unbelievable. Of all the concerts I've attended in my lifetime, I would rank this concert second only to Elvis concerts that I attended in Little Rock, Arkansas, and Memphis, Tennessee, in 1973 and 1974, respectively.

As of this writing (October 2010), Sid Herring lives in Tennessee close to Nashville. He still writes songs, plays the guitar, and sings. Sid is, in my opinion, good enough to make a big splash in Nashville. I hope he does. Johnny Sanders is a medical doctor in Tupelo, Mississippi, Johnny Freeman lives in Greenwood, Mississippi, where he runs the family-owned cotton gin business, Charles Hall owns and operates a music store in Greenwood, Mississippi, and I've heard that Don Wood lives in Kilmichael, Mississippi. Vince Montgomery was a practicing attorney for a number of years in Clarksdale, Mississippi, before his untimely death in 2001.

I hope the remaining Gants continue performing from time to time. Further, I would like to make a 21st century Gants' performance. I'm sure it wouldn't equal the 1965 gig, but you never know. Anyway, it would be a special treat for me in my sunset years.

During the writing of this book, Don Wood died on May 14, 2011, He was 61 years old.

Chapter 71
John Hughey

John Hughey was born December 27, 1933, in Elaine, Arkansas. He died November 18, 2007, in Hendersonville, Tennessee.

In 1968 Larry Rogers recorded a song entitled "The First Thing I Tried" on me for release on his Younger label. The flip side was "My Woman." Larry brought in John Hughey to play steel guitar on "The First Thing I Tried". Larry told me to get there early in the morning because the steel player had to catch a flight at 11:00 A.M. so he could play a gig in Oklahoma with Conway Twitty. At the time, I had never heard of John Hughey, but after that session, I knew him well as the best steel guitar player I had ever heard. I might add that I haven't heard one since who could play like John Hughey. This 1968 session was recorded at Lyn-Lou Recording Studio at 1518 Chelsea Avenue in Memphis, Tennessee.

Information about John's musical career is presented as follows:

John began playing guitar at age nine, when his parents bought him an acoustic guitar from Sears. In the seventh grade, he befriended a classmate named Harold Jenkins, who would later become a prominent country singer under the stage name Conway Twitty (Hughey and Jenkins also attended high school together).

While in high school, John Hughley, along with Harold Jenkins and other high school friends, performed in a local band called The Phillips Country Ramblers. By then, John had talked his father into buying him a lap steel guitar.

John Hughey first played professionally as a member of Slim Rhodes and The Mother's Best Mountaineers, a Memphis, Tennessee based-band. After leaving this band, John joined Conway Twitty on the road as his pedal steel guitarist. He backed Conway from 1968 to 1988. He also recorded with various acts such as Marty Stuart, Willie Nelson, Elvis Presley, and Dickey Betts.

Besides Conway, John played for Loretta Lynn, then moved on to play for Vince Gill for twelve years. Vince Gill cited Hughey as giving "definition" to his music, while Marty Stuart described John Hughey as "a top drawer statesman who helped define the whole 20th century sound of country music." John Hughey's method of steel guitar playing was known as the "crying steel" method because of his use of tremolo on the instrument's higher range.

In the 2000s, John and several other Nashville musicians formed a western swing band called The Time Jumpers, who performed every month at a club in Nashville. The "crying steel" became silent on November 18, 2007, when John Hughey died from heart complications, one month after having had a stint put in his heart. His funeral was held on November 21, 2007, at the First Baptist Church in Hendersonville, Tennessee.

For 45 years, John Hughey was married to his wife, Jean, who often sat in the audience during his performances. Together, they had one daughter. John also has four brothers and four sisters.

John Hughey is gone, but his "crying steel" will live on through the numerous recordings he made throughout his long, successful career.

Chapter 72
Kenny Loftin

Kenny Loftin was born September 30, 1954, in Miami, Florida. The Loftin family later moved to Vaiden, Mississippi. In 1973, Kenny graduated from Vaiden High School, after which he attended Holmes Junior College at Goodman, Mississippi, and Wood Junior College at Mathiston, Mississippi.

Kenny was mentioned in Chapter 24 which highlighted Magnolia Blue, but he was kind enough to provide me with additional information, so I am glad to highlight him with his own chapter.

According to Kenny, he met Van Simpson in a pool hall in Vaiden in 1965. He stated that Van was seven years older than he was but could not beat him in pool. He further stated that Van learned he could play guitar, and he learned that Van could sing, so they decided to form a band.

Their first band was Cold Fire and their first gig was in 1968 at the VFW Club in Kosciusko, Mississippi. They then became the Key Notes, and in 1970 became Magnolia Blue. As noted in Chapter 24, Magnolia Blue played some of the same clubs we did during the 70s, and we had several battles of the bands with them.

Kenny stated that he quit playing in 1991 and went "off-shore" as a crane operator for 15 years. Kenny said that he still loves music and plays a little from time to time. Kenny has two sons, Leith and Devin, who are both musicians. Leith lives in Nashville, Tennessee, where he plays and writes. He also hits the road occasionally and has performed in Greenwood, Mississppi, as well as other towns in North Mississippi like Carrollton, Winona, and Grenada, to name a few. Kenny's younger son, Devin, also plays but has chosen the Army as his career. As of this writing (October 2010), he has been in the Army over six years. He is currently a Green Beret. He is stationed in Afghanistan. Kenny stated that both of his sons have really made him proud. Kenny should be proud of them, and they should be proud of Kenny. I'm sure they are, and I wish them all the best that life has to offer.

Chapter 73
James O'Gwynn

James O'Gwynn, known as the smiling Irishman of country music, was born January 26, 1928, at Winchester, Mississippi, a small community in Wayne County. He learned guitar as a child from his mother, and his earliest influences were Jimmy Rodgers and Hank Williams. James dropped out of grade school to help out at his father's mechanic shop, and later joined the U. S. Marines for four years.

In 1977, I recorded a song I had written entitled, "If Only I Could Get One Hit". I sent a copy to Martin Hawkins in England who was releasing some recordings on me at that time. He told me to send the song to his friend, John Singleton, in Nashville, Tennessee, and he would call John and tell him to be on the lookout for the tape. To make a long story short, they recorded my song on James O'Gwynn and released a single on Plantation Records. The title was changed to "If I Could Only Get One More Hit".

I had never heard of James O'Gwynn in 1977 but learned that he had six chart records from 1956 through 1962 on the country charts. During this period of time, my primary focus was on rock-a-billy, blues, and rock and roll. Country wasn't even in my vocabulary. Nonetheless, I was excited to have my song recorded on Plantation Records, because during the 1960s they had released a song entitled "Harper Valley PTA" on Jennie C. Riley which had become one of the top country recordings of all time.

Sanford Horton told me about attending a Jerry Lee Lewis gig at the 45 Club near Starkville where they were announcing that Jennie C. Riley would be there the next month. Sanford said that one of Jerry Lee's band members stated that Jennie C. Riley only had one song, to which Jerry Lee replied, "Yeah man, but that one song was a mother."

After my song was released on James O'Gwynn in 1977, I finally got to meet him in Vaiden, Mississippi, at the Country Music Palace. In fact, my band (The Flames) backed James on his one- hour set. He did a fantastic job. As Jerry Lee would say, "Man, that one hour set was a mother."

Highlights of James' performing career include stints on the Houston Jamboree, the Louisiana Hayride, and Grand Ole Opry. While on the Louisiana Hayride, James performed with such greats as Johnny Horton, Claude Gray, Webb Pierce, Faron Young, and even a newcomer named Elvis Presley. With the help of Jim Reeves, James debuted on the Grand Ole Opry. He moved to Nashville in 1961 and appeared on the Opry for the next two years.

Labels that James recorded for are: D, Mercury, United Artists, Hickory, Starday, Sparton, and Plantation. He charted six times on the Hot Country Songs charts. Songs that made the singles charts are as follows: "Talk To Me Lonesome Heart" was number 16 on the charts in 1956. This song, which was also written by James

O'Gwynn, was featured in the hit movie "61," the story of Roger Maris' setting his long standing record in the final game of the season in 1961 with his 61st home run. To date, this song has, according to James' son, Robert, been recorded 28 times by different artists.

Robert gave me James' telephone number, so I called him in Hattiesburg (11/5/10) and thanked him for recording my song in 1977. He invited me to come visit him in Hattiesburg, and, if possible, I plan to do so.

In 1958 "Blue Memories" was number 28. Two songs hit the charts in 1959 ("How Can I Think of Tomorrow" was number 13 and "Easy Money" was number 26). In 1961, "House of Blue Lovers" rose to number 21, and in 1962, "My Name is Mud" peaked at number 7.

All of James' hits were years behind him when he recorded my song in 1977. But I appreciate him recording it. It was nice to get one on Plantation Records, even if it did start off slow and then taper off like all of my records did. HA!

Update: I'm sad to report that before I could make my trip to Hattiesburg, James O'Gwynn died on January 19, 2011. He was 83. If he had lived one week longer until his birthday on January 26, James would have been 84.

Chapter 74
Rick, Jimmy and Dan

Why did I include three giants like Rick Hall, Jimmy Johnson, and Dan Penn in the same chapter? Because of a common denominator. The common denominator: Fame Recording Studio in Muscle Shoals, Alabama.

I met all three of the above giants at Fame Recording Studio in Muscle Shoals, Alabama. In 1963, Dominic Fratesi changed from Hi in Memphis to Fame in Muscle Shoals for our third single. Rick Hall, owner of Fame, was also engineer on this recording which was released on Statue Records. My first two singles, which were recorded at Hi in Memphis, were on Vee-Eight Records. My next Statue record was recorded in 1964 at Fame and, again, Rick Hall, was the engineer. For details see the Appendix. For my fifth single, one side was recorded in 1964 at Fame with Jimmy Johnson the engineer, and the other side was recorded at Hi in Memphis. In 1965, my sixth and final Statue single was recorded at Fame with both Jimmy Johnson and Dan Penn in the control room. In 1966, I cut my last session at Fame. The single from this session ("Big Silver Tears" and "Not Strong Enough") was released on Mariteen Records in Memphis. The single was later reissued to Jab Records, a subsidiary of Atlantic Records. Again, Jimmy Johnson was the engineer.

As previously discussed in other chapters, I moved to Memphis where I spent 1967, 1968, and until August of 1969 at Lyn-Lou studio trying to cut something resembling a hit record. While I was starving, Dan Penn was down the street cutting his records at American Recording Studio. I saw Dan several times while I was in Memphis, and he always spoke and was friendly even though he was definitely on a higher level. Musically speaking of course. Otherwise, I may have been higher. HA!

It would take an entire book to present the careers of Rick, Jimmy, and Dan. Therefore, a brief recap of their careers is presented as follows:

<u>Roe Erister (Rick) Hall</u> was born January 31, 1932, in Tishomingo County, Mississippi. He was raised in Franklin County, Alabama. After meeting saxophonist Billy Sherrill, the pair began playing songs together and formed an R&B band, the Fairlanes, fronted by Dan Penn with Rick playing bass. Rick had his first songwriting successes in the late 1950s when George Jones recorded his song, "Aching Breaking Heart." Brenda Lee recorded "She'll Never Know," and Roy Orbison recorded "Sweet and Innocent".

In 1959, Rick Hall, Billy Sherrill, and Tom Stafford formed a new music publishing company in Florence, Alabama, called Florence Alabama Music Enterprises or FAME. However, in 1960, Sherrill and Stafford dissolved the partnership, leaving Hall with rights to the studio name. Rick then set up a studio at Muscle Shoals, where one of his first recordings was Arthur Alexander's "You Better Move On." The commercial success of this record gave Rick the financial resources to establish a new, larger, Fame Recording Studio. To use an old worn out phrase, "The rest is history."

After "You Better Move On," Rick produced hits for Tommy Roe, Joe Tex, Jimmy Hughes, Percy Sledge, Wilson Pickett, Aretha Franklin, Clarence Carter, Otis Redding, Arthur Conley, and others. He gained a reputation as a white southern producer who could produce and engineer hits with black southern soul singers.

In the early 1970s, Rick turned his attention from soul music to mainstream pop, producing hits for the Osmonds, Paul Anka, Tom Jones, and Donny Osmond. In 1971, he was named Billboard Producer of the Year. Later in the decade, Rick moved back towards country music, producing hits for Mac Davis, Bobbie Gentry, Jerry Reed, and The Gatlin Brothers. Rick's publishing company and in-house songwriters also became responsible for some of the biggest country hits for artists like John Michael Montgomery and The Dixie Chicks.

Rick Hall was inducted into the Alabama Music Hall of Fame in 1985, his citation referring to him as the "Father of Muscle Shoals Music."

<u>Jimmy Johnson</u> was born February 4, 1943, at Sheffield, Alabama. Jimmy began his recording career at Fame Recording Studio in Muscle Shoals, Alabama. He worked sessions as a producer, engineer, and guitarist. Jimmy later was a founder of Muscle Shoals Sound Studio located at first on 3614 Jackson Highway in Sheffield, Alabama, and at a second site on 1000 Alabama Avenue, also in Sheffield, Alabama. A few highlights of Jimmy's career include performing with Wilson Pickett and Aretha Franklin, and engineering The Rolling Stones album, "Sticky Fingers."

Recordings where Jimmy Johnson either worked as producer, engineer, or guitarist are too numerous to list, as a list on Wikipedia shows over 400 recordings. A few that include Jimmy in some capacity follow: "Road Runner" (The Gants), "Sweet Soul Music" (Arthur Conley), "When A Man Loves a Woman" (Percy Sledge), "Land Of a Thousand Dances" (Wilson Pickett), "Mustang Sally" (Wilson Pickett), "Respect" (Aretha Franklin), "Brown Sugar" (Rolling Stones), "Bloody Mary Morning" (Willie Nelson), "Misty Blue" (Dorothy Moore), and many, many, many, many more. Needless to say, Jimmy Johnson is also in the Alabama Music Hall of Fame.

<u>Wallace Daniel (Dan) Pennington</u>, known as Dan Penn, was born November 16, 1941. He grew up in Vernon, Alabama, and spent much of his teens and early twenties in the Quad Cities/Muscle Shoals area. Dan was a regular at Rick Hall's Fame Studios as a performer, songwriter, and producer. At Fame, Dan cut his first record, "Crazy Over You," in 1960, and wrote his first hit, "Is a Bluebird Blue?" which was recorded by Conway Twitty the same year, and was later covered by James Brown.

Though Dan is considered to be one of the great white soul singers, he has a meager recorded output, preferring the relative anonymity of songwriting and producing. His early success as a songwriter convinced Dan that songwriting was a worthwhile (and lucrative) career choice. Dan Penn co-wrote many soul hits of the 1960s including "Dark End of the Street" and "Do Right Woman" (with Chips Moman) and "Out of Left Field" and "Cry Like a Baby" (with Spooner Oldham). He also produced hits such as "The Letter" by the Box Tops and many more. Dan had moved to Memphis in early 1966, so "The Letter" and his subsequent hit "Cry Like a Baby" were recorded at American Recording Studio in Memphis.

The first Dan Penn/Chips Moman collaboration resulted in the enduring classic "Dark End of the Street" which was first a hit for James Carr and has since been recorded by Aretha Franklin, Clarence Carter, Elvis Costello, Emmy Lou Harris, and Linda Ronstadt, to name a few. It was also used in the movie "The Commitments."

Dan continued writing and producing hits for numerous artists during the 1960s and finally released a record of his own, "Nobody's Fool," in 1972. In 1993, he recorded the acclaimed "Do Right Man" with many of his friends and colleagues from Memphis and Muscle Shoals. Dan now lives in Nashville and continues to write with Oldham and other writers such as Donnie Fritts, Gary Nickolson, Norbert Putnam, and Carson Whitsett. He and Oldham also tour together as their schedules permit.

I don't have the expertise to rate the impact that Rick, Jimmy, and Dan have had on the music recording industry. However, I know it's enormous.

Chapter 75
Ray & Hershel

As in Chapter 74, where I highlighted more than one person, I'm doing it again in this chapter. Also, I'm doing it for the same reason. Because of a common denominator. The common denominator: Hi Recording Studio in Memphis, Tennessee. That is where I first met Ray Harris and Hershel Wiggington.

In 1962, my band and I recorded our first single ("I Got My Mojo Working" and "I'm A Lover") at Hi Recording Studio in Memphis, Tennessee. The engineer was Ray Harris and the producer was Hershel Wiggington. The single was released by Dominic Fratesi on his Vee-Eight record label. Our second single ("Hobo Man" and "Old Man River") was also recorded in 1962 at Hi Studio with Ray Harris the engineer and Hershel Wiggington the producer. This single was also released by Dominic Fratesi on his Vee-Eight record label.

A brief recap of the careers of Ray and Hershel is presented as follows:

<u>Ray Harris</u> was born September 7, 1927, in Tupelo, Mississippi. He died November 13, 2003, in Mooreville, Mississippi, at age 76.

Before becoming engineer at Hi, where he also worked as producer, he recorded several songs that he had written for Sam Phillips at Sun Records. After joining Hi Records in the late 1950s, Ray worked as engineer/producer throughout the 1960s. During this period of time he recorded hit records on The Bill Black Combo, Ace Cannon, Gene Simmons, and many more.

Eventually Ray relinquished his position as engineer/producer to the legendary Willie Mitchell. After Willie took over, Ray moved back to Mississippi. John Mihelic told me that Ray came by his and Dominic Fratesi's studio (Statue Records) quite often and helped out with a number of recordings. Statue studio was located in Tupelo.

Besides my first two singles, which were recorded in 1962 at Hi, we returned to Hi in 1964 to record "Skeleton Fight" with Ray Harris the engineer and Hershel Wiggington the producer. After this session, I never saw Ray Harris again.

<u>Hershel Wiggington</u> was born January 28, 1938, in Hamilton, Alabama. Hershel attended Hamilton High School where he graduated in 1956.

Besides the recordings at Hi in Memphis, Hershel produced eight recordings for us at Fame Recording Studio in Muscle Shoals, Alabama. On six of the eight recordings at Muscle Shoals, Hershel's vocal group, comprised of Hershel, Jerry Eddleman, Darlene Eddleman, and Sandy Posey, did the backup vocals.

After our last session with Hershel and his vocal group in 1966 at Fame Recording Studio, I never saw Hershel and his group up close and in person again. However, I saw them hundreds of times on TV where they performed as the backup group on Hee-Haw for many years.

With the help of Sanford Horton (my research detective) in Jackson, Mississippi, I obtained Hershel's telephone number and gave him a call November 16, 2010. He provided me with the following information:

When the Memphis and Muscle Shoals days were over for Hershel, he relocated to Nashville, Tennessee. Hershel stated that he and his vocal group appeared on Hee-Haw for 25 years. During this period of time, he also did vocal work on numerous recordings. Before talking to Hershel, my wife had searched the internet and told me that the Hershel Wiggington Discography disclosed too many recordings to list unless I planned to write another book with nothing but Hershel Wigginton recordings. Hershel verified Lois' assumption when he told me that in 1973, he had provided the vocal work on fourteen number one records. He probably also did the vocal backup on hundreds of Hot 100 records that didn't make number one. Say that times 25 years and what do you have? A book of Hershel Wigginton recordings.

Hershel told me that he retired from his backup vocal group in 1994. He is now living in Hermitage, Tennessee. Hershel said that he misses singing, but has no plans for making a comeback. He did say that there is a karaoke place close to his home where he goes and sings some to keep his voice in shape. I wonder why he wants to keep his voice in shape. Possibly a comeback perhaps? Stay tuned.

To Ray and Hershel I say: "Thanks for everything. I will never forget your contributions to my recordings."

Chapter 76
Richard (Ricky) Lynburgh Mabry

Ricky Mabry was born October 4, 1958, at Grenada County Hospital in Grenada, Mississippi. The Mabry family was living in Carroll County, Mississippi, near Holcomb. Ricky attended Grenada High School in Grenada, Mississippi, where he graduated in 1975.

When I retired from the honky-tonk circuit in 1984, I had never heard of Ricky Mabry, but since coming out of retirement in 2002, I have heard a lot about Ricky Mabry. In fact, my band and I have appeared on a number of shows with Ricky at the Black Hawk school house, the Carrollton Community House, and the Gore Springs school house. In addition, Ricky and I have performed for several Legends shows. Ricky is always Elvis and, on occasion, has also been Conway Twitty, Charlie Rich, and Ronnie Milsap. He has a very strong voice and can really do it all.

Even though Ricky can do it all, his reputation is primarily as an Elvis impersonator. I have read that there are thousands of Elvis impersonators in the world which are rated as follows: Most are not very good and some are downright pathetic. However, a few are really good. Ricky Mabry is one of really good ones.

Pertinent information on Ricky's career in music and his day jobs is presented as follows:

In 1985, Ricky sang for a while with a band called Moody Blues. From 1986 to 1992, Ricky performed as an Elvis impersonator. One year he won second place at the annual show in Memphis where Elvis impersonators from all over the world appeared. Then, in 1992, he pulled one of my stunts and retired from the music business. Ricky stayed retired ten years, then in 2002, he came out of retirement. Since 2002, hundreds of people have been blessed by this man with one of the best voices you will hear anywhere. Besides the gigs I previously mentioned, Ricky sings in church, at nursing homes, and at funerals.

Regarding Ricky's day jobs, his main gig was as a salesman with Frito-Lay where he stocked stores with potato chips, nabs, and other goodies. Ricky retired from Frito-Lay in 2005 after 21 years of service as the singing potato chip man. Reportedly, you could hear Ricky coming from miles away. HA! Since retiring from Frito-Lay, Ricky has kept busy as a cook for his daughter at Tally's Convenience Store in Grenada. When he's not cooking at Tally's, Ricky is cooking on stage all over North Mississippi. If you get a chance to hear Ricky sing and perform, then do it. You'll be glad you did.

Chapter 77
Edward (Eddie) Lee Alderman

Eddie Lee Alderman was born February 19, 1931, in Carroll County, Mississippi. The Alderman residence was located in the northern section of Carroll County. The general area is known as Little Texas. Eddie Lee died February 6, 1972. He is buried at Bethel Methodist Church cemetery which is located 14 miles northeast of Carrollton, Mississippi.

As discussed in Chapter 50 (Grover Duke), I got my first taste of sin at the Grenada VFW when I was 15 years old. Also, as mentioned, Eddie Lee Alderman was playing steel guitar with Grover Duke and the Delta Rhythm Boys.

Fast forward three years to 1956 when I'm all grown up at the ripe old age of 18. Enter Eddie Lee Alderman again. This time he's playing lead guitar with me and my band (Mack Allen Smith & The Flames). I attended Holmes Junior College in the fall of 1956 and, on weekends, we played at the 51 Club in Durant and the VFW clubs in Kosciusko and Greenwood. This only lasted a few months before I lost my mind and joined the Marines, but thanks to Eddie Lee Alderman, I will remember those few months forever. I had been singing for several years, but this was my first time to sing with a real seasoned professional like Eddie Lee.

After returning from the Marines in 1959, our paths crossed a few times, but Eddie Lee was never a member of my band again. He did sit in with us a few times on lead guitar and steel guitar, and it was always a special occasion for me when he did.

Chapter 78
Bobby Joe Alford

Bobby Joe Alford was born July 18, 1941, in the Gravel Hill community of Carroll County, Mississippi. He attended Greenwood High School in Greenwood, Mississippi. On September 28, 1962, Bobby married Kay Overstreet. They have two children, Michael and Christopher.

I didn't know Bobby Alford before coming out of my 18-year retirement in 2002. Since then, most of my singing has been at the old Black Hawk school house where Bobby is the head man in charge. Bobby started the shows at Black Hawk in 2000, and the place is usually packed every third Saturday - March through December. He shuts it down in January and February so we can all sit by the fire and drink coffee.

At Black Hawk the show starts at 6:00 PM and features country, gospel, bluegrass, and Carroll County's ole rock-a-billy, which Bobby calls me and my band. As they say, "It don't pay nothing, but we have lots of fun." To get paid, I would have to go back on the honky-tonk circuit; however, I told my wife, Lois, that I wouldn't sing in honky-tonks anymore. So, I just keep on singing for fun at Black Hawk.

Without a doubt, Bobby's shows at Black Hawk each month have given hundreds of musicians and singers an opportunity to pick and grin who otherwise wouldn't have had an opportunity to do so.

Information on Bobby's music career and his day jobs is presented as follows:

Bobby Alford told me that he strummed rhythm guitar and sang around the house for several years before joining his first band in 1968. This band was called The Country Strings, and they played together for ten years. Band members were Bobby Alford (rhythm guitar and singer), James Carpenter (lead guitar), Terry Carpenter (bass), Robert Alexander (steel guitar), and Bobby Bruce (lead guitar and singer).

From 1978 to 1993 Bobby played rhythm guitar and sang alone at several churches and nursing homes in Greenwood and surrounding areas. Then, from 1994 to 2000, he played rhythm guitar and sang with the Mississippi Ramblers from Grenada, Mississippi. Members were Bobby Alford (rhythm guitar and singer), Neil Wrenn (guitar, fiddle, and mandolin), Luke Borderlong (dobro), Marvin Lemley (bass), Bushy Martin (fiddle), and Butch Mooneyham (dobro).

Bobby's day jobs over the years consisted of five years with Baldwin Piano, five years with National Picture Frame company, and thirty four years (1972-2006) as owner and operator of Alford Carpet. When Bobby retired in 2006, his two sons (Michael and Christopher) took over the carpet business.

According to Bobby, he is busy enough growing vegetables and muscadines to say he is semi-retired. In addition, he makes muscadine wine, and he owns a molding plant.

I hope Bobby Alford keeps the Black Hawk school house gig going until I get ready to hang up my rock-a-billy shoes again for the last time. I don't believe that will be much longer. We'll see!

Chapter 79
Robert Alexander

Robert Alexander was born May 9, 1926, at Glendora, Mississippi. Most of his adult life he lived in Greenwood, Mississippi, with his wife Nita. Robert died October 1, 1993, while residing in Greenwood. He is buried in Odd Fellows cemetery in Greenwood.

I have to give Robert Alexander a chapter in my book, if for no other reason than he is my wife's uncle. However, even if he wasn't my wife's uncle, he would get a chapter because he was a great steel guitar man. Bobby Alford says that Robert was the best steel guitar player he ever heard. I may not go that far, but I believe he was among the best around these parts.

Robert's wife, Nita, and James Minyard both told me that the first band Robert played with was Slim Douglas and the Delta Drifters. Robert played with them in the late 1940s and early 1950s. In 1951, they had a weekly radio show in Greenwood. Members of the band were Slim Douglas (rhythm guitar and singer), Robert Alexander (steel guitar), Eddie Eubanks (lead guitar), Willie Narmour (fiddle), and James Minyard (fiddle). Nita mentioned two other members - Hi Water Harris and Alvin Keith, but doesn't remember what they played.

As discussed in Chapter 78 (Bobby Alford), Robert played steel guitar with the Country Strings for ten years (1968-1978). During Robert's music career, he also played with D. G. Williams and the Delta Raiders.

Robert's day job was as a plumber. Reportedly, he made a good living for himself and his family doing plumbing work.

Chapter 80
Richard Dennis Corder

Richard Corder was born April 21, 1947, at Greenwood Leflore Hospital in Greenwood, Mississippi. The Corder family was living in Carroll County, Mississippi, about five miles from North Carrollton. Richard attended J. Z. George High School in North Carrollton. Richard married Judy Lemley on November 7, 1965. They have two children, Richie and Dickie.

Richard has owned and operated his own business (Richard Corder Auto Repair) in Greenwood since 1978. He has been working on my cars since 1978, but I didn't know he was a singer until I came out of my 18-year retirement in 2002. Since then, Richard has sung with my band at Black Hawk school house and the Carrollton Community House a number of times.

One of Richard's employees at his repair shop said that Richard was a better mechanic than he was a singer, and he wasn't much of a mechanic. Everyone there laughed. However, if the truth be told, Richard Corder is a very good mechanic and he ain't a bad singer. His songs range from Marty Robbins "Begging To You" to Chuck Berry's "Johnny Be Good". Richard sings for fun, and everyone has fun when he sings.

Besides sitting in with my band, he has a band that usually backs him at shows around this area. They are Sue Duke (piano), Jessie McCrory (lead guitar), George McCrory (bass), and Pete Miskelly (drums and vocals).

Richard, keep on rockin' and try to find me a good cheap pickup truck.

Chapter 81
Jerry Masters

Jerry Masters was born December 11, 1939, at Little Rock, Arkansas. He attended high school at Little Rock Central High where he graduated in 1957.

I met Jerry Masters for the first and last time in 1969 at Lyn-Lou Recording Studio in Memphis. I was recording "Riding Home to Judy" for Larry Rogers, and he had hired Jerry to play bass on the session. I learned real fast that I was in the studio with a professional bass man; however, little did I know what a giant he would become in the music business.

Jerry Masters started his music career playing bass with Charlie Rich. Later, he played with Ronny and the Daytonas who had the hit song "Little GTO." From the musicians in that group, Jerry formed The Hombres who had the hit song "Let It All Hang Out," a song that has experienced a revival on You Tube and on the hit TV show "Cold Case".

In the seventies Jerry went from playing music to creating music as an engineer in the studio. He became one of the best recording engineers to sit at a console. The list of stars he has recorded is too long to present here. A few are Rod Stewart, Paul Simon, Jerry Lee Lewis, Mac Davis, etc., etc., etc.

On 12/11/10 I received a questionnaire from Jerry that I had sent him a while back. He said that he had just moved back to Muscle Shoals, Alabama, after working 20 years for Malaco Records in Jackson, Mississippi. While at Malaco he recorded 122 albums. Jerry made a statement that I'm presenting verbatim as follows: "I'm currently preparing to marry the love of my life whom I met at Muscle Shoals Sound in 1973. Her name is Jan Stevenson and, after 37 years, we want to live in this area where we met and fell in love and spend the rest of our lives. I'm currently working at Big Star Grocery Store for $7.25 per hour. Never been happier."

Jerry further stated: "It's an honor to be included in your publication. I do remember your session and I'm humbled to be a part of your life once more."

I want to say thank you to Jerry for playing on my 1969 session in Memphis, and for returning my questionnaire with information on your career and current status. Good luck with your marriage and the rest of your life. As they say: "Ain't love grand?"

Chapter 82
Lisa Cook McNamara

Lisa was born June 2, 1964, in Lexington (Holmes County), Mississippi. She graduated from Central Holmes Academy in 1982. After high school, Lisa attended Mississippi Delta Community College (MDCC) at Moorhead, Mississippi. In 1996, Lisa graduated from MDCC with a medical lab technician's degree. She currently works for the North Central MS Regional Cancer Center at the Greenwood Leflore Hospital in Greenwood, Mississippi. In addition, Lisa has taken courses from Ole Miss and is pursuing a degree that will enable her to teach.

Lisa, who is the step-daughter of my long time lead guitar picker, Laney O'Briant, sang with my band (The Flames) in the late 1970s and early 1980s. In 1980, we were the opening act for a concert in Vicksburg, Mississippi, which featured the Kendalls and The Bellamy Brothers. For months after the Vicksburg concert, Laney would proudly introduce Lisa as the highlight of the big concert in Vicksburg. I never heard anyone disagree with the assessment. Lisa came on before me and, I must admit, she was a hard act to follow.

After I hung up my rock-a-billy shoes in 1984, Lisa continued singing. First, she sang with the Black River Band which consisted of Laney O'Briant (lead guitar), Bill Jones (drums), Mike Lovelace (bass), and Doug Walker (rhythm guitar). Lisa sang with Black River for several months then formed her own band with Tiger Coleman (lead guitar), Robby Browning (drums), Billy Miller (bass), and Obie Atkins (piano).

I talked to Lisa this past year (2010) and she stated that she had been singing with a band called Trykes for about six months. She also told me that her husband, Johnny McNamara, composes contemporary Christian music, and they have recorded three songs.

On December 18, 2010, Lisa and her husband came to the old Black Hawk school where we were playing. We invited her to sing with the band and she obliged. Guess what? As usual, she was the highlight of the show.

Chapter 83
Other Known & Unknown Stars

The previous chapter (82) concluded the chapters where stars are highlighted with their own chapters. The fact that 82 is the number of counties in Mississippi is purely coincidental. Jamie Isonhood reminded me that Highway 82 runs through Greenwood where I live and through Carroll County where I was born and raised. That has nothing to do with anything either.

A number of people in this chapter would have been highlighted with their own chapter if they had provided me with a little requested information to go with the information I had in my head. But, as Elvis might say, "That's the way the mop flops or the way the cookie crumbles."

Instead of an index for these stars, they are presented in substantial alphabetical order as follows:

Larry Acy - Larry, also mentioned in Chapter 3, played piano in my band for about three years (1977-1980). Larry played on a couple of my records that were recorded at Lyn-Lou recording studio in Memphis. See Appendix for details. After leaving the band in 1980, Larry served in the Army and then had a career with the post office in Texas. As of this writing (February 2011), Larry has retired from the post office and moved back to Carroll County, Mississippi.

Billy Adams - Based in Memphis, Billy played the clubs there for many years. He was a great drummer described by many as master of the shuffle beat. I booked Billy and his band during the seventies (1971-1976) at my club (Mack Allen Smith's Town & Country Night Club) outside Greenwood. We even did a few battles of the bands. Besides playing drums, Billy was a singer. In the 1950s he recorded such hits as "Ruby Jane," "Betty and Dupree," "Reconsider Baby," "Looking for my Mary Ann," "Got My Mojo Working," and "Rock Me Baby" on the Sun record label. Billy died December 3, 1984, in Memphis. He was 47.

Billy Ainsworth - In the summer of 1956 Billy and I both sang at the VFW club in Greenwood, Mississippi. One Saturday I would sing with Kenny Minyard, and the next Saturday Billy would sing with another band. We both sang on radio shows each Saturday that were broadcast by the VFW. Billy did mostly Carl Perkins type rock-a-billy and some country. He had a great voice, but didn't keep up the honky-tonk grind like I did. Probably because he was smarter than me. Over the 50+ years since we sang together, Billy has made a living working as a mechanic. Reportedly, he's a good one. I see Billy once in a while around town, and occasionally we'll stop and talk about those bygone years.

Alton Alderman - Alton played rhythm guitar and sang harmony in the FFA band (the first band I every sang with). I saw Alton at Wal-Mart not long ago. He is retired. Alton says that after high school, he only played music around the house. He worked

46 years as a salesman for Henderson & Baird Hardware Company in Greenwood, Mississippi.

Junior Bailey - Junior sang harmony vocals in the FFA band. He finished high school in 1955, one year ahead of me. I was honored to be best man at his wedding. We played football together and double dated together. After high school, Junior moved to Louisville, Kentucky, where he wound up owning his own manufacturing plant. I have seen Junior a few times over the years. His brother, M. C. Bailey, was in my graduating class in 1956. I have seen him at several class reunions. M. C. became a PhD and is retired. He and his family live in Newport News, Virginia.

Johnny Baker - Johnny played trumpet with me some in the honky-tonks in the early years. He also played on both sides of my second Vee-Eight record in 1962. On one side he played trumpet, and one the other side he played harmonica. See Appendix for details. Johnny later got a college degree in music and became a band director in South Mississippi. After he left my band in the early sixties, I never saw him again.

Scott Barretta - I met Scott sometime after coming out of my 18-year retirement in 2002. He wrote the liner notes for my Big Legal Mess CD that was released and distributed by Fat Possum Records in 2009. Scott also did an article on me and my Fat Possum CD in his weekly newspaper article for *The Clarion Ledger* in Jackson. At the conclusion of his weekly article is the following: "Scott Barretta is an Oxford-based writer and music critic. He is host of the Highway 61 blues radio show on MPB on Saturday nights. He blogs about the blues at the website for the MPB show at www.highway61radio.com". Scott wrote a book entitled *Mississippi, State of the Blues*, which was released in 2010, and he is one of the main writers for the blues markers throughout Mississippi and other states.

Jim Bickerstaff - Jim released two songs I had recorded at Muscle Shoals, Alabama, on his label, Mariteen Records in 1966. He leased the single ("Big Silver Tears" and "Not Strong Enough") to Atlantic Records. They reissued the single on their subsidiary, Jab Records. In 1967 Jim moved to Arizona because of his wife's health. I never saw him again. I've been told that Jim died many years ago. I don't know when, but believe it was in the 1970s or the 1980s.

Black River Band - Popular during the 1980s, the band members were Laney O'Briant (lead guitar), Bill Jones (drums), Bubba Calhoun (singer), Mike Lovelace (bass), and Doug Walker (guitar).

Bill Bole - Bill played trumpet in my band for six years (1963-1969). He played on all the songs I recorded at Muscle Shoals, Alabama, which included all eight songs on my four Statue Records, plus others released and unreleased. See Appendix for complete details. I have not seen Bill since sometime in the 1970s, but I have talked to him on the phone several times. Bill became a Jehovah's Witness preacher and preached in Oklahoma over 25 years. As of this writing (3/4/11), Bill is living in Sherman, Texas.

Michael Bole - Michael is the son of Bill Bole. He played drums with me several times since I came out of my 18-year retirement in 2002. The gigs were at old school houses in Black Hawk and Gore Springs, Mississippi, and the Community House in Carrollton, Mississippi. In addition, Michael played several years with the popular band, Crossin' Dixon, who recorded in Nashville and went on a national tour. As of this writing (3/4/11), Michael is back on his day job as a salesman of office equipment and supplies.

    Robert Box - I had heard of Robert Box for many years before he played lead guitar with me in 1982 at the Country Music Palace in Vaiden, Mississippi. He only played with my band and me one time, but he made a lasting impression. As of this writing (3/4/11), Robert lives in Ackerman, Mississippi, and is still pickin' and grinnin.'

    Alan Bridges - Alan, the owner of Grape Records in Jackson, Mississippi, released two singles (four songs) on me. One was in 1980 and the other in 1981. He also released at least one single on Bubba Calhoun from Vaiden, Mississippi. At the time, he was married to Bubba's sister (Linda). I haven't seen Alan since the early 1980s. When I started this project in June 2009, I tried to call Alan, but the number I have is no longer in service. Bubba Calhoun is dead, and so far my contacts have been unable to provide me with information on Alan's whereabouts and what he is doing.

    Wayne Brown - Wayne played piano with the Nite-Liters who are highlighted in Chapter 53. He played piano with the Nite-Liters on all our battles of the bands, as well as their great recordings. Reportedly, Wayne is still living in the Tupelo, Mississippi, area.

    Butch Carter - Butch played piano with Shylo, the band that is highlighted in Chapter 67. He played with Shylo at my club in Greenwood, Mississippi, and played on several of my recordings at Lyn-Lou Studio in Memphis, Tennessee. In reviewing my Discography, I noted that my last recording at Lyn-Lou Studio with Butch playing piano was in 1980. I haven't seen Butch since 1980, and don't have a clue what happened in his life during the last 30+ years. He was a great piano player and person. I hope he has enjoyed good health and much success.

    Bubba Calhoun - John C. "Bubba" Calhoun, III, a lifelong resident of Vaiden, Mississippi, was a very good singer. Besides singing in local nightclubs, he recorded a song in Nashville entitled "Gennie in the Bottle" that got local play and was quite popular in this area. My band and I (Mack Allen Smith & The Flames) had the privilege of engaging in several battles of the bands with Bubba and his band at clubs located in Vaiden and surrounding areas. Bubba died November 27, 2009, at age 59. He is buried in the Vaiden cemetery in Vaiden, Mississippi.

    Clyde Campbell - Clyde and I attended school together at J. Z. George High School in North Carrollton, Mississippi, and at Holmes Junior College in Goodman, Mississippi. We also left Holmes Junior after one semester and joined the Marines. While at Holmes Junior, Clyde helped out with the singing. He did Pat Boone and Fats Domino. Clyde had a great voice but, to my knowledge, never sang again with a band. Clyde died on May 17, 1996.

    Tommy Cathey - Tommy played bass on one song "Don't Be Cruel" that I recorded in 1972 at Lyn-Lou Studio in Memphis. He did a great job. After the 1972 session I never saw Tommy again and have no information about his career.

    Alton Cheek - The first time I sang in a nightclub was in 1956 at the VFW in Greenwood, Mississippi. The band was the Kenny Minyard Band, and Alton Cheek was the lead guitar man. Alton was primarily a country picker, but he had heard "That's All Right, Mama" and was able to get us going by beating the crap out of it in the key of "A." Throughout the 1950s, Alton was regarded as one of the best lead guitar pickers in this area. Besides playing with Kenny Minyard, Alton also played with Grover Duke, Jenkins Ruscoe and several other bands. He died September 21, 1985.

<u>Van Cook</u> - Van was a bass man in my band for a while during the late 1970s at the old Country Music Palace in Vaiden, Mississippi. He and his family currently live in Bandera, Texas.

<u>David Lee Cox, Jr.</u> - Junior was born March 1, 1960, in Greenwood, Mississippi. His dad, who is highlighted in Chapter 16, was playing piano in my band when Junior was born. As noted in Chapter 3, my final honky-tonk band from January 1983 to October 20, 1984, included David Lee Cox on keyboards and Junior Cox on drums. I talked to Junior recently, and he said that he sold his drums several years ago and quit the rat race. Junior and family currently live in Richland, Mississippi, where he owns a janitorial service.

<u>Charlie Davis</u> - Charlie was one of my drummers during the 1970s, and he was a good one. Since the 1970s, I have seen Charlie a few times in Jackson, Mississippi, where he works. Charlie is a computer expert for the State of Mississippi at the Mississippi Board of Health. According to Sanford Horton, Charlie is a better computer man than he was a drummer.

"Toad" Donahoo - I met "Toad" at Black Hawk after coming out of my 18-year retirement in 2002. Later, we did some shows together at the school houses in Black Hawk, Carmack, and Gore Springs, and at the Carrollton Community House. "Toad" spends several months each year at Mountain View, Arkansas, and he promotes a festival each year at Grenada Lake called "Pickin' on the Lake." The rest of his time is spent doing benefit shows and singing in nursing homes in North Mississippi. "Toad" has a 12-song CD entitled "Back to the Oldies" that was recorded at Lighthouse Recording Studio in Mountain View, Arkansas.

"Duff" Dorrough - "Duff" is a guitar picker from Ruleville, Mississippi. I first met "Duff" in 1980 when we did a battle of bands with him and his band at the Delta Queen in Vaiden, Mississippi. Since coming out of my 18-year retirement in 2002, I have seen "Duff" a couple of times and in 2009, I sang on a show with "Duff" at the Ribeye in Yazoo City, Mississippi. Without a doubt, "Duff" Dorrough is one of the best guitar pickers in these parts (the Mississippi Delta).

<u>Bridge Downs</u> - During the late 1970s and early 1980s, Bridge played lead guitar with me and my band on a few gigs. Also, my band and I did several battles of the bands with Bridge and his band. Last year (2010), I saw Bridge at my dentist's office in Carrollton, Mississippi. I was there to get my teeth worked on, and Bridge was there to do some electrical work, which is his full time job now. No more picking with a day job. Bridge told me that he hasn't picked up a guitar in over 20 years. Bridge and his family now live in Grenada, Mississippi.

<u>Duck Hillbillies</u> - See Chapter 56, which highlights Doc Herbert.

<u>Sue Duke</u> - After my coming out of retirement in 2002, Sue Duke has played piano with me and my band several times at the old school houses in Black Hawk and Gore Springs, and at the Carrollton Community House. She played with her husband, Grover Duke, for many years before his untimely death in 1982. Sue is a fine piano player, and many people are blessed by her playing. When she plays with a band these

days, it is usually with the McCrory brothers (Jessie and George) and Pete Miskelly. I hope she keeps on playing for years to come.

Mike Ellis - I started hearing about Mike Ellis and the Hometown Band during the 1970s. They were very popular throughout the Mississippi Delta. In 1980, we finally got around to doing a battle of the bands with them at the Delta Queen in Vaiden, Mississippi. I don't remember who won the battle, but I think it's safe to say that they were worthy opponents.

Johnny Freeman - Johnny was one of the original members of Curb Service, which is highlighted in Chapter 37. Curb Service was formed in 1978. Johnny still plays lead guitar with the popular band. Besides Curb Service, Johnny was also an original member of the world famous Gants, who are highlighted in Chapter 70. For his day job, Johnny is owner and operator of cotton gins in Mississippi and other southern states.

Leman Gandy - I first met Leman in 2003 at the old Black Hawk school house where we both were performing. After this, we were on shows together at Carmack and Carrollton. He had a fine gospel group called the Deltones. Before settling in Greenwood, where he worked as an attorney, he had played bass with some more pickers in California. Also, in 1975, he ran for governor of Mississippi.

Good Times Express - See Chapter 56, which highlights Doc Herbert.

Charles Hall - Charles plays keyboards with Curb Service, a local band that is highlighted in Chapter 37. He also owns and operates a recording studio and music store in Greenwood, Mississippi.

Jimmy Harrell - A brother-in-law to Sonny Strohm who played saxophone in my band during the early 1960s. Jimmy recorded for Sun Records in the 1950s, after which he had a career as an officer in the Navy. He is now retired and living in Jacksonville, Florida. In 2000, Jimmy sponsored an update to my listing on the Rock-A-Billy Hall of Fame Website (rockabillyhall.com).

Gloria Hathcock - Gloria is a fine harmonica player now living in Durant, Mississippi. Since ending my 18-year retirement, Gloria has played a number of gigs with me and my band.

Clovis Harbin - In high school Clovis played bass tub in our FFA band which is highlighted in Chapter 2. Clovis graduated one year ahead of me, and I have not seen him since his graduation.

Rusty Hobgood - Rusty and I attended Holmes Junior College in the fall of 1956. He was manager of Mack Allen Smith & The Flames and did a good job of getting us gigs. Also, like me and Clyde Campbell, he joined the Marines in January 1957. I have seen Rusty several times over the years. He now lives in Grenada, Mississippi.

Danny Hogan - Danny played bass with Shylo who is highlighted in Chapter 67. He played at my club in Greenwood, as well as on some of my recordings at Lyn-Lou Studio in Memphis, Tennessee.

Hershel Hood - Hershel played drums with the Nite-Liters who are highlighted in Chapter 53.

Jerry Hood - Jerry, brother of Hershel, played lead guitar with the Nite-Liters in the 1960s and into the 1970s. Jerry still plays, and I heard him a couple of times in 2010 with the Silver Eagle Band. He still picks as good as he ever did - maybe better.

MACK ALLEN SMITH

<u>Barry Hopkins</u> - Barry played keyboards with me during the 1970s. He was living in Kosciusko then, but last I heard, he was living in Tennessee.

<u>Roger Humphries</u> - Roger and his great band, the Cherry Pickers, backed me on my tour of England in 1979. Roger later sent me a 12-song album that DTS Records, a British label, has released on him and his band. I lost touch with Roger in the mid-1980s and don't know what happened to this talented bunch.

<u>The Ivories</u> - Mentioned in Chapter 19, which highlighted Laney O'Briant, the Ivories were quite popular in North Mississippi during the early to mid-sixties. Members of the Ivories were as follows: Laney O'Briant (lead guitar), Jimmy Smith (singer and piano), Doug Steen (sax), and Norman Freeland (drums).

<u>Terry Jenkins</u> - Terry is mentioned in Chapter 3 (Mack Allen Smith & The Flames). Terry's tour of duty with the Flames was 1963-1969. He played trumpet on a bunch of my recordings. For details see the Appendix. After leaving the Flames, Terry lived in Jackson for 20+ years where he worked for Morrison Music until his death.

<u>Gilruth Johnson</u> - Gilruth played with me and my band for a few months in 1961 after Keith Worrell left for college. Gilruth is now retired and living in Carrollton, Mississippi.

<u>Ronnie Korner</u> - Originally from Corpus Christi, Texas, Ronnie moved to Memphis in 1970 with Billy Wayne Herbert and Pete Bartosch to do studio work at Lyn-Lou Studio. As noted in Chapter 6, which highlights Billy Wayne Herbert, Ronnie also played the nightclub circuit which included my club in Greenwood, Mississippi. In reviewing my Discography, I found that Ronnie played drums on one of my Lyn-Lou sessions in 1970. After over ten years in the rat race, Ronnie went to college and got a degree in accounting. He's now a CPA living in Navasota, Texas.

<u>Leo LeBlanc</u> - Leo worked Memphis sessions for many years and was considered one of the best steel guitar players around. In 1976, Leo played on one of my Ace recordings ("Angel Face, Body Full of Sin") which was recorded at Lyn-Lou Studio in Memphis. Thanks to Leo, this turned out to be one of my best recordings.

<u>Gerald Little</u> - Gerald played bass with the Nite-Liters who are highlighted in Chapter 53. After my association with the Nite-Liters, I never saw Gerald again.

<u>Robert Loers</u> - Robert was born March 23, 1943, in The Netherlands where he still lives. For 30+ years Robert has owned and operated Redita Records. In 1979, he released an 18-song album of my recordings entitled "The Sound of Mack Allen Smith." For details see the Appendix. Then, in December 2010, he released a 33-song CD of my recordings which included my 1959 Sun recordings. The CD is entitled "Mack Allen Smith-Gotta Rock Tonight." The unreleased 1959 Sun recordings and 28 other vintage recordings. Robert had a heart attack several years ago and has slowed down some in recent years. He also had hip and knee replacements and calls himself the bionic man. I hope he can go many more years. Robert has done a lot over the years to keep rock-a-billy alive outside the United States of America. If anyone would like to order a copy of my December 2010 CD, you may write: Robert Loers, Dalfsenstraat 20, 2541VS Den Haag - The Netherlands.

<u>Allen Malone</u> - I sang several times with Under the Gun when Allen was playing lead guitar. Allen and the band were always good and a real pleasure to perform with. Allen told me that a large part of his learning to play lead guitar came from coming to the Greenwood Moose Lodge with his daddy (Nelson Malone) when he was a small boy

and watching my lead man (Murry Moorman). Murry was the best lead man I ever had, and Allen learned his lesson well because today Allen is one of the best around.

Charles Martin - Charles played lead guitar in the J. Z. George FFA band which is highlighted in Chapter 2. As noted, this was the first band I ever sang with. I talked to Charles today (4/26/11) and learned that he was born October 27, 1936, at McCarley (Carroll County), Mississippi. He is retired and still lives in Carroll County at 1223 Highway 51 in Vaiden, Mississippi.

Paul Melton - Paul played bass in my band about three years (1977-1980). He played on a couple of my records which were recorded at the Lyn-Lou Studio in Memphis. His day job for around 40 years has been as a furniture salesman for several stores in Greenwood, Mississippi.

John Mihelic - John's career is highlighted in Chapter 53 (The Nite-Liters/John Mihelic). John was a unique individual and a great musician. He has been dead several years now, but his legacy lingers. I really enjoyed all the battles of bands we had at the Greenwood Moose Lodge during the 1960s.

Chris Mims - Chris played keyboards with me two and one-half years (1980-1982). He played on my 38-song CD entitled "Live On Halloween," which was recorded at the Country Music Palace in Vaiden, Mississippi, on October 31, 1981. When Chris played with me, his day job was as purchasing agent with Lewis Grocery in Indianola, Mississippi. Since 1982, I have lost touch with Chris and don't know where he is or what he is doing. I do know that when he played with me, he was one great keyboard player.

Pete Miskelly - In the early 1960s, Pete played drums with me once at the old Moose Lodge (before the lodge was enlarged) in Greenwood, Mississippi. Over the years our paths have crossed a number of times when my band and I shared a stage with Pete and his band at the Carrollton Community House and other places. Also, in the early 1960s, Pete played with the local legend, Jenkins Ruscoe. As for day jobs, Pete worked for many years in law enforcement, which included his service as constable and prison warden. As of this writing (4/27/11), Pete is the mayor of North Carrollton, Mississippi. Besides being a fine singer and musician, he is also an excellent stand-up comedian.

Charlie McCarty - Charlie played drums with me and my band in the fall of 1956 while we were both students at Holmes Junior College in Goodman, Mississippi. The last I heard, Charlie was retired and living in a condo on Ross Barnett Lake in Jackson, Mississippi.

McCrory Brothers (Jessie & George) - Jessie plays lead guitar and George Plays bass. They have both been playing in the local area since the 1960s. My band and I have performed on shows with them and their bands a number of times over the years. In addition, I remember George playing bass with me and my band once during the 1960s at Al's Supper Club in Greenville, Mississippi. The McCrory brothers still live in their home county (Carroll County, Mississippi), and they still pick and grin occasionally.

Jackie McIlwain - Jackie was an original member of Under the Gun which was formed in 1995. He is still a member of Under the Gun. Jackie plays rhythm guitar and sings, and does a fine job on both. As previously noted, I have sung with Under the Gun a few times and have heard them on other occasions.

Don McMinn - I know Don through a mutual acquaintance, Billy Wayne Herbert, my first cousin. Don and Billy Wayne worked the Memphis scene over 30 years with their own group or as single acts. Don and I know each other well enough that he gave me a free copy of his CD on Ice House Records entitled "Painkiller Blues." I talked to Don on the phone in 2010, and he told me that he tours The Netherlands each year and is still active on the Memphis scene where he had a 20+ year run on Beale Street. Some highlights of Don's successful career are as follows: 1974-79 - guitarist with Jerry Lee Lewis, "The Killer," 1975-79 - guitarist and recording partner with "Memphis Slim," 1981-85 - toured with "The Memphis Blues Revue," and 1985 - opened on Beale Street in Memphis and has been a mainstay in Memphis music until the present day. A note from "Painkiller Blues" CD follows: "Don is a veteran blues artist (guitar and vocals) who has paid his dues. Though his schedule is highly demanding, he still makes time for the younger musicians and artists who need advice or assistance."

Sidney Nabors - Sidney played rhythm guitar and sang with the J. Z. George FFA band. As previously mentioned in Chapter 2, which highlighted the FFA band, this was the first band I ever sang with. After high school, I had no further contact with Sidney, and have no knowledge of his future participation in music.

Alan Pace - Alan was a great lead guitar picker and singer who is no longer with us. He died several years ago. I first met Alan in 1959, and in 1960 my band and I shared a stage with Alan and his band (Alan Pace and the Bad Habits) on WABG TV shortly after the TV station opened in Greenwood. Alan later played with other bands and was always in great demand.

Gary Page - Gary played saxophone with the Nite-Liters who are highlighted in Chapter 53. He played with the Nite-Liters when we battled them at the Greenwood Moose Lodge in the 1960s, as well as on the Jimmy Gilreath and Nite-Liters records. During his heyday, few sax players in this area could compete with him. Since the 1960s, I have not been in touch with Gary Page.

Gene Parker - The name Gene Parker may not be a household name, but to well known sax players the name Gene Parker is a well known name. I booked Gene Parker at my club several times during the early 1970s. They were then known as the Gene Parker Quintette. Besides playing my club, Gene played many gigs in Memphis, as well as around the country and overseas. He played with top Memphis drummer, Danny Ivy, as well as with the world famous Memphis Horns. Gene played sax on a number of hit records that will be remembered for many years to come.

Dewey Phillips - He was born May 13, 1926, and he died September 28, 1968. In high school I listened to Dewey Phillips "Red Hot & Blue" radio show on WHBQ in Memphis, where he introduced Elvis Presley's first record "That's All Right, Mama" and "Blue Moon of Kentucky." Little did I know that he would one day play one of my records. In 1966 while working for a radio station in Middleton, Tennessee, Dewey played both sides of my record, "Big Silver Tears" and "Not Strong Enough." Subsequently, he got me and my band booked on Eddie Bond's TV show and then on George Klein's TV show on WHBQ TV. Getting to know this great radio personality was one of the super highlights of my career.

Prime Cut - This fine band, which played about four years in the early 1990s, consisted of the following members: Ronnie Stone (lead singer), Laney O'Briant (lead guitar), Mike Lovelace (bass), Joel Anderson (rhythm guitar), and Elliott Crawford (drums).

The Phantoms - In 1964 when my record "Only Make Believe" was number one on the Dan's BBQ chart in Greenville (HA!), my band and I did a battle of bands with the Phantoms in Greenville at a big hall close to the river downtown. The only band member I remember in the Phantoms was Charlie Ross who sang and played lead guitar. I do remember that the Phantoms were one good band. In fact, they were so good we never battled them again.

Rhythm Aces - For two years (1960-1962) the Rhythm Aces were popular in North Mississippi around Greenwood and the surrounding areas. Band members were as follows: Jessie Yates (singer and rhythm guitar), Laney O'Briant (lead guitar), Chuck Ivy (bass), Doug Steen (sax), Jamie Isonhood (piano), and Leroy Sylvester (drums).

Charlie Ross - Besides playing and singing with the Phantoms, who are discussed above, Charlie Ross has been associated with other bands over the years. The most popular of all the groups that Charlie has been a member of would have to be the Cracker Jacks. They have been rockin' and rollin' for 30+ years and are considered to be "The Party Band of the South." Charlie's day job over the years has been as a radio announcer or, if you prefer, disc jockey. No matter what you call it, he's a good one. That also applies to his pickin', grinning, and singing.

Ronnie Scaife - Some information on Ronnie is presented in Chapter 67, which highlighted Shylo. As noted, I learned during the writing of this book that Ronnie Scaife died on November 3, 2010, in Nashville. He was 63 years old. Besides playing lead guitar and singing with Shylo at my club in Greenwood and doing battles of the bands with us in Vaiden, Ronnie played lead guitar on some of my best recordings at Lyn-Lou Studio in Memphis. In addition, Ronnie was later a hugh success in Nashville where he wrote hit songs for Marty Stuart, Travis Tritt, Johnny Paycheck, Ricky Skaggs, Conway Twitty, and Garth Brooks, to name a few. Ronnie also won BMI awards for "Men" (Charlie McClain, 1980), "Wrinkles" (Diamond Rio 2003), and "I Couldn't See You Leavin'" (Conway Twitty 1991).

Southern Five - This group made their mark in the 1970s playing some of the finest music you could find anywhere. Members of the original band are as follows: W. C. Taylor (lead guitar), Sanford Horton (bass), Gary Lee Worsham (drums), Albert Morrison (sax), and Steve (Reno) McGregory (piano).

Ken Spencer - Ken was born June 4, 1961, at the hospital in Greenville, Mississippi. The family lived in Sunflower County. Ken attended Indianola Academy in Indianola, Mississippi, where he graduated in 1980. Then, he attended Mississippi Delta Junior College in Moorhead for one semester. Ken played with Southern Breeze for nine years (1987-1996), and since 1996, has played lead guitar and sang with Under the Gun, a band I have sang with on several occasions. Ken's day job for the past 28 years has been in law enforcement. His jobs have been with the Greenville Police Department, Sunflower County Sheriff's Department, and the Leflore County Sheriff's Department. Ken has been a detective with the Leflore County Sheriff's Department for the past 16 years. It has been said that he chases crooks all day and picks a guitar all night. Reportedly, he's good at both jobs. I know for sure that his guitar pickin' is good. In fact, it's super good or better.

<u>Sonny Strohm</u> - Sonny played saxophone with me and my band during the early 1960s. In 1963, Sonny played on my recordings of "Such A Night" and Please Don't Fall In Love With Me" which were recorded at Fame Recording Studio in Muscle Shoals, Alabama. These two songs were released as a single on Statue Records. After finishing college, Sonny worked 30+ years as a high school band director. He is now retired and living in Fayetteville, Georgia, where his hobby is collecting guitars. The last count I had, his collection totaled over 300 guitars. Why he collects guitars instead of saxophones, I don't have a clue.

<u>Under the Gun</u> - One of the top bands in Mississippi for over 15 years now shows no signs of slowing up anytime soon. They were formed in 1995. As of this writing (5/10/11), members of Under the Gun are: Ken Spencer (lead guitar and singer), Jackie McIlwain (rhythm guitar and singer), Robbie Browning (drums), Robert Ray (bass), and Marty Hardin (keyboards). I have had the opportunity to sing with Under the Gun on several occasions, and it has been a real pleasure.

<u>George O. Vernon</u> - George was born October 27, 1942, at Avalon (Carroll County), Mississippi. George attended Valley High School in Carroll County where he graduated in 1961. After high school, he played drums with a number of local bands including the Casuals who are highlighted in Chapter 23. George was an original member of the Casuals. He also played drums with the Nightcaps, a popular band from Greenville. In addition, George played drums for a while with Jimmy Gilreath, who had a million selling record with "Little Band of Gold." Jimmy is highlighted in Chapter 52. Further, George played drums with Grand Ole Opry star, Johnny Russell, when Johnny operated The Rising Sun Club outside Greenwood. I see George quite often at the Greenwood Wal-Mart. He is retired and claims that he goes to Wal-Mart everyday to walk. Every time I see George he is sitting on a bench. HA! According to George, he has just finished walking every time I see him. HA! George lives on Highway 7 between the Teoc turn off and Avalon. I asked him if he lived in Carroll County and he said, "No, I live in Leflore County, but I can stand in my yard and throw a rock into Carroll County." My conclusion: From George's yard to Carroll County is not very far. I'm glad I get to see George from time to time at Wal-Mart. I hope we will both be able to get to Wal-Mart for years to come.

<u>Bruce Watson</u> - Bruce is one of the owners of Fat Possum Records and their subsidiary, Big Legal Mess Records. In 2009, Bruce released twenty-one of my early recordings on Big Legal Mess Records. The CD is entitled "Mack Allen Smith, the Early Years 1962-1967." The main office and warehouse for Fat Possum Records are located in Oxford, Mississippi, and the recording studio is located in Water Valley, Mississippi. Bruce lives in Water Valley and does the producing and engineering on sessions at their studio. He is also active in promotion, distribution, and all areas of operation. Bruce was born and raised in Missouri, but I'm glad that he wound up in Mississippi. I'm also glad that he called me in 2008 about my recordings, which wound up in 2009 on Big Legal Mess Records.

<u>Joel Williams</u> - Joel, a popular drummer on the Memphis scene during the late sixties and early seventies, played drums on a song "Don't Be Cruel" that I recorded at Lyn-Lou Studio in 1972.

Allen Wood, Jr. - Allen, considered one of the best jazz drummers around, could also play rock-a-billy. He played several gigs with me in 1960 which included a concert at the high school auditorium in Greenwood, Mississippi, and a fraternity party at Ole Miss in Oxford, Mississippi. Allen also played with some big name stars like Dave Gardner and Bobbie Gentry. Allen was born August 20, 1943, in Greenwood, Mississippi. He graduated from Greenwood High School in 1961. In 1965, Allen graduated from Mississippi State University with a degree in accounting. He married Charlene Eskridge on March 11, 1960. They have three children, seven grandchildren, and one step grandchild.

Charlie Worsham - Charlie is the son of Gary Lee Worsham who is highlighted in Chapter 40. Charlie currently lives in Nashville where he writes songs and plays on recording sessions. He also tours with big name artists like Taylor Swift.

Perry York - Perry (Dumpy) York played with Shylo who are highlighted in Chapter 67. As previously mentioned, Dumpy played at my club in Greenwood and other Mississippi clubs, and he played on some of my songs that were recorded at Lyn-Lou Studio in Memphis. Whatever happened to Dumpy, I don't know.

Chapter 84
Winding It Up

The purpose of this chapter is to recognize stars that were not highlighted with their own chapter in 1 through 82, nor were they highlighted with a section in Chapter 83. Some listed in this chapter may have been mentioned in preceding chapters, while others have not been mentioned anywhere in the book. This chapter will simply list the stars' names in Whatchamacallit Order with no comment about them. Some of these stars I have known and/or heard, others I have not known or heard - just heard about. They are, of course, stars who have graced many Mississippi stages. The list is presented as follows:

Cecil Abels, Burt Aldridge, Scotty Aldridge, Joe Allen, Andy Anderson, Joe Arnold, Obie Atkins, Alan Abbott, Jewell Bass, Bud Bays, Dave Belcher, Earl Bishop, Larry Blakely, Blue South, Martha Britt, David Browning, Robbie Browning, Butch Buck, Boundless Love, Jimmy Beck, Back Porch Pickers, Burton Family, Delisa Brown, C. C. Junction, David Calhoun, Catawa Brothers, Eddie Causey, Sammy Cook, Felix Costilow, Count Downs, Cracker Jacks, Olan Crout, PeeWee Costilow, Roger Cox, Ken Cooper, Billy Daly, Johnny Dickens, Delta Raiders, Dawnbreakers, Chuck Estes, Randy Everett, D. D. Frecca, Bill Fears, Joe Frank & the Knights, Ed Forsythe, Buddy Flowers, Norman Freeland, Fox & the Raiders, Flower Power, Allison Fraiser, Carl Griffin, Donnie Gullett, Tommy Gray, Generations, Levi Gentry, Hamp Gentry, Chris Hall, Bill Haney, Robert Haney, Jack Harper, Jimmy Harrell, Heardsmen, His Majesty, Carl Hopkins, Brandon Hyde, Michael Hyde, Minyard Hill, Deanna Hooper, Jerry Hughes, Jimmy Hamilton, Boots Harris, Imperials, Mike Jacks, James Gang, Jack Jones, Bobby Jones, Buddy Key, Keynotes, Kicks, Kelts, George Lawrence, T. R. Lancaster, Judy Ledford, Marvin Lemley, Rodney Lippencott, Benny Long, Bud Long, J. D. Long, Steve Long, Lost Cords, Lancers, Steve LaVere, Randy Martin, Sayles Martin, Freddie Matthews, Jimbo Mathus, Mike Mihelic, Jamie Mitchell, James Minyard, Larry Morrisey, Freddy Mullen, Albert Morrison, Larry McClellan, Kenny McCrory, Warren Lee McNeer, Prentiss McPhail, Frank Montgomery, Sara McClure, Missing Links, Bob Morrison, Mike Morgan, Billy McGarrity, Magic Cowboy Band, Danny McGregory, Terry Moxley, Carty McMullan, Leonard McIntosh, Mississippi Rain, New Born, Malone Newsom, Tyanne Newsom, Night Caps, Brad Noah, One Way Street, Okra Tones, Ricky Parker, Sidney Pearson, Rodney Polk, Alan Purdy, Lisa Purdy, Jimmy Purdy, Phinx, Hal Pleasants, Will Pleasants, Rebels, Riviaires, Brady Roberts, Billy Robertson, Tina Robinson, Rockin' Rhythm Band, Rolling Stones, Robert Ray, Johnny Russell, Rain' Blue, Rick's Continentals, Benny Simmons, Ronny Smith, Allen Smith, Southern Blend, Southern River, Spades, Silver Eagle Band, Southern Breeze, Jim Slocum, Jimmy Smith, Soul Survivors, Sandpypers, Strags, Soul Shakers, Substantial Evidence, Souls For Christ, Bill Tackett, Murry Tingle, Ronnie Turner, Doug Thomas, Michael Thorn, Undertakers, Eddie Vail, Charlie Watts, Wanders, D. G. Williams, Roger Wade, Scottie Winters, Kenny Whitfield, Randy Williamson, Stacy Wren, Doug Walker, Jimmy Williams, Billy Womble, Glen Walker, Travis Wammack, Tim Whitsett, Jerry Waugh, Jim White, Ricky Wages, Judy Williamson, Booker Walker, and Jessie Yates, Jr.

Biography

MACK ALLEN SMITH
814 W. CLAIBORNE AVENUE
GREENWOOD, MS 38930
662-453-3302 & 662-455-4061

Mack Allen Smith was born in Carroll County, Mississippi, on October 20, 1938. He is the son of Malcolm Alonzo Smith and Fannie Mae (Herbert) Smith. Mack Allen has a younger brother, Herbert Barry Smith, who was born on January 25, 1940. Years later Barry played bass in Mack Allen's band, "The Flames." The place of Mack Allen's birth and childhood years through the second grade were spent in a general area known as "Little Texas," which is out in the country about 10 miles from North Carrollton, Mississippi. They lived with Mack Allen's grandparents (Lum and Sally Herbert) in an old log house about two miles from Hickory Grove Baptist Church. The specific location is known as the Hickory Grove Community of Little Texas. As with many singers, some of Mack Allen's first singing was in church. Each Sunday would find the Smith family at Hickory Grove Baptist Church.

Mack Allen attended grammar school in Carrollton his first two years, then moved to Camp McCain at Elliott, Mississippi, where his father was in charge of the sheet metal department of the German Prison Camp. While at Camp McCain, Mack Allen attended the third grade in Grenada, Mississippi. His brother, Barry, was in the first grade at Grenada. After Mack Allen completed the third grade, the Smith family moved to Carrollton, Mississippi, where Mack Allen's parents opened a grocery store. Mack Allen returned to grammar school in Carrollton in the fourth grade. They had living quarters in the grocery store until Mack Allen was in the 8th grade, when his father purchased an old two-story house on the banks of Big Sand Creek between Carrollton and North Carrollton. The old house, which was the Smith residence for over 40 years, is on the Carrollton side of Big Sand Creek. Mack Allen graduated from J. Z. George High School in North Carrollton, Mississippi, in 1956.

Mack Allen was exposed to country and blues music at an early age, and this exposure provided the foundation for his unique style which in later years was defined as the "Delta Sound." Mack Allen's early exposure to country music came from his mother and her family (the Herberts). Mack Allen's mother, Fannie Mae, played guitar and sang old Jimmie Rodger's songs, while her brothers, Jimmy and Archie Herbert, both played guitar, fiddle, and bull bass and sang all the country songs that were popular at the time.

Most Saturday nights would find the Herbert's playing for country dances, which were at Lum and Sally Herbert's house. Lum and Sally were the parents of Fannie Mae, Jimmy, and Archie, and the grandparents of Mack Allen. Before Mack Allen even started to school, he remembers sitting in one corner of the living room of his grandparent's old log house on Saturday nights listening to the Herbert's play country music while everyone else danced.

Mack Allen was also exposed to blues music before he started school, but this exposure occurred in North Carrollton, Mississippi. North Carrollton is on the North side of Big Sand Creek and Carrollton is on the South side. The population of Carrollton and North Carrollton combined was somewhere around 800, and each Saturday, Mack Allen's mother and father would bring him and his brother, Barry, to this great Metropolis for a day of shopping and good old city fun.

On one side of the railroad tracks in North Carrollton, you could hear country and western music coming from the cafes where the white folks were drinking beer. On the other side of the railroad tracks, you could hear rhythm and blues music coming from the cafes where the Black people were drinking beer. Back then, Mack Allen figured the whites and blacks went to different cafes because they just liked different kinds of music. Personally, Mack Allen always liked the blues music better than he did the country music.

In 1954, while in high school, Mack Allen became lead singer in his first band (The J. Z. George FFA Band). This band consisted of Mack Allen Smith (lead singer), Charles Martin (lead guitar), Alton Alderman (rhythm guitar and harmony vocals), Sidney Nabors (rhythm guitar and harmony vocals), Junior Bailey (harmony vocals), and Clovis Harbin (bass tub). The J. Z. George FFA Band won the State FFA Band Championship contest two years in a row (school years 1954-55 and 1955-56).

After graduating from high school in 1956, Mack Allen joined the Kenny Minyard band as lead singer and performed with this band at the VFW in Greenwood, Mississippi, until September 1956, when he left for college at Holmes Junior College in Goodman, Mississippi. The Kenny Minyard band was a traditional country or hillbilly band, but Mack Allen was hired to do the Elvis and other Rock-a-billy stuff that was sweeping the country at that time.

Just prior to leaving for college, Mack Allen formed a band called The Carroll Country Rock & Roll Boys which consisted of Mack Allen Smith (lead singer and rhythm guitar), Ellis Hopper (lead guitar), and Billy Wayne Herbert (rhythm guitar). After entering college at Holmes Junior College in September 1956, Mack Allen hired Charlie McCarty from Kosciusko, Mississippi, to play drums, and Eddie Lee Alderman from Carroll County to play lead guitar. Mack Allen then changed the name of the band to Mack Allen Smith and the Flames. They performed on weekends at the 51 Club in Durant, Mississippi, and the VFW in Kosciusko and Greenwood, Mississippi.

In January 1957, Mack Allen joined the Marines and left for a two-year tour of duty in California. After three months of boot camp at San Diego, Mack Allen was transferred to Camp Pendleton at Ocean Side, California, where he was stationed until completion of his tour of duty in January 1959. While in the Marines, Mack Allen sang some weekends at the USO Club in Ocean Side, California. He also sang with a Black band at the Figure-Eight Club in Los Angeles.

In January 1959, Mack Allen returned to Carrollton, Mississippi, and immediately re-formed Mack Allen Smith and the Flames. This group was comprised of: Mack Allen Smith (lead singer), Keith Worrell (lead guitar), Red McGregor (rhythm guitar), David Lee Cox (piano), and Durwood Herbert (drums). Later, in 1959, Laney O'Briant was hired to play lead guitar, which gave the Flames two lead guitars for a while. Mack Allen Smith and the Flames recorded three songs (Kansas City, Mean Woman Blues, and Sandy Lee) for producer Ernie Barton at Sun Records in 1959; however, Mr. Barton left Sun Records shortly thereafter to form Barton Records in Little Rock, Arkansas. After 50 years the Sun masters have been found and are in my possession.

After re-forming the band in January 1959, Mack Allen Smith and the Flames performed for 25 more years (until October 1984) throughout Mississippi and surrounding states. Mack Allen owned his own nightclub (Mack Allen Smith's Town & Country Night Club) in Greenwood, Mississippi, for five years (1971-1976), and the Flames performed mostly at clubs throughout the Mississippi Delta during his performing career.

Mack Allen has had a number of singles and albums released overseas, and in 1979, was booked by Martin Hawkins on a two-week tour of England. Overseas releases have been on the following record labels: Redneck, Checkmate, Charly, Redita, and Country Groove.

Record releases in the United States have been on the following labels: Vee Eight, Statue, Mariteen, Jab (a subsidiary of Atlantic), Cynthia, Younger, Delta Sound, Ace, Grape, Cindy Boo, and QMC.

During his career Mack Allen Smith has recorded over 150 songs at various studios in Mississippi, Alabama, and Tennessee. Many of these studio recordings have not been released; however, Mack Allen is hoping for a contract overseas that will result in a CD box set of all his studio recordings.

In addition to his studio recordings, Mack Allen has a number of live recordings that were made at nightclub performances. One of the live performances that is considered worthy of CD is "Mack Allen Smith - Live on Halloween" which was recorded at the Country Music Palace in Vaiden, Mississippi, on October 31, 1981. This Halloween recording consists of 38 songs and a great performance by Mack Allen Smith.

Mack Allen completed a novel in 2001 entitled *Looking Back One Last Time, A Memoir*. This book was published in 2004.

Mack Allen and his wife of 50 years, Lois Bennett Smith, live in Greenwood, Mississippi, where he is currently writing songs, tracing his family roots, and working on his second novel. Mack Allen and Lois have two children: Cynthia Alan (Smith) Brown (born January 29, 1961) and Malcolm Allen Smith, Jr. (born March 11, 1967). They also have two grandchildren: Stephanie Karen Blackburn (born June 28, 1980) and Jerry Dale Blackburn, III (born April 24, 1983). In addition, Mack Allen and Lois have two great grands - Lucas Lormand (born 9/8/2002), and Ansleigh Lormand (born 4/18/2005).

In October 2002, Mack Allen came out of his 18 year retirement with a gig at the old school house in Black Hawk, Mississippi. Since then he has performed throughout north Mississippi. His wife, Lois, predicts that he won't quit again until he drops dead with a microphone in his hand.

Discography

MACK ALLEN SMITH - SUN RECORDINGS

DATE	TITLE OF SONGS	RECORDED AT
1959	Kansas City Mean Woman Blues Sandy Lee Musicians: Mack Allen Smith (lead singer), Keith Worrell (lead guitar), Billy Wayne Herbert (lead guitar), Red McGregor (rhythm guitar), David Lee Cox (piano), and Durwood Herbert (drums) Engineer/Producer: Ernie Barton	Sun Recording Studio Memphis, Tennessee

MACK ALLEN SMITH - 45 RPM VINYL RECORDS

RELEASE DATE RECORD LABEL & NO.	TITLE OF SONGS	RECORDED AT
1962 Vee Eight - 1005	I Got My Mojo Working I'm a Lover Musicians: Mack Allen Smith (lead singer), Arthur Browning (lead guitar), Barry Smith (bass), Red McGregor (rhythm guitar), Doug Steen (saxophone), Hardin Browning (piano), Durwood Herbert (drums) Engineer: Ray Harris Producer: Hershel Wiggington	Hi Recording Studio Memphis, Tennessee
1962 Vee Eight - 1006	Hobo Man Old Man River Musicians: Mack Allen Smith (lead singer), Arthur Browning (lead	Hi Recording Studio Memphis, Tennessee

	guitar), Barry Smith (bass), Hardin Browning (piano), John Mihelic (trumpet), Johnny Baker (trumpet & harmonica), Durwood Herbert (drums), Buddy Millett (drums) Engineer: Ray Harris Producer: Hershel Wiggington		
1963 Statue - 602	Such A Night Please Don't Fall In Love With Me Musicians: Mack Allen Smith (lead singer), Murry Moorman (lead guitar), Barry Smith (bass), Hardin Browning (piano), Bill Bole (trumpet), Sonny Strohm (saxophone), Buddy Millett (drums) Engineer: Rick Hall Producer: Hershel Wiggington	Fame Recording Studio Muscle Shoals, Alabama	
1964 Statue - 603	Only Make Believe Guess I've Been a Fool All the Time Musicians: Mack Allen Smith (lead singer), Murry Moorman (lead guitar), Barry Smith (bass), Hardin Browning (piano), Bill Bole (trumpet), Terry Jenkins (trumpet), John Mihelic (trumpet), Hershel Wiggington Singers (backup vocals), Buddy Millett (drums) Engineer: Rick Hall Producer: Hershel Wiggington	Fame Recording Studio Muscle Shoals, Alabama	
1964 Statue - 606	Skeleton Fight Don't Let Me Treat You That Way Musicians: Mack Allen Smith (lead singer), Murry Moorman (lead guitar), Barry Smith (bass), Hardin	Hi Recording Studio Memphis, Tennessee Fame Recording Studio Muscle Shoals, Alabama	

	Browning (piano), Bill Bole (trumpet), Terry Jenkins (trumpet), Hershel Wiggington Singers (backup vocals), Jimmy Gilreath (harmony vocals), Buddy Millett (drums) Eng: Ray Harris Producer: Hershel Wiggington	
1965 Statue - 607	Mean Old Frisco Daniel, Blow Your Horn Musicians: Mack Allen Smith (lead singer), Murry Moorman (lead guitar), Barry Smith (bass), Hardin Browning (piano), Bill Bole (trumpet), Terry Jenkins (trumpet), Hershel Wiggington Singers (backup vocals), Buddy Millett (drums) Producer: Hershel Wiggington	Fame Recording Studio Muscle Shoals, Alabama
1966 Mariteen - 6602 Reissued by Atlanta Subsidiary Jab - 9001	Big Silver Tears Not Strong Enough Musicians: Mack Allen Smith (lead singer), Murry Moorman (lead guitar), Barry Smith (bass), Hardin Browning (piano), Bill Bole (trumpet), Terry Jenkins (trumpet), Hershel Wiggington Singers (backup vocals), Buddy Millett (drums) Producer: Mack Allen Smith	Fame Recording Studio Muscle Shoals, Alabama
1967 Cynthia - 1961	Lonely Weekends (Recorded 1966-Fame) Baby Pink Rose (Recorded 1967 - Lyn-Lou) Musicians: Mack Allen Smith (lead singer), Murry Moorman (lead guitar), Barry Smith (bass), Hardin Browning (piano), Bill Bole (trumpet), Terry Jenkins (trumpet), The Lyn-Lou Singers (backup vocals), Buddy Millett (drums) Producer: Mack Allen Smith	Fame Recording Studio Muscle Shoals, Alabama Lyn Lou Recording Studio Memphis, Tennessee
1968	My Woman	Lyn-Lou Recording

Younger - 1568	The First Thing I Tried Musicians: Lyn-Lou Studio Band plus John Huey on steel guitar Producer: Larry Rogers	Studio Memphis, Tennessee
1969 Younger - 323	Riding Home To Judy Treat Me Nice Musicians: Lyn-Lou Studio Band Producer: Larry Rogers	Lyn-Lou Recording Studio Memphis, Tennessee
1970 Delta Sound - 2869	I'm Not Drunk I'm Just Drinking Do It To Them First Musicians: Mack Allen Smith (lead singer), Billy Wayne Herbert (lead guitar & rhythm guitar), Pete Bartosch (bass), Ronnie Korner (drums) Producer: Billy Wayne Herbert	Lyn-Lou Recording Studio Memphis, Tennessee
1972 Cindy Boo - 1001	Never Ending Song of Love Carroll County Blues Musicians: Mack Allen Smith (lead singer), Murry Moorman (lead guitar), Barry Smith (bass), Jessie Yates (keyboards), Lawrence Stacy (drums), Laney O'Briant (fiddle), Gene Simmons/Jamie Wood (backup vocals) Engineer/Producer: John Mihelic	Statue Recording Studio Tupelo, Mississippi
1972 Delta Sound - 1956	Don't Be Cruel Mean Old Frisco Musicians: <u>Don't Be Cruel</u> - Mack Allen Smith (lead singer), Billy Wayne Herbert (lead guitar), Tommy Cathey (bass), Don Chandler (organ), Joel Williams (drums), Memphis Horns (horn section) Producer: Billy Wayne Herbert <u>Mean Old Frisco</u> - Mack Allen Smith (lead singer), Murry Moorman (lead guitar), Barry Smith (bass), Hardin Browning (piano), Bill Bole	Lyn-Lou Studio Memphis, Tennessee Fame Recording Studio Muscle Shoals, Alabama

	(trumpet), Terry Jenkins (trumpet), Hershel Wiggington Singers (backup vocals), Buddy Millett (drums) Producer: Hershel Wiggington	
1973 Delta Sound - 1938	Sweet Becky Walker Lodi Musicians: Mack Allen Smith (lead singer), Murry Moorman (lead guitar), Laney O'Briant (bass), Jessie Yates (keyboards and harmony vocals), Lawrence Stacy (drums) Producer: Mack Allen Smith	Statue Recording Studio Tupelo, MS
1975 Delta Sound - 1 Reissued and distributed by World Wide Sound - Memphis	I'm Dog Tired of Cattin' Around I See the Want To In Your Eyes Musicians: <u>I'm Dog Tired of Cattin' Around</u> - Mack Allen Smith (lead singer), Ronnie Scaife (lead guitar), Danny Hogan (bass); Butch Carter (piano), Perry York (drums) <u>I See the Want To In Your Eyes</u> - Mack Allen Smith (lead singer), Laney O'Briant (lead guitar), Sanford Horton (bass), Steve McGregory (piano), Gary Lee Worsham (drums) Producers: Larry Rogers & Mack Allen Smith	Lyn-Lou Recording Studio Memphis, Tennessee
1975 Ace - 3011	King Of Rock and Roll Lonely Street Musicians: Mack Allen Smith (lead singer), Laney O'Briant (lead guitar), Sanford Horton (bass), Steve McGregory (piano), Gary Lee Worsham (drums) Executive Producer: Johnny Vincent	Ace Recording Studio Jackson, Mississippi
1976 Ace - 3014	Angel Face, Body Full of Sin Mama, When I'm Gone Don't Cry For Me	Lyn-Lou Recording Studio Memphis, Tennessee

	Musicians: Mack Allen Smith (lead singer), Ronnie Scaife (lead guitar), Danny Hogan (bass), Butch Carter (piano), Perry York (drums), Leo LeBlanc (steel guitar) Executive Producer: Johnny Vincent	
1977 Ace - 3022	Who the Heck Is Bob Wills Shake Your Money Maker Musicians: <u>Who the Heck Is Bob Wills</u> - Mack Allen Smith (lead singer), Ronnie Scaife (lead guitar), Bobby Neal (lead guitar), Danny Hogan (bass), Butch Carter (piano), Perry York (drums) <u>Shake Your Money Maker</u> - Mack Allen Smith (lead singer), Laney O'Briant (lead guitar), Paul Melton (bass), Larry Acy (piano), Lawrence Stacy (drums) Executive Producer: Johnny Vincent	Lyn-Lou Recording Studio Memphis, Tennessee Ace Recording Studio Jackson, Mississippi
1977 Country Groove - 100 England	Sweet Becky Walker Dog Tired of Cattin' Around Musicians: Previously listed (See 1973 - Delta Sound - 1938 and 1975 - Delta Sound - 1)	Lyn-Lou Recording Studio Memphis, Tennessee
1979 Grape - 2003	Gonna Turn Your Brown Eyes Black Toast to the Talk of the Town Musicians: Mack Allen Smith (lead singer), Ronnie Scaife (lead guitar), Danny Hogan (bass), Butch Carter (piano), Perry York (drums) Executive Producer: Alan Bridges	Lyn-Lou Recording Studio Memphis, Tennessee
1979 QMC - 5001	Natural Gas Natural Gas Musicians: Studio pickers from Nashville, Tennessee	Lyn-Lou Recording Studio Memphis, Tennessee

	Producer: Quinton Claunch	
1981 Grape - 2009	Memphis, You Ain't Nothing But the Best (Recorded 1979) I Don't Do Disco (Recorded 1981) Musicians: <u>Memphis, You Ain't Nothing But the Best</u>: Mack Allen Smith (lead singer), Laney O'Briant (lead guitar), Ronnie Scaife (lead guitar), Paul Melton (bass), Larry Acy (piano), George Thomas (drums) <u>I Don't Do Disco</u>: Mack Allen Smith (lead singer), Billy Wayne Herbert (lead guitar, rhythm guitar, bass, and drums) Producers: Mack Allen Smith and Billy Wayne Herbert	Lyn-Lou Recording Studio Memphis, Tennessee Billy Herbert Studio Memphis, Tennessee

MACK ALLEN SMITH - ALBUMS - UNITED STATES & OVERSEAS

RELEASE DATE RECORD LABEL & NO.	TITLE OF ALBUM	RECORDED AT
1972 Delta Sound 1061 A & B 1649 A & B Greenwood, Mississippi	Saturday Night With Mack Allen Smith and the Flames (A double album) <u>1649-A</u> 1. Boogie Children 2. Don't Worry About Me 3. Don't Leave Me Now 4. Maybelline 5. Lawdy, Miss Clawdy <u>1649-B</u> 1. Shake Your Money Maker 2. Blue Money 3. Proud Mary 4. Then You Can Tell Me Goodbye 5. Carroll County Blues	Statue Recording Studio Tupelo, Mississippi <u>1061-A</u> 1. Help Me Make It Through the Night 2. Me and Bobby McGee 3. Begging To You 4. Have You Ever Seen the Rain 5. Never Ending Song of Love <u>1061-B</u> 1. Hello, Darling

	Musicians: Mack Allen Smith (lead singer), Murry Moorman (lead guitar), Barry Smith (bass), Jessie Yates (keyboards), Lawrence Stacy (drums), Gene Simmons/Jamie Wood (backup vocals) Engineer/Producer: John Mihelic	2. Memphis 3. Joy to the World 4. Promised Land 5. For the Good Times
1977 Ace - 2022 Jackson, Mississippi	The King of Rock and Roll Side One 1. Flip, Flop and Fly (1975 Lyn-Lou - Memphis) 2. Blue Suede Shoes (1975 - Lyn-Lou - Memphis) 3. You Can Have Her (1975 - Lyn-Lou - Memphis) 4. I See the Want To In Your Eyes (1975 - Lyn-Lou - Memphis) 5. Brown Eyed Girl (1975 - Lyn-Lou - Memphis) 6. My Baby Left Me (1975 - Lyn-Lou - Memphis) 7. Maybelline (1972 - Statue - Tupelo) 8. Mean Old Frisco (1965 - Fame - Muscle Shoals) Side Two 1. Don't Be Cruel (1972 - Lyn-Lou - Memphis) 2. Red Rooster Blues (1964 - Fame - Muscle Shoals) 3. Lonely Weekend (1966 - Fame - Muscle Shoals) 4. Me and Bobby McGee (1972 - Statue - Tupelo) 5. Never Ending Song of Love (1972 - Statue - Tupelo) 6. Memphis (1972 - Statue - Tupelo) 7. Sick and Tired (1975 - Ace - Jackson) 8. You Better Move On - (1975 - Ace - Jackson)	Ace Recording Studio Jackson, Mississippi Lyn-Lou Recording Studio Memphis, Tennessee Fame Recording Studio Muscle Shoals, Alabama Statue Recording Studio Tupelo, Mississippi

	9. King of Rock & Roll (1975 - Ace - Jackson) Musicians: Mack Allen Smith (lead singer), Billy Wayne Herbert (lead guitar), Murry Moorman (lead guitar), Laney O'Briant (lead guitar), Barry Smith (bass), Tommy Cathey (bass), Sanford Horton (bass), Jessie Yates (keyboards), Don Chandler (organ), Steve McGregory (keyboards), Buddy Millett (drums), Lawrence Stacy (drums), Gary Lee Worsham (drums), Hershel Wiggington Singers (backup vocals) Executive Producer: Johnny Vincent	
1976 Redneck - 500 England	Redneck Rock - The Delta Sound <u>Side One</u> 1. Shake Your Money Money (1972 - Statue - Tupelo) 2. Hobo Man (1962 - Hi - Memphis) 3. Flip Flop and Fly (1975 - Lyn-Lou - Memphis) 4. Promised Land (1972 - Statue - Tupelo) 5. My Baby Left Me (1975 - Lyn-Lou - Memphis) 6. Don't Worry About Me (1972 - Statue - Tupelo) 7. Blue Suede Shoes (1975 - Lyn-Lou - Memphis) 8. It's Only Make Believe (1964 - Fame - Muscle Shoals) <u>Side Two</u> 1. Maybelline (1972 - Statue - Tupelo)	Ace Recording Studio Jackson, Mississippi Hi Recording Studio Memphis, Tennessee Lyn-Lou Recording Studio Memphis, Tennessee Statue Recording Studio Tupelo, Mississippi Fame Recording Studio Muscle Shoals, Alabama

	2. Don't Leave Me Now (1972 - Statue - Tupelo) 3. Memphis (1972 - Statue - Tupelo) 4. Blue Money (1972 - Statue - Tupelo) 5. Begging To You (1972 - Statue - Tupelo) 6. Lodi (1973 - Lyn-Lou - Memphis) 7. Proud Mary (1972 - Statue - Tupelo) 8. Carroll County Blues (1972 - Statue - Tupelo) Musicians: Mack Allen Smith (lead singer), Murry Moorman (lead guitar), Laney O'Briant (lead guitar), Arthur Browning (lead guitar), Barry Smith (bass), Sanford Horton (bass), Jessie Yates (keyboards), Steve McGregory (keyboards), Buddy Millett (drums), Lawrence Stacy (drums), Gary Lee Worsham (drums), Durwood Herbert (drums), Johnny Baker (harmonica), The Hershel Wiggington Singers (backup vocals), Gene Simmons/Jamie Wood (backup vocals) Producers: Hershel Wiggington, John Mihelic, and Mack Allen Smith	
1978 Checkmate - 1032 England	Delta Country Side One 1. If Only I Could Get One Hit (1977 - Lyn-Lou - Memphis) 2. Angel Face, Body Full of Sin (1975 - Lyn-Lou - Memphis) 3. Mama, When I'm Gone (1975 - Lyn-Lou - Memphis) 4. Do It To Them First (1970 - Lyn-Lou - Memphis) 5. I'm Not Drunk, I'm Just Drinking (1970 - Lyn-Lou -	Ace Recording Studio Jackson, Mississippi Lyn-Lou Recording Studio Memphis, Tennessee Fame Recording Studio Muscle Shoals, Alabama

	Memphis) 6. Rag Mama (1966 - Fame - Muscle Shoals) <u>Side Two</u> 1. The Only King I Know (1977 - Lyn-Lou - Memphis) 2. Sick and Tired (1977 - Lyn-Lou Memphis) 3. I See the Want To In Your Eyes (1975 - Lyn-Lou - Memphis) 4. Snake-eyed Woman (1966 - Fame - Muscle Shoals) 5. Treat Me Nice (1968 - Lyn-Lou Memphis) 6. Don't Be Cruel - (1972 - Lyn-Lou - Memphis) Musicians: Mack Allen Smith (lead singer), Murry Moorman (lead guitar), Billy Wayne Herbert (lead guitar), Laney O'Briant (lead guitar), Ronnie Scaife (lead guitar), Barry Smith (bass), Sanford Horton (bass), Danny Hogan (bass), Butch Carter (piano), Hardin Browning (piano), Steve McGregory (piano), Leo LeBlanch (steel guitar), Perry York (drums), Lawrence Stacy (drums), Buddy Millett (drums), Gary Lee Worsham (drums) Producers: Larry Rogers, Billy Wayne Herbert, and Mack Allen Smith	
1979 Redita - 105 Holland	The Sound of Mack Allen Smith <u>Side A</u> 1. Skeleton Fight (1964 - Hi - Memphis) 2. You Can Have Her (1975 - Lyn-Lou - Memphis) 3. Please Don't Fall In Love With Me (1963 - Fame - Muscle Shoals) 4. Stop and Go 5. I Need You So (1965 - Fame -	Hi Recording Studio Memphis, Tennessee Lyn-Lou Recording Studio Memphis, Tennessee Fame Recording Studio Muscle Shoals, Alabama Statue Recording

	Muscle Shoals) 6. Me and Bobby McGee (1972 - Statue - Tupelo) 7. Then You Can Tell Me Goodbye (1972 - Statue - Tupelo) 8. Lonely Weekends (1965 - Fame Muscle Shoals) 9. Don't Let Me Treat You This Way (1964 - Fame - Muscle Shoals) Side B 1. Mean Old Frisco (1965 - Fame Muscle Shoals) 2. Don't Be Cruel - 1972 - Lyn-Lou - Memphis) 3. Railroad Rock 4. Lawdy Miss Clawdy (1972 - Statue - Tupelo) 5. Red Rooster Blues (1964 - Fame - Muscle Shoals) 6. I See the Want To In Your Eyes (1975 - Lyn-Lou - Memphis) 7. Free, Single, and Disengaged (1965 - Fame - Muscle Shoals) 8. Daniel, Blow Your Horn (1965 Fame - Muscle Shoals) 9. Guess I've Been A Fool (1964 - Fame - Muscle Shoals) Musicians: Mack Allen Smith (lead singer), Billy Wayne Herbert (lead guitar), Murry Moorman (lead guitar), Laney O'Briant (lead guitar), Barry Smith (bass), Sanford Horton (bass), Hardin Browning (piano), Steve McGregory (piano), Don Chandler (organ), Jessie Yates (organ), Buddy Millett (drums), Joel Williams (drums), Lawrence Stacy (drums), Gary Lee Worsham (drums), The Hershel Wiggington Singers (backup vocals), Gene Simmons/Jamie Wood (backup vocals) Producers: Hershel Wiggington,	Studio Tupelo, Mississippi

	John Mihelic, Billy Wayne Herbert, and Mack Allen Smith	
1982 Charly - 30201 England	Gotta Rock Tonight <u>Side One</u> 1. Gotta Rock Tonight (Red Rooster Blues) (1964 - Fame - Muscle Shoals) 2. You Got Me Running (1979 - Lyn-Lou - Memphis) 3. My Baby Left Me (1975 - Lyn-Lou - Memphis) 4. Shake Your Money Maker (1972 - Statue - Tueplo) 5. Hobo Man (1962 - Hi - Memphis) 6. Skeleton Fight (1964 - Hi - Memphis) 7. Mean Old Frisco (1965 - Fame Muscle Shoals) 8. Treat Me Nice (1968 - Lyn-Lou Memphis) <u>Side Two</u> 1. If Only I Could Get One Hit (1977 - Lyn-Lou - Memphis) 2. Hey, Clyde (1979 - Lyn-Lou - Memphis) 3. Tulsa Time (1979 - Lyn-Lou - Memphis) 4. Who the Heck Is Bob Wills (1977 - Lyn-Lou - Memphis) 5. Memphis, You Ain't Nothing But the Best (1979 - Lyn-Lou - Memphis) 6. Ain't Got No Business Doin' Business Today (1979 - Lyn-Lou - Memphis) 7. Rag Mama (1966 - Fame - Muscle Shoals) 8. Flip, Flop, and Fly (1975 - Lyn-Lou - Memphis) Musicians: Mack Allen Smith (lead singer), Laney O'Briant (lead guitar), Murry Moorman (lead	Lyn-Lou Recording Studio Memphis, Tennessee Statue Recording Studio Tupelo, Mississippi Hi Recording Studio Memphis, Tennessee Fame Recording Studio Muscle Shoals, Alabama

	guitar), Arthur Browning (lead guitar), Barry Smith (bass), Jerry Masters (bass), Paul Melton (bass), Sanford Horton (bass), Larry Acy (piano), Steve McGregory (piano), Don Chandler (organ), George Thomas (drums), Gary Lee Worsham (drums), Joel Williams (drums), Buddy Millett (drums) Silver City Band of Memphis played on Hey, Clyde	

MACK ALLEN SMITH - UNRELEASED STUDIO RECORDINGS - SONGS WRITTEN BY MACK ALLEN SMITH

YEAR RECORDED	TITLE OF SONGS	RECORDED AT
1964	Listen to the Bells	Tupelo, Mississippi
1968	A Heart Full of Sorrow	Memphis, Tennessee
1968	Please, Mr. D. J.	Memphis, Tennessee
1968	I'm Gonna Leave	Memphis, Tennessee
1968	I Couldn't Pick a Winner	Memphis, Tennessee
1968	Any Place Away From Here	Memphis, Tennessee
1968	That's Why I Pray	Memphis, Tennessee
1971	I Can't Stand to See Mama Cry	Greenwood, Mississippi
1971	Keeping Up the Family Name	Greenwood, Mississippi
1971	She May Not Be An Angel	Greenwood, Mississippi
1978	I Don't Wanna See Them Cotton	Jackson, Mississippi

	Fields Again	
1980	Short End of the Stick	Memphis, Tennessee
1980	Nobody Cares Who I Am	Memphis, Tennessee
1980	She Wasn't Near as Good	Memphis, Tennessee
1981	She Broke My Heart At Walgreen's	Memphis, Tennessee
1982	I Hate Trains	Memphis, Tennessee
1982	Too Poor To Leave	Greenwood, Mississippi
1982	I'm Not Broke But I'm Badly Bent	Greenwood, Mississippi
1982	Anything That Turns You On	Greenwood, Mississippi
1982	It's Never Too Late for Jesus	Greenwood, Mississippi
1982	I Made A Deal With Jesus	Greenwood, Mississippi
1983	Bloody Mary Morning	Greenwood, Missisippi
1983	Budweiser Morning	Greenwood, Mississippi
1983	P. S., I Love You, Santa	Greenwood, Mississippi
1988	If I Can't Have You For Christmas	Jackson, Missisippi
1989	Take Your Disposition and Shove It	Jackson, Mississippi
1989	If It Hadn't Been For Chasing Skirts	Jackson, Mississippi
1991	I Went Out Walking in the Woods	Memphis, Tennessee
1991	Too Long In Them Cotton Fields	Greenwood, Mississippi
1991	Only the Strong Survive	Greenwood, Mississippi

1991	Whatever Happened to Warren Smith	Greenwood, Mississippi
1991	Daddy's Sweet Darling	Jackson, Mississippi
1992	The Jig Is Up	Memphis, Tennessee
1992	Sick and Tired of Texas	Memphis, Tennessee
1992	Eighteen Wheeler Blues	Memphis, Tennessee
1992	Zydeco Boogie	Memphis, Tennessee
1992	I See You Everywhere	Memphis, Tennessee

MACK ALLEN SMITH - OTHER UNRELEASED STUDIO RECORDINGS

YEAR RECORDED	TITLE OF SONG	RECORDED AT
1964	Everything I Do Is Wrong	Muscle Shoals, Alabama
1964	Boogie Children	Muscle Shoals, Alabama
1965	Mama Luchi	Muscle Shoals, Alabama
1983	Mr. President, Have Pity on the Working Man	Jackson, Mississippi

Inadvertently omitted from single recordings :

DATE	TITLE OF SONGS	RECORDED AT
1980 Grape	**All the Praises** Musicians: Mack Allen Smith (lead	Lyn-Lou Recording Studio Memphis, Tennessee

	singer) Ronnie Scaife (lead guitar) Danny Hogan (bass) Butch Carter (piano) Perry York (drums) Executive Producer: Alan Bridges	

MACK ALLEN SMITH - LIVE RECORDINGS

MACK ALLEN SMITH - LIVE ON HALLOWEEN

RECORDED AT COUNTRY MUSIC PALACE IN VAIDEN, MISSISSIPPI ON OCTOBER 31, 1981

1. Hello, Vaiden
2. Loving Arms
3. Elvira
4. Old Flame
5. On the Road Again
6. Just Because You Asked Me To
7. Matilda
8. I Can't Stand It
9. Redneck Mother
10. True Love Ways
11. Josephine
12. Memphis
13. He Stopped Loving Her Today
14. Older Women
15. Party Time
16. Wasn't That a Party
17. Hell Yes I Cheated
18. Blue Eyes Crying In the Rain
19. Giving It Up For Your Love
20. Johnny Be Good
21. Cherry Pie
22. I Got the Hoss
23. Feel So Right
24. Leroy Brown
25. Leona
26. Lovers Live Longer
27. Flip, Flop, and Fly
28. Fiddle (Shortening Bread)

29. More fiddle (Orange Blossom Special)
30. South's Gonna Do It Again
31. All the Praises
32. Cocaine
33. Haunted House
34. Looking for Love
35. Red Rooster Blues
36. Smoky Mountain Rain
37. Baby, Let's Play House
38. Rock and Roll Medley

Daddy and Mama: Malcolm (Mack) Alonzo Smith and Fannie Mae (Herbert) Smith.

Jimmy Herbert Band - Jimmy Herbert, second from left

L to R: Eddie Lee Alderman, Franklin Ricks, Archie Herbert and James McDonald

MACK ALLEN SMITH

Mack Allen Smith - November 1956 - 51 Club in Durant, Mississippi. Charlie McCarty (drums). Not visable: Eddie Lee Alderman (lead guitar), Billy Wayne Herbert (rhythm guitar) and Ellis Hooper (lead and rhythm guitar).

Mack Allen Smith - 1956

1959 - Carrollton Community House - Mack Allen Smith (lead singer) L to R: David Lee Cox (piano), Laney O'Briant (lead guitar), Durwood Herbert (drums), Keith Worrell (lead guitar), and Red McGregor (rhythm guitar).

1959 - VFW in Greenwood, Mississippi - L to R: David Lee Cox, Mack Allen Smith, Durwood Herbert, Keith Worrell and Laney O'Briant.

Mack Allen Smith and guitar in lap - 1960.

1962 - Front row L to R: Arthur Browning, Hardin Browning, Buddy Millett. Back row L to R: Barry Smith, Mack Allen Smith and Red McGregor. Showing off first Vee Eight Recording "I've Got My Mojo Working" and "I'm a Lover".

1965 - Moose Lodge in Greenwood, Mississippi. From L to R: Terry Jenkins (trumpet), Hardin Browning (piano), Bill Bole (trumpet), Buddy Millett (drums), Mack Allen Smith (lead singer), Barry Smith (bass), and Murry Moorman (lead guitar).

1960 - High School Auditorium in Greenwood, Mississippi. From L to R: Red McGregor (rhythm guitar), Billy Wayne Herbert (bass), Keith Worrell (lead guitar), Mack Allen Smith (lead singer), Allen Wood (drums) and David Lee Cox (piano).

1972 - Town & Country Night Club - Greenwood, Mississippi. L to R: Jessie Yates (keyboards), Lawrence Stacy (drums), Mack Allen Smith (lead singer), Murry Moorman (lead guitar), and Barry Smith (bass).

1979 Reunion of 1959 Flames at the Holiday Inn in Greenwood, Mississippi. L to R: Red McGregor (rhythm guitar), Keith Worrell (lead guitar), Mack Allen Smith (lead singer), and David Lee Cox (piano).

1974 - Mack Allen Smith and the Flames at Mack Allen Smith's Town & Country Night Club. Center: Mack Allen Smith (lead singer). L to R: Laney O'Briant (lead guitar), Steve McGregory (piano), Gary Lee Worsham (drums) and Sanford Horton (bass).

Christmas 1976 - Grenada Golf Club in Grenada, Mississippi. L to R: Laney O'Briant, Sanford Horton, Mack Allen Smith, Gary Lee Worsham and Steve McGregory.

1978 - Country Music Palace, Vaiden, Mississippi. Front row L to R: Lawrence Stacy (drums), Mack Allen Smith (lead singer), Larry Acey (piano). Back row L to R: Paul Melton (bass), Laney O'Briant (lead guitar).

Rock-a-Billy Rebel

1980 - At the Delta Queen in Vaiden, Mississippi. Center: Mack Allen Smith. L to R: Paul Melton (bass), George Thomas (drums), Lary Acey (piano) and Laney O'Briant (lead guitar).

1983 - L to R: David Lee Cox, Mack Allen Smith, David Lee Cox, Jr. and Laney O'Briant.

1975 - Getting down at Mack Allen Smith's Town & Country Night Club. Pickers visable L to R: Sanford Horton, Mack Allen Smith and Laney O'Briant.

December 2006 - "Old Burnt Out Flames" get together at Carrollton Mississippi Community House. L to R: Laney O'Briant (lead guitar), Sanford Horton (bass), Mack Allen Smith (lead singer), Buddy Millett (drums), Murry Moorman (lead guitar) and Barry Smith (bass).

Late 1950's - L to R: Marcus Van Story (bass), Warren Smith and Al Hopkins (lead guitar).

The 1960's - Warren Smith.

Late 1970's - Warren Smith with bottle.

The 1970's - Billy Wayne Herbert playing guitar with Chuck Berry at the Coliseum in Memphis, Tennessee.

Late 1970's - Warren Smith smiling.

Basin Street Club, El Dorado, Arkansas - Early 1990's. Middle three L to R: Billy Wayne Herbert, Ace Cannon and Jim Rorie.

L to R: Billy Wayne Herbert, Merle Travis and Jim Rorie.

June 2, 2007 - Carrollton, Mississippi Community House.
Billy Wayne Herbert - final gig.

June 2, 2007 - Billy Wayne Herbert with fans at the Community House in Carrollton, Mississippi.

June 2, 2007 - Fans buying CD's from Billy Wayne Herbert at the Community House in Carrollton, Mississippi.

Under the Gun - L to R: Scottie Winters, Robert Ray, Jackie McIlwain, Ken Spencer and Terry Herbert.

2005 at CG's in Oakland, Mississippi - Under the Gun, L to R: Robert Ray (guitar), Jackie McIlwain (guitar), Scottie Winters (drums), Ken Spencer (guitar) and Terry Herbert (bass).

2003 - Terry Herbert getting ready to fly off the stage at Horseshoe Bar & Grill in Yazoo City, Mississippi.

May 2009 - Mack Allen Smith at first and last Yall Fest in Carroll County, Mississippi.

May 2009 - Yall Fest - L to R: Ken Spencer (lead guitar), Scottie Winters (drums), Mack Allen Smith (lead singer) and Terry Herbert (bass).

Charlie Pride and Jim Rorie.

Carl Perkins and Jim Rorie.

December 2006 - "Old Burnt Out Flames" get together at Carrollton Mississippi Community House. L to R: Laney O'Briant (lead guitar), Sanford Horton (bass), Mack Allen Smith (lead singer), Buddy Millett (drums), Murry Moorman (lead guitar) and Barry Smith (bass).

Jerry Lee Lewis and Jim Rorie.

L to R: Billy Earheart, Jeff Davis, Jim Rorie, Don McMinn and Mike Gardner.

Jim Rorie and his guitar.

The Southern Five - Seated: Bill Daly (drums). L to R: Sanford Horton (bass), W. C. Taylor (lead guitar), Steve McGregory (piano) and Albert Morrison (saxophone).

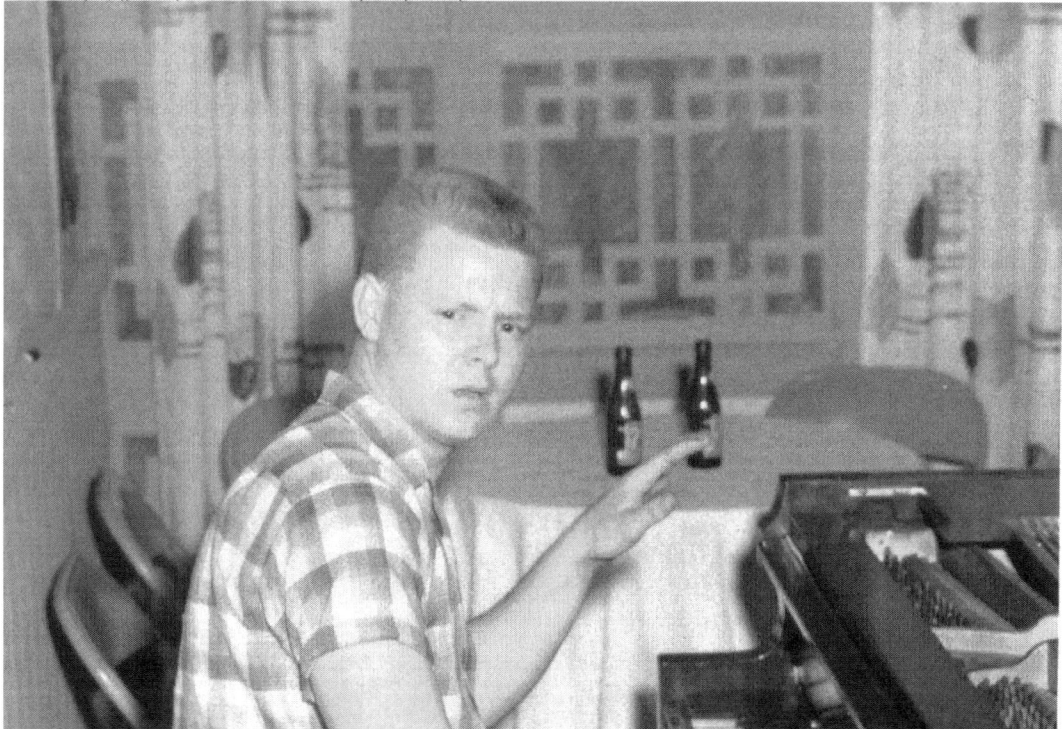

Teenage Jamie Isonhood.

L to R: Ace Cannon and Sanford Horton.

L to R: Sanford Horton and Jamie Isonhood.

L to R: W. S. Holland (drummer for Johnny Cash) and Jamie Isonhood.

L to R: Jamie Isonhood and Travis Wammack.

1972 in Memphis Club - L to R: Jamie Isonhood, Billy Adams, Bobby Stewart and Buck Hutchinson.

Jamie Isonhood and Ace Cannon.

Jamie Isonhood and Jason D. Williams.

L to R: Richard Ray, Jamie Isonhood, Doyle Nelson, Bubba Feathers and Prentiss McPhail.

L to R: unknown lady, Travis Wammack, T. M. Van Eaton, and Jamie Isonhood.

The Rib Eye in Yazoo City, Mississippi - Center: Jamie Isonhood. L to R: Travis Wammack (guitar), Sanford Horton (bass), Chris Hall (drums), Donnie Gullett (guitar), Leonard McIntosh (saxophone) and Carty McMillen (keyboard).

The Casuals: L to R: Ray Hall, Kelly Hall, Tony Browning and Keith Worrell.

1969 - George Vernon (drums). Original drummer with the Casuals.

1970 - The Casuals. L to R: Charlie Watts (piano), George Vernon (drums), Doug Steen (saxophone), Keith Worrell (lead guitar) and Tony Browning (bass).

1975 - In front of Ace Recroding Studio - Jackson, Mississippi. L to R: Steve McGregory, Johnny Dickens, Mack Allen Smith, and Martin Hawkins.

1975 - Ace Recording - Jackson, Mississippi. L to R: Mack Allen Smith and Steve McGregory.

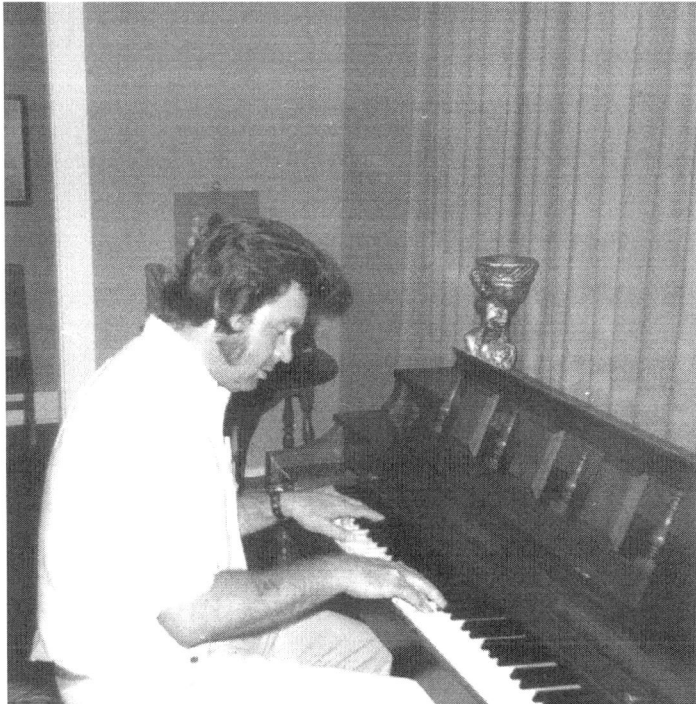

1975 - Mack Allen Smith pretending to play the piano at home in Greenwood, Mississippi.

Steve McGregory after he grew up some and put on a little weight.

L to R: Arthur Browning and Hardin Browning.

August 31, 2011 - Grenada, Mississippi. Arthur Browning and John William (Man) Hurt.

1966 - Mississippi John Hurt at Cook's Cabin - Avalon, Mississippi.

1966 - Mississippi John Hurt at Cook's Cabin - Avalon, Mississippi.

1966 - Cook's Cabin - Avalon, Mississippi. L to R: Kitty Cook, Jessie Hurt, John Hurt and Virgil Cook, Jr.

2008 - Stephen Winters at Earnest Tubb Record Shop in Nashville, Tennessee, with Rhonda Vincent.

2008 - Stephen Winters with Marty Stuart's band "the Fabulous Superlatives". L to R: Paul Martin, Kenny Vaughn, Stephen Winters and Harry Stinson.

2009 - L to R: Bill Cody of WSM, CMT and GAC Fame and Stephen Winters.

2009 - Old Black Hawk School House, Black Hawk, Mississippi. L to R: Barry Smith (bass), Laney O'Briant (lead guitar), Jamie Winters (rhythm guitar - behind Mack Allen), Mack Allen Smith (lead singer), Stephen Winters (drums) and Benny Rigby (piano).

2003 - Bob Timmers, Burns Tennessee.

December 2006 - L to R: Charlie McCoy, Mike Leech, Bob Timmers and Gene Chrisman.

November, 2003 - Margie Perkins with Bob Timmers.

L to R: James Carr and Quinton Claunch.

L to R: Percy Sledge, Quinton Claunch and Rufas Thomas.

Dock Carpenter and Willie Harmour.

The Deltones - Front L to R: Leman Gandy and Ray Hall. Back L to R: Vicki Carsile, Shirley Barton and Yavone Gandy

L to R: Glen Glover, Doc Herbert, Ray Cummings, Bob Barnett and Al Hauggy.

L to R: Dusty Rainey, Doc Herbert, Ricky Windham, Curley Rainey, James Winter and George Timbs.

L to R: Charles Carroll, Shirley Carroll, Doc Proctor, Neil Wrenn, Jimmy Hamilton and Doc Herbert.

Susie James

Dean Faulkner Wells and Susie James.

Susie James and Mack Allen Smith.

L to R: Johnny Vincent and Martin Hawkins.

Sonny Burgess and the Pacers.

Sonny Burgess and the Pacers autographs - courtesy of Joe Gary.

Allen Wood, Jr.

1-03-08 Kenny Minyard, Jim Minyard, Bobby Alford, Glen Walker and Jimmy Hamilton.

James O'Gwynn - Early 1960's

James O'Gwynn on stage at the Grand Ole Opry.

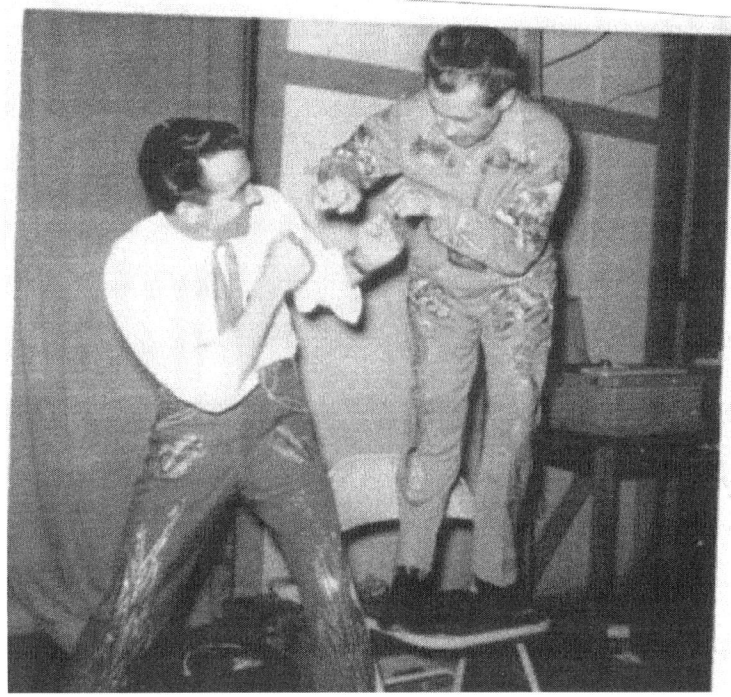
James O'Gwynn backstage at the Opry horsing around with 4 foot 7 inch Little Jimmy Dickens.

1967 - In front of Sun Records. L to R: Dickey Lee and Robert Loers.

1977 - England. Charlie Feathers and Robert Loers.

1999 - Hamburg, Germany. L to R: James Burton and Robert Loers.

1980 - Holland. L to R: Sleepy LaBeef, Joop Visser, Martin Hawkins and Robert Loers.

1996 - Belgium. Bo Diddley and Robert Loers.

1997 - Rotterdam, Holland - backstage. L to R: Little Richard and Robert Loers.

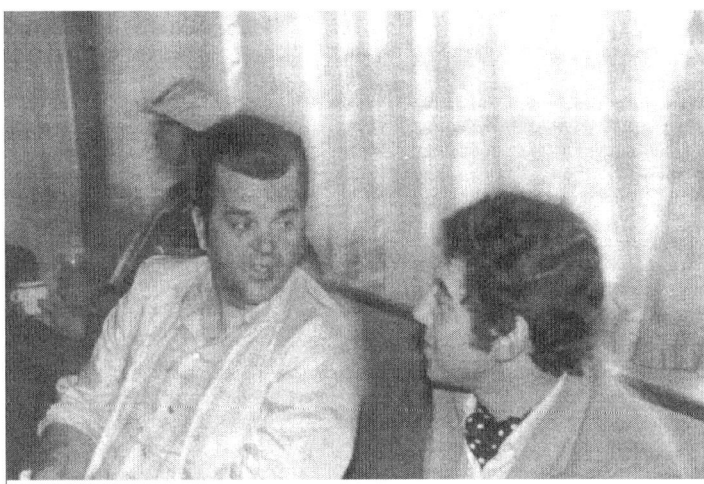

1968 - Amsterdam Airport-Press Room. L to R: Conway Twitty and Robert Loers.

1996 - Essex, Germany. L to R: Robert Loers and Jerry Lee Lewis.

Stone Blue - L to R: Don Chandler, James Govan, Billy Wayne Herbert, Ronnie Korner and Pete Bartosch.

May 1, 1971 - Mack Allen Smith. Grand Opening of Mack Allen Smith's Town & Country Night Club - Greenwood, Mississippi.

May 1, 1971 - Mack Allen Smith. Grand Opening of Mack Allen Smith's Town & Country Night Club - Greenwood, Mississippi.

January 22, 2011. L to R: Richard McLaughlin and Joe Max Blakely. Richard's induction into the Gore Springs Country Music Hall of Fame.

Billy Wayne Herbert singing and pickin' with House Band at Basin Street Club in El Darado, Arkansas.

May 15, 2010 - Black Hawk School House. L to R: Laney O'Briant (lead guitar), Jamie Winters (rhthym guitar), Stephen Winters (drums), Mack Allen Smith (singer) and Jamie Isonhood (piano). Not shown: Terry Herbert (rhthym guitar), Barry Smith (bass).

1984 - Curb Service. L to R: Duff Dorrough, John Elliott, Fish Michie, Joe Searight, Charlie Jacobs and Johnny Jennings.

May 15, 2010 - Black Hawk School House. L to R: Terry Herbert (rhythm guitar), Barry Smith (bass), Laney O'Briant (lead guitar), Jamie Winters (rhythm guitar), Mack Allen Smith (singer), Stephen Winters (behind Mack Allen on drums) and Jamie Isonhood (piano).

Printed in Great Britain
by Amazon.co.uk, Ltd.,
Marston Gate.